GENDERED STRUGGLES AGAINST GLOBALISATION IN MEXICO

Gender in a Global/Local World

Series Editors: Jane Parpart, Pauline Gardiner Barber
and Marianne H. Marchand

Gender in a Global/Local World critically explores the uneven and often contradictory ways in which global processes and local identities come together. Much has been and is being written about globalization and responses to it but rarely from a critical, historical, gendered perspective. Yet, these processes are profoundly gendered albeit in different ways in particular contexts and times. The changes in social, cultural, economic and political institutions and practices alter the conditions under which women and men make and remake their lives. New spaces have been created – economic, political, social – and previously silent voices are being heard. North-South dichotomies are being undermined as increasing numbers of people and communities are exposed to international processes through migration, travel, and communication, even as marginalization and poverty intensify for many in all parts of the world. The series features monographs and collections which explore the tensions in a 'global/local world', and includes contributions from all disciplines in recognition that no single approach can capture these complex processes.

Also in the series

Series titles continued at the back of the book.

Gendered Struggles against Globalisation in Mexico

TERESA HEALY
Canadian Labour Congress, Canada

ASHGATE

Parts of Chapter 4 were previously published in Healy, T. (2006), 'The Condition of Hegemony and Labour Militancy: The Restructuring of Gender and Production Patterns in Mexico', in Davies M. and Ryner, M. (eds), *Poverty and the Production of World Politics: Unprotected Workers in the Global Political Economy* (Houndmills, Basingstoke, UK; New York: Palgrave Macmilllan), pp.178–203.

Published by
Ashgate Publishing Limited
Gower House
Croft Road
Aldershot
Hampshire GU11 3HR
England

Ashgate Publishing Company
Suite 420
101 Cherry Street
Burlington, VT 05401-4405
USA

Ashgate website: http://www.ashgate.com

British Library Cataloguing in Publication Data
Healy, Teresa, 1962-
    Gendered struggles against globalisation in Mexico. -
    (Gender in a global/local world)
    1. Automobile industry workers - Labor unions - Mexico
    2. Globalization - Mexico 3. Working class men - Mexico
    I. Title
    331.8'8129222'0972

Library of Congress Cataloging-in-Publication Data
Healy, Teresa, 1962-
    Gendered struggles against globalisation in Mexico / by Teresa Healy.
        p. cm. -- (Gender in a global/local world)
    Includes bibliographical references and index.
    ISBN 978-0-7546-3701-1
    1. Automobile industry workers--Labor unions--Mexico. 2. Globalization--Mexico. 3. Working class men--Mexico. I. Title.

    HD6534.A8H42 2008
    331.20972--dc22

                                                                          2008003432

ISBN 978-0-7546-3701-1

Printed and bound in Great Britain by TJ International Ltd, Padstow, Cornwall.

Contents

This book is dedicated to the Mexican men and women
whose movements are chronicled here.
No se olvide.

Series Editors' Preface

Teresa Healy's *Gendered Struggles against Globalisation in Mexico* is the thirteenth volume in the *Gender in a Global/Local World* series by Ashgate Publishing. In this book we turn our gaze to the complexities of globalisation or global restructuring in a country that has undergone profound changes as a result of such forces. Focusing on the processes of restructuring and their resistances in a crucially important sector, the automotive industry, Healy reveals the gendered dynamics of such processes, in particular in the realm of the internationalisation of production. Starting with two ideal types of masculinity, partially enshrined in the revolutionary nationalism of post-colonial Mexico, Healy suggests that these types have undergone profound transformations with globalisation. She identifies *caudillismo* as the revolutionary nationalist hegemonic masculinity in Mexico, while the worker-father identity was identified as a form of subordinate masculinity. It is in particular the worker-father masculinity around which workers in the automotive industry mobilise when contesting globalisation. As Healy argues, many workers felt threatened by the protracted (economic) crisis in Mexico which started in the late 1960s or early 1970s and which set the stage for a fundamental restructuring of its political economy. Being faced with transformations affecting their livelihoods and (masculine) identities, workers in the automotive industry have resorted, unsuccessfully, to contestations in the form of radical labour organising outside of the government co-opted labour union, the CTM (*Confederación de Trabajadores Mexicanos*). A key element of their struggles has been to fight the feminisation of their work and the automotive industry.

Healy's book forms an important contribution to the literatures on globalisation, social movements and resistance, as well as developmental states and their nationalist underpinnings. As other contributions to this series have demonstrated, gender is an important power dimension that permeates all facets of social relations. Moreover, in order to better understand the workings of gender, it is important to include the ways in which masculinity/ies are constructed, exercised and transformed. *Gendered Struggles against Globalisation in Mexico* is a 'must read' not only for those interested in the trappings and workings of masculinity/ies in the context of globalisation, but also for those who are primarily concerned with the very gendered, particularly masculinist, nationalist underpinnings of postcolonial states.

Marianne H. Marchand
Pauline Gardiner Barber
Jane L. Parpart

Acknowledgements

I hardly know where to begin, now that I'm at the end. I'm not sure how one could possibly sum up what it means to love and be loved, to be welcomed, to be supported and know the meaning of solidarity, to be accompanied, to walk in community, to have finally found the peaceful, sustained, energetic conditions needed for writing. There is so much life to acknowledge. There was so much labouring that took place. To Alejandro Álvarez I owe a great debt of gratitude not only for sharing his analysis, but for the gift of his friendship over the years.

A great many people laboured with me and I would like to begin by recognising the contribution of Rianne Mahon, who, in her uncompromising commitment to the argument was able to help me say what I wanted to say. Jane Jenson and Laura Macdonald worked overtime to ensure clarity and I thank them for the enormous support when this project first emerged.

For welcoming me into their activism and analysis so that I might understand some of the complex dynamics of their struggles, I am grateful to Joan Atlin, Elain Burns, Mary McGinn, Viky Villanueva, and Lynda Yanz of *Mujer a Mujer*- Woman to Woman; Alfredo Domínguez, Benedicto Martínez and Berta Lújan of the *Frente Auténtico del Trabajo*; Héctor de la Cueva, *Centro de Investigaciones Laborales y Acción Sindical*; Alberto Arroyo, *Red Mexicana de Acción frente al Libre Comercio*; Arturo Alcalde and Manuel Fuentes of the *Asociación Nacional de los Abogados Democráticos*; the leaders of the *Movimiento Democratico de la Ford* and the organisers of *Alianza Cívica*.

For their generosity in welcoming me into a vibrant community of scholars and friends, I am most grateful to Arnulfo Arteaga, Maria de la Luz Arriaga Lemus, Jaime Avilés, Jennifer Cooper, Teresina Gutiérrez-Haces, Huberto Juarez; Gabriel Mendoza Pichardo, Jordy Micheli, Sergio Sandoval Godoy, Jussara de la Peña and Edur Velasco Arregui. I would like to acknowledge the quiet presence of the late Sergio de la Peña in my historical work.

I gratefully acknowledge the generous financial support of the Social Sciences and Humanities Research Council, the International Development Research Council and the Political Science Department at Carleton University. I thank *Facultad de Economía-Posgrado, Universidad Nacional Autónoma de México (UNAM)* for generously allowing me to affiliate as a visiting researcher. I am also grateful to the *Facultad de Economía*, UNAM as well as the *Fundación Friedrich Ebert-México* for sharing their published materials with me.

I would also like to thank Buzz Hargrove and the Canadian Autoworkers union for allowing me an extended period of time as writer-in-residence at the CAW Family Education Centre in Port Elgin Ontario. Over the years, I have learnt from many insightful discussions with intellectuals within the CAW. In particular, I thank Bruce Roberts and Sam Gindin.

I acknowledge how much I have learned by working with Common Frontiers and other networks on free trade over the years due to the solidaristic efforts of Ken Traynor, John Foster, Lorraine Michael, John Dillon, the late Michelle Swarnechuk, Tony Wolfarth, Judith Marshall, Fran Arbour, Bruce Campbell, Sheila Katz, Rick Arnold, Tony Clarke, Sandra Sorensen and Bob Carty.

Thank you to the students at Trent University, Peterborough with whom I tried out many of the ideas found here. In Toronto, I was given much needed encouragement by members of the "Mexico Group" under the energetic leadership of Judy Adler Hellman and Dick Roman. Their friendship means a great deal.

When I finally came to Ottawa to put down roots, I was welcomed into a wonderful political community at CUPE National and later, at the Canadian Labour Congress. My analysis has been sharpened and my heart blessed by the friendship and commitment of Jane Stinson, Morna Ballantyne, Heather Farrow, Blair Redlin, Julie White, Geoff Bickerton, Andrew Jackson, Shanaz Moloo, Tamara Levine, Penni Richmond and Karl Flecker.

What would I have done without the care of everyone who brought be back from the brink and nursed me through chemo-brain? Much love to the Seven Sisters of the Dragon! In the same way, I thank my musical community and Ottawa's song-writers' collective, Writer's Bloc, for opening the flood-gates.

I am forever grateful for the confidence shown by most wonderful series editors Marianne Marchand, Jane Parpart and Pauline Gardiner Barber, as well as Kirstin Howgate of Ashgate. It was an honour to have worked with them and to have felt their warm and welcome support for the book.

I thank Rick Eagan for the many years during which we accompanied one another as this research came to life. I thank him, my friends and my family for staying connected with me along the way. For the profound ways in which each has shaped my life and this manuscript I thank Susan Attenborough, Ann Bjorseth, Sergio Cabrera, Jenny Cafiso, Susie Chater, Bob and the late Jessie Cox, Susan Crofts, Stephen Dale, Karen Doyle, Brian Edgecombe, Danielle Fontaine, Kathleen Gollogly, Karen Hadley whom I miss very much, Anne Healy, Emma Heffernan, Tracy Heffernan, Colleen O'Manique, Joe Mihevc, Treasa NiÉalaithe, Yasch Neufeld, Viviana Patroni, Cathy Remus, and Katherine Scott.

Most of all, I thank Tom Juravich who lovingly helps me remember that it is all about the voice, about listening and being heard, around a table, on a picket line, in the streets or at a border. It's the blend of spices, the palette of sound, the range of possibilities, and the sheaf of proposals. It's all the life that can happen in one day, the restless harmony and the adamant, defiant, glorious embrace in spite of everything else.

To all of these friends, colleagues, comrades, *compañeros y compañeras* and loved ones, thank you.

Chapter 1

Introduction

This book is concerned with globalisation and its gendered contestations. Globalisation is often defined in material terms as the liberalisation of international trade, the deregulation of international finance and the internationalisation of production. It may also be defined in ideological terms as the discourse which limits the range of legitimate political activities. The ideology of globalisation is captured in the refrain that 'there is no alternative' to restructuring along neo-liberal lines. Globalisation may also be defined in institutional terms as the consolidation of neo-liberal restructuring within agreements such as the North American Free Trade Agreement (NAFTA). It has meant the restructuring of states in the wake of struggles between social forces at the workplace, in the community, at the national level, and at the level of world order. We have also come to understand globalisation by definitions of what it is not. In general, definitions of globalisation do not include 'Fordist' trade union rights and forms of work organisation, state support for public services, import-substitution industrialisation, or the 'family' wage. In a broad sense, we can identify a globalising dynamic that had its genesis in the crisis of the 'postwar settlement' beginning in the late 1960s.

Each of these statements opens up its own world of inquiry. Why did the transformation to globalisation take this path and not another? What was the role of contestation and repression? Which social forces are most implicated? What are the variations between and within countries? What happened to the people involved? Who has benefited and who is losing? This book approaches this great global transformation as it has been located in one country, Mexico; one economic sub-sector, auto assembly; and one gender, men. None of these can actually be contemplated in isolation, and so the stories which follow are also relational. Neither can these dynamics be understood without an historical account, so I will locate this period of crisis and transformation in a longer perspective.

In the following chapters, I trace the ways unequal power relations between men and women were written into Revolutionary Nationalism in an epic struggle to re-draw the post-colonial map at the beginning of the twentieth century. Revolutionary Nationalism drew from the stability of gender relations in society and became aspects of the way Mexico intersected with the world economy. In this period, *caudillismo* came to define a particular combination of masculinised practices and ideas which served to legitimise the leadership of certain men in powerful positions, and de-legitimise dissent. Whether it was through the presidency, or other lesser forms of political leadership, including trade unionism loyal to the ruling party, the hegemonic masculinity of *caudillismo* became a framework of power within which working-class movements for democracy, independence and autonomy were either co-opted or repressed and sometimes both. As movements of working-class men tried to disrupt these relationships they ran the risk of reproducing *caudillismo* in their own movements, but for the most part, the collective actions of rebel 'worker-fathers' could not gain institutional legitimacy and were crushed. Women's subordination in the gendered division of labour is clearly part of this story, insofar as women workers were 'protected' by the institutions of Revolutionary Nationalism, prevented from becoming full participants in the economic and political life of the country, and active in organising against their disenfranchisement.

This book examines three key movements of resistance among trade unionists in the Mexican auto industry. These movements emerged during the period of crisis in Mexico spanning the years 1968-94. Each movement represents an effort by trade unionists to transform the character of labour representation in Mexico. Each was defeated and through each case, a significant moment in the deepening crisis is illuminated. This book explores how radical labour movements became both protagonists and casualties in the crisis which ushered globalisation into Mexico. Through their gendered struggles we can understand important aspects of the *restructuring* of the economy and production; the crisis in *representation*, including the political sphere and labour's own institutions; and changes in forms of *resistance*.

While social scientists have done much to illuminate the way in which a particular pattern of class relations came to be temporarily institutionalised in mid-twentieth century Mexico, the gendered dimension of this stability, and subsequent crisis is often not seen. I have set out to analyse how working-class men organised to fight for the recognition of their citizenship rights and how they defended those rights when faced with repression, economic restructuring and *maquilisation*. They contested the terms of globalisation as it wrested from them their masculine identity of 'worker-fathers'. They fought other groups of men who tried to usurp their claims for self-representation. They battled employers and masculinised political power at every level within the state to maintain their livelihoods and resist the feminisation of their work and their own identities. These were gendered struggles against globalisation as they were experienced and carried out by men. Sometimes they involved solidarity with women's movements. At times, the concerns of women workers remained invisible.

I will tell well-known stories of oppositional movements of working-class men within the unions at *Nissan Mexicana*, *Ford de México* and *Volkswagen de México* (Aguilar García 1982; Arteaga 1992; Bizberg 1990; Carillo 1990a; Micheli 1994; Middlebrook 1995; Molot 1993; Montiel 1991; Roxborough 1984; Shaiken and Herzenberg 1989). Here they are revisited through a gendered lens and an analysis of crisis and struggles for transformation. By reflecting on these experiences, I hope we may come to an understanding of the specific context of crisis and change in Mexico that led to the signing of the North American Free Trade Agreement (NAFTA). While *caudillismo*, a highly illiberal form of political leadership grew out of Mexico's particular history, transnational capital also played a significant role in strengthening and maintaining the model. Similarly, as Mexico became increasingly open to the world economy in the period after 1968, the specifically gendered ways in which power relations were constructed conditioned the country's relationship with 'globalisation'. Gendered social relations infused labour's sense of collectivity, the organisation of its institutions and its relationship to the state. The globalising dynamic did not so much diminish inequalities between men and women, as bring about a significant 're-gendering' of the economy. This had a profound impact on working-class politics.

We only come to understand moments of crisis in their historical context. Crises emerge out of contradictions rooted in history. They also emerge from the struggles of social forces based in past experiences, constrained by pre-existing institutional arrangements, bound by material conditions and given vitality by options considered to be within the realm of possibility.[1] Despite crisis, social forces will struggle on a terrain marked by a certain amount of continuity. In other words, if we are going to understand Mexico's present, we must understand Mexico's past. We must also appreciate the very concrete ways in which workers experience the terms of production in which they are engaged, in order to understand the strategies they choose in their resistance. Globalisation in Mexico cannot be understood without an appreciation of the history of social struggle initiated well before the transition to the new order.

Hegemonic Masculinity

One of the main concepts I will use to discuss these stories is the concept of 'hegemonic masculinity' which comes from R.W. Connell who defines it as the dominant masculine ideal of a culture to which all others are subordinated (Connell 1987, 183). Hegemonic masculinity problematises the concept of patriarchy as a universal or essential category by identifying a hierarchy of relations between different groups of men. Instead of pointing to a set of role expectations or an identity, the concept shifts our focus to changing practices that maintain men's dominance over women and on devalued groups of men (Connell 1987, 183; Connell and Messerschmidt 2005; Hooper 2001, 28–53). As the 'currently most honored way of being a man', a specific masculinity becomes hegemonic through culture, institutions and persuasion, although at times is supported by force (Connell and Messerschmidt 2005, 832). It is possible for a hegemonic masculinity to be transformed in struggle and for a new masculinity to take its place. If a certain form of masculinity attains hegemony in a society, it cannot be built upon coercion only. It must elicit consent as well. Once it emerges, a hegemonic masculinity is not self-sustaining and requires 'the policing of men as well as the exclusion or discrediting of women' to be maintained (Connell and Messerschmidt 2005, 844).

One of the benefits of this way of looking at gender and power is that it suggests a wide range of possible definitions of masculinity and femininity and, correspondingly, many possible responses to issues of inequality. It is a one way of doing the 'careful, politically focused, local analyses' which may replace monolithic notions of patriarchy which Chandra Talpade Mohanty sees as leading to similarly reductive ideas about women's oppression in post-colonial societies (Talpade Mohanty 1991 53–4, 65). Michael Kaufman has developed the argument that hegemonic masculinity takes different forms in different places and among different cultures at different times (Kaufman 1993). Similarly, Matthew Gutmann, who studied masculinity in a neighbourhood in Mexico City concludes that 'claims about a uniform character of

---

1   This starting point is influenced by the work of Robert Cox (1987).

Mexican masculinity, a ubiquitous *macho mexicano* should be put to rest' (Gutmann 1996, 263). These approaches suggest it would be fruitful to investigate the effect of hegemonic masculinity on various societal and global transformations. Some are less convinced of a concept based power relations that makes the powerlessness of individual lives invisible. Siedler, for example, would prefer explorations of masculinities which address the ambiguities and contradictions individual men experience (Seidler 2006, 13). On the other end of the spectrum, Ann Tickner uses the concept as a way to understand transformations in international security issues at the level of world order (Tickner 1992). It has also been suggested that by investigating masculinities, we immediately undermine their 'naturalness'. As Steve Smith says, this in itself is an act that challenges centuries of privilege (Smith 1998, 65).

In the work that follows, my questions will consider whether the masculinity in question is hegemonic or not, but I will also explore how hierarchies of masculinities contributed to the hegemonic projects of dominant classes. Masculine power can and does reproduce the dominance of one class of men over another class of men and women. Rather than using an absolute notion of power, however, we can look for the ways subordinated groups of men, as well as women, resist and work to transform their situation. In Mexico, the 'worker-father' emerged as a very important masculinity in twentieth century Revolutionary Mexico, but it never attained hegemonic status. I would argue it was subordinated to the hegemonic masculinity of *caudillismo*, which itself experienced moments of construction, destruction, and reconstruction. As ideal-types, these two masculinities will help us understand some of the central ways gendered inequalities have been created and re-created in ideological, institutional and material terms.

Unequal gender relations were maintained in Mexico, despite the cataclysmic social impacts of the Revolution which began in 1910. Revolutionary Nationalist masculine authority was reproduced in the image of the *caudillo* who is often referred to a 'strong man' or as 'a leader on horseback'. The best translation, however, is 'chieftain' (Wolf and. Hansen 1967). Historically, *caudillos* were not necessarily hereditary rulers, but *criollo* or *mestizo* leaders who gained power as a result of the Wars of Independence in Latin America. As Eric Wolf and Edward Hansen argue, *caudillos* were men who could assert their masculinity before other men by demonstrating their dominance over women, as well as their willingness to use violence to control others. Both of these dynamics led to conflict with other men. The *caudillo* was a leader who could gain authority by forming coalitions and commanding the loyalty of other leaders who would 'declare' their support for him any time he was challenged.[2] The *caudillo* was constantly aware of his need to mobilise support for his leadership among his followers. Wolf and Hansen argue that, whether through trading or in pillage, it was crucial for the *caudillo* to use good judgment in the acquisition and distribution of

---

2 So as not to introduce another term, I am avoiding the use of the term 'cacique'. These 'other leaders' were actually 'caciques' who had already attained power in the hierarchy of locally based elites and maintained it through clientelistic relationships with other men, including traditional elders in the pueblos. As Paul Garner argues, the 'caudillo' is simply a 'cacique' who has subordinated other caciques to his will in order to fulfill his broader aspirations (Garner 1985, 120; see also Díaz and Álvarez 1972).

the wealth obtained by the band so as to conserve the loyalty of these other leaders (Wolf and Hansen 1967, 169). There was instability in this form of leadership, as competition between men, disability, death or treachery could seal the fate of an individual caudillo. The system was, however quite diffuse, given the relatively large number of *caudillos* who developed regional power bases and kept each other in check (Wolf and Hansen 1967, 177). As a system of power, the *caudillaje* was by definition anarchic, and anti-institutional. Berthea Lerner and Susana Ralsky describe the *caudillo* in this way:

> The regional *caudillo* is a military strong man, capable of offering a certain amount of protection to his followers. By means of his paternalism he attains internal loyalty to his persona and the dependence of his followers. As well, his leadership depends on the kind of strength that characteristically projects an image of exaggerated masculinity and heroism. He is a leader that ascends to power for his qualities of invulnerability and not by virtue of his education, his political vision with respect to the future or his social propositions at the national level. In general, he depends more upon his ample military intuition and on personal valour than on strategy or educated manoeuvring. (Lerner and Ralsky 1976, 26; Translated by the author)

There are many different determinations of when *caudillaje* as a system came to an end, but to the extent that it was a political form of a struggle for finite resources derived from the control of peasants, the expansion of land holdings and mercantilist trade, it survived only until the late nineteenth century (Wolf and Hansen 1967, 178). As political practice, however, *caudillismo* continued without much interruption. Despite the centralisation and institutionalisation of state power during the dictatorship of Porfirio Díaz, and the increasingly important role of foreign investment, the *porfiriato* was stabilised through co-optation and alliances with *criollo caudillos* and state governors. This was very much in the tradition of *caudillo* politics (Garner 1985).

This idealised masculinity was rooted in the family where gender hierarchies were heavily guarded. Women's subordination to her husband, the church, her in-laws, and her own parents and community was designed to preserve the honour of her husband. Women's virtue and sexual purity were controlled by keeping women chaperoned and at home. There they were seen to be responsible for the upbringing of their children and attending to their husbands (Carne 1987, 97). This was, however, an idealised femininity. Contrary to the nineteenth-century myths suggesting women were confined to the home, there were many women who worked in small businesses, domestic service and in all activities related to the production of food and clothing. Women were teachers. Women on ranches worked in both the house and the farm, and peasant women were heavily involved in agricultural production and artisanal work, as well as household production. At the beginning of the twentieth century women were employed in offices, and in textiles and cigarette factories (Carne 1987, 105). Miserable working conditions and low wages and sexual harassment were not mitigated by the right to join unions. Nevertheless, there were moments in which women's resistance resulted in strikes (Ramos Escandón 1987, 158).

The argument advanced here is that much of the 'code of *caudillo* behaviour' survived the transition to capitalism and the Revolution (Wolf and Hansen 1967, 178).

Certainly *caudillismo* as 'militarised factionalism' was evident in the Revolutionary period and in the crisis that followed (Garner 1985). It is quite common for scholars to identify the Revolutionary generals in Mexico as *caudillos*, and to identify *caudillismo* in the actions of Revolutionary presidents in their dealings with regional leaders (Martínez-Assad 1978). Indeed, the apparently 'individualistic' leadership of strong men continued through the mid-century to be rooted in a system of power tied to 'groups' of other powerful men and regional interests. As will be argued below, *caudillismo* has played an important role in the history of trade unions in Mexico. It is this continuity of practice which is most salient. *Caudillismo* became the 'hegemonic masculinity' with dire consequences for working-class emancipation.

This particular masculine framework of power has been so long-lived because of the way it combines paternalism and authoritarianism. Paternalism may be understood as a set of social practices in which social inequality is legitimated and reproduced in ways similar to those of a patriarchal family. In this image of family, the father may be benevolent but commanding. He exercises decision making power by arguing that it is in family members' best interests to defer to the internal hierarchy (Jary and Jary 1991). To the outside, the family is presented as a homogeneous entity while the unequal power relationships within it are legitimised. The privileging of such structures of masculine authority enables one actor to emerge in relation to a number of other 'pre-actors' having no legitimate role in representing their own interests within or without the collectivity.[3] In this sense, paternalism may refer to the usurping of rights to self-representation legitimised by the dominant group.

Within patriarchal relations, authoritarianism may underlie this paternalistic effort to legitimise relations of social inequality. Authoritarianism is the means by which the subordinated are threatened with the possible withdrawal of resources, or the application of violence if they challenge the relationship. The authoritarianism of patriarchal social relations is relatively easy to identify, but when authoritarianism is joined with paternalistic relationships built on the acquiescence and consent of the subordinated, unequal gendered relations of power attain a resilience that is much more difficult to contest. If we are to assume that the gendered dimensions of hegemony rest upon paternalism as well as authoritarianism, then we can expect to see an interplay between the two in the hegemonic masculinity in question. In the Mexican case we witness the ebb and flow of paternalism and authoritarianism within capitalist society.

As I will argue in Chapter 2, victorious and authoritarian Revolutionary leaders sought to conclude the civil war and re-establish stability, by promoting a model of progressive capitalism which incorporated into the Mexican Constitution through Article 123; the article dedicated to issues 'of labour and social provision'. The chapter continues on to explore how the transition from the crisis of the Revolution to a more stable order depended upon three dimensions of gender that developed in succession. These included: 1) a paternalistic ideology incorporated into the Constitution of 1917, in which the family, rather than the individual or class, was constructed as the basic unit of society; 2) institutionalised *caudillismo* as the hegemonic masculinity within the state and expressed in the federal executive and official union leadership,

---

3　I am grateful to Janine Brodie for her reflections on this point in conversation.

and the universal father-worker; 3) the masculinised character of state corporatism which was the productive mode favoured by the state, exemplified by the automotive industry and in which the worker-father played a central role.

Each of the three cases under consideration in Chapters 3, 4 and 5 offers an insight into how oppositional movements *within* Mexican trade unions attempted to contest the terms of crisis and restructuring by transforming the established basis of labour representation. In this context, the auto industry remained key to state priorities within the context of North American restructuring, but the relative position of male auto workers and the privileged place of their traditional corporatist forms of representation deteriorated dramatically. Since the auto industry in Mexico has always been an internationalised site of production relations to some extent, resistance from labour movements brings overlapping relations of power into focus. As we shall see, the state remained the crucial site of struggle for oppositional movements, although it was not always the first target of contestation. As production was restructured along continental lines in Mexico beginning in the 1960s, the state became increasingly authoritarian. The discourse of international competitiveness undermined the myth of the 'gradually perfecting Revolution', while the highly feminised and coercive character of export-oriented production took hold.

The ability of the official labour central, the *Confederación de Trabajadores de México* (CTM), to represent its members worsened as the crisis of state legitimacy deepened during the years 1968–94. As we shall see in the first instance, an atrophied CTM played no innovative role during the onset of crisis. Later, it attempted to reassert its presence as the legitimate interlocutor with the restructured state. Nevertheless, the CTM's traditional core supporters accused it of acquiescence in the face of attacks on their acquired rights. In response, the CTM resorted to violence against its own members to maintain union discipline. This strategy did not restore the CTM's close relationship with the ruling party and, as the NAFTA negotiations were concluded, the CTM was displaced from its central position by new institutions of labour.

In Mexico, the CTM was one of the most important corporatist institutions developed within the Revolutionary Nationalist project. The radical movements of working-class men discussed here sought independence from the CTM. Whether or not they were successful, they tried to democratise both official and 'independent' labour institutions. When they were unsuccessful there, they fought their battles on legal grounds with the argument that it was the state itself that was the problem. They formed political organisations and they demanded both individual and social rights within the legal system. They sought to build alliances with other social movements at the local, national and international levels in order to press their demands for democratic representation in the workplace, within trade unions, and within the state more generally. They participated in national movements that challenged the lack of democracy at the federal level. These movements included, but were not confined to, demands for electoral transparency. Their struggles had a material dimension to them, but their struggles were also about their rights to be represented and to represent themselves in the life of their society. This reading of history shows that oppositional movements of working-class men, acting collectively to transform the conditions of their subordination, must, and in fact do, engage political projects that problematise questions of representation in a new form of state. Their struggles are some of the many gendered contestations of globalisation in Mexico.

Chapter 2

'Of Labour and Social Provision': Gender, Production and Revolutionary Nationalism

It is at the beginning of the twentieth century that we will search for the gendered roots of globalisation in Mexico. In the Revolution we will look for the ideology and the political practices which were to shape dominant ideas about the gender division of labour. In mid-century the Federal Labour Law institutionalised the masculinised power of state and union leaders over women and working-class men. Later, while working men were disciplined in the areas of the economy most favoured by the state, women were excluded. The auto industry offers one example of the contradictions of this strategy for the national economy and the efforts of state leaders to keep Revolutionary Nationalism immune from dissent.

Ideology, the Family and the Mexican Constitution of 1917

For most observers of the Mexican Revolution, Article 123 'Of Labour and Social Provision' has been an ambiguous document which was both a triumph for workers, as well as a mechanism for ensuring their continued subordination (Carr 1976). This ambiguity has been explained by giving weight to a variety of state, society and international factors. It has been argued that, in guaranteeing the right of workers to strike and to associate, and in providing corresponding rights for employers, Article 123 codified historic gains for workers, but elevated the role of the state as mediator between labour and capital and justified state intervention in socioeconomic development from that moment onward (Carr 1976, 86; LaBotz 1992, 43). The Constitution became therefore, the ideological legitimation of an authoritarian state, as well as the institutional grounding of an alliance between the labour movement and the governing elite; both of which assisted in bringing lasting stability to the Revolutionary regime (Middlebrook 1995). Other observers emphasise the lack of correspondence between the progressive aspects of the Constitution and the economic conditions facing the country in the early twentieth century (Hellman 1983, 22). In this view, Article 123 committed governing elites to an ideology of ongoing reform, and encouraged mass movements of workers and peasants to accept incremental change in the Revolutionary Nationalist project. Some observers propose that Article 123 was the product of deal-making that went on during the Constituent Assembly when it appeared the Revolutionary context would provide no simple return to a Constitutional order. For others, the progressive labour provisions of the Constitution coincided with the 'corporate liberalism' of the United States and England, and expressed at the same time, the Revolutionary Nationalist view that internal conflict should not be permitted to distract from fighting foreign domination (Roman 1976, 143–4).

Each of these explanations recognises the imperfect promise of Article 123 for labour rights in Mexico and the contradictory role of the state envisioned there. Article 123 is significant for working-class politics not only because it recognised working-class collective identities in the Revolution, but because it recognised those of owners of capital as well. The problem, as I shall argue here, was not that Constitutional promises to workers were left unfulfilled. The problem was that they were *unfulfillable* given the unequal structures of representation underpinning Revolutionary ideology. As a result, twentieth-century Revolutionary Nationalism emerged as contested terrain upon which both dominant and subordinate social forces would continue to struggle. They would do so on gendered terrain.

Throughout the twentieth century, Mexican labour movements justified their activities in light of their Constitutional rights to form unions, to strike, to share in profits and benefit from the social wage. For their part, employers made demands of the state to intervene on their behalf when they felt the social 'balance' had been upset by trade union militancy. The state, by no means a neutral arbiter, did indeed intervene. Throughout the century, the official trade union leadership also intervened to reassert the balance in favour of its own position within the Revolutionary Nationalist project when it was threatened by internal movements for democracy, autonomy and independence. These conflicting claims made 'Of Labour and Social Provision' reveal the ideological power of the Revolutionary Constitution.

Ideological stalemate is, however, insufficient as an explanation of labour's subordination within the Revolutionary project. Here I argue that there were gendered assumptions written into the Constitution which reinforced unequal relations between men and women workers, and between groups of men. These assumptions contributed to the creation of unequal structures of representation within Revolutionary Nationalism. As expressed in part through the Constitution, *caudillismo* reproduced unequal gendered relations which limited the autonomy of working-class politics and provided an alternative to democratic forms of leadership. In making this argument, I will revisit Article 123 by looking at the gendered dynamics of both the text itself, as well as the context in which it was written.

It is through the discourse of the family and the protective elements of the Article, together with the vision of society as an organic and corporate whole which suggests the gender conservatism played a significant role in the struggle to define the scope of individual and social rights. Yet, the politics of gender were not confined to questions about women's role in the family and the economy. For example, in 1915 divorce was legalised. What appeared to be a radical intervention on behalf of women's rights, had much more to do with a direct challenge by governing elites to the authority of the Catholic Church (Macías 1982, 35). In 1916, the Convention Assembly was presented with a proposal to give women equal political rights. It was rejected with the argument that women continue to be located in the domestic sphere and their interests are linked with those of men in the family. The Assembly did not wish to challenge the 'unity' of the family and because they saw no collective response indicating otherwise, they argued women themselves did not want to participate in public affairs (Tuñón 1987, 184). It was also thought that the church would have undue influence over women's votes so female suffrage was not seriously entertained (Macías 1982, 337). As a result, Article 34 was not modified. Women were not defined as citizens and continued to be denied the right to vote and hold public office. While women gained rights of parental authority (guardianship), and women's rights to draw up contracts and engage in business were also recognised by a change in the Law of Family Relations of 1917, they were not allowed to do so without their husband's consent. Thus, argues Anna María Alonso, patriarchy was rationalised and reinscribed as modern in law (Alonso 1995; see also Varley 2000, 241).

Furthermore, in the story of how Article 123 came to be presented to the Constituent Congress we have an example of the role that gender, and hegemonic masculinity in particular, played in establishing state – labour relations in Revolutionary Mexico. As the hegemonic masculinity, *Caudillismo* was a form of political practice that legitimised the transition of General to President, allowed him to assert his leadership over women and other men who were regional leaders, as well as the men who led the trade unions. This was accomplished with the use of violence, by appealing to their shared masculinity, by forming coalitions and by making deals. It was the context within which Article 123 was written which expressed the continuation of *caudillo* politics as Revolutionary Nationalism was constructed. Despite women's active role in the Revolution, the masculine order prevailed in the institutions and practices of the new regime (Molyneux 2000, 51). Thus, in both text and context, these two gendered aspects of the Constitution subordinated women to the Revolutionary project and justified unequal social relations between men and women, and between groups of men.

Article 123: 'Of Labour and Social Provision'

Article 123 of the Mexican Constitution of 1917 is first and foremost, an effort to accommodate nineteenth century liberal economic objectives within an organic, corporate construction of society. It assumes the family is the basic unit of society and builds from the 'natural' assumptions of a gendered division of labour. It portrays a model of labour relations in which both men and women are defined more in terms of family identity rather than class identity. As part of the effort to direct the creation of free wage labour, Article 123 elaborates a protective mandate, especially for women and children, but also for men. It favours local communities, tripartite governing bodies and a limited role for the state in social provision. In Article 123 there are many important positive declarations of labour's collective rights, but these are set within an explicit charge to preserve a balance between labour and capital. Thus, for every assertion of a labour right, there is a corresponding statement of employers' rights. The state authorities reserved for themselves the power to arbitrate between capital and labour through labour boards. Employers were expected to shoulder many of the responsibilities for the social wage required by workers, their families and the local community.

The protective elements of Article 123 assumed a gendered division of labour within the family that would be extended as the labour market developed. In the way they regulated working conditions for workers in general, working-class men, women and children, these provisions did not simply reflect a gendered division of labour but imposed a gendered framework as the labour market was constructed. Article 123 included a clear statement of the right of women to equal pay for work of equal value, as well as a prohibition on discrimination based on sex or nationality. Women workers, however, were not seen as fully adult workers and their role in the workplace was restricted. As generally the case in juridical environments which granted 'protection' to women, they were not seen as complete citizens (Molyneux 2000, 44). Women were referred to in clauses that also considered the situation of children under 16. Like children, women were prohibited from working overtime, from participating in unhealthy or dangerous work, from working past ten at night in commercial establishments and from doing industrial night shifts. Children under the age of 12 were not to be hired and those between the ages of 12 and 16 were restricted to six-hour shifts. Recognising the prevalence of child labour, the Article only limited the practice.

As well as special provisions based on women-as-workers, there were other provisions for women-as-mothers. Women workers were protected from engaging in physically demanding work in the three months prior to giving birth and they were guaranteed their jobs after one month of maternity leave, during which time they were to receive their wages and other benefits. Nursing mothers were to be provided with two extra half-hour breaks during the day for feedings, apart from a regular meal break.

The commitment to a vision of workers as family members was reflected in the protective articles concerning women workers, but also in the provisions for a minimum wage. It was decided that minimum wages should be sufficient, 'depending on the conditions of each region, to satisfy the normal necessities of life of the worker, his education and honest pleasures, according to his role as the head of the family.'[1] Thus, in a somewhat contradictory fashion, the Mexican constitution provided for both an equal pay clause as well as for the right to a family wage.[2] This may be explained by the fact that the Constitution was not meant to challenge the gendered division of labour within production. Men and women were not expected to work in the same jobs, so an equal pay provision would refer to wages within workplaces that were, effectively, segmented. Equal pay provisions responded to the complaint during the Porfiriato, that Mexican men were paid less than American men in the same workplace. This was one of the main issues driving the strike at Cananea in 1905.

In certain respects, Article 123 dealt with the protection of working-class men as well. The Constitution limited the workday of men to eight hours during the day and seven hours at night. One day of rest per week was made mandatory and the Article restricted overtime to three hours per day, with 100 per cent overtime premiums. While there was no right to refuse overtime, it was limited to three consecutive

---

1   'Título VI, Del Trabajo y de la Previsión Social: Artículo 123', as reproduced in Moreno (1967, 47).

2   That the Mexican Constitution encompassed both of these provisions suggests an unusual combination when compared with the British and French cases in which two different social structures may be seen as having created divergent political demands around issues of social and biological reproduction. For a discussion of early twentieth-century politics of the family wage in the British case and equal pay for work of equal value in the French case, see Jenson (1992).

shifts. Although it appeared that the Constitution established the 48-hour week, the over-time provisions were a significant limitation, insofar as it left the whole issue of the length of the working day a matter for individual or collective negotiation. As well, the Article restricted those labour practices recognised as having made men victims to outright swindling at the hands of their employers. These provisions set down specific protections that applied to working-class men. Alcohol and gambling were not allowed on work sites and all employment pools were to be set up without charge to the workers. Employers could not establish stores at which workers had to shop, thus outlawing the infamous *tienda de raya,* or company store. Employers were prohibited from paying workers inside of any sort of commercial establishment and wages were to be paid in legal currency. In the event of bankruptcy, it was declared that workers would be the first to be reimbursed.

The Article ended by stating that all previously accumulated work-related debts would be cancelled with the proclamation of the Constitution. The fact that the Article forbade any employer from holding workers' families responsible for acquired debt was one of the most important contributions to the creation of free wage labour in Mexico. This provision ended one of the most pernicious aspects of traditional labour relations through which workers had become indentured to their employers for generations.

Although the Article provided for a family wage, the male worker was not seen as solely responsible for maintenance of the family. The worker-father existed in relation to the family, but the family existed within a community. The health of the community was seen to depend to a certain extent on the employer. Employers with establishments in town, and employing more than 100 workers were responsible for providing clean and comfortable housing at a regulated rental rate. Since establishments of over 100 employees were rare indeed, this provision would be rarely fulfilled. Rural employers were responsible for housing as well as the provision of community services such as health care centres and schools. This was meant to ensure that new communities set up around mines, for example, would have to be provided with the necessary social infrastructure. All employers had to establish public spaces for markets, municipal buildings and recreation centres.

Whether due strictly to questions of state resources, or perhaps because of the Revolutionary ambition for national economic development under the leadership of an emerging capitalist class, the new governors were unwilling and perhaps unable to take over tasks that employers might be made responsible for. Indeed, in the aftermath of the Revolution, the *Porfirian* state was in a shambles. Not only had its institutions been undermined by seven years of civil war and foreign interventions, but there was at best only a very tenuous alliance between military victors, the landed classes and middle-class professionals who advanced this a new nationalist project.

One of the most celebrated characteristics of Article 123 is the declaration of workers' rights to form 'coalitions'. Under this provision, it was recognised that both workers and employers hold equal rights 'to group themselves in defence of their respective interests, by forming unions, professional associations, etcetera' (XVI). It is crucial to notice that the same right to organise applies to both workers and employers. Similarly, Article 123 declared that a strike by workers, or a halt in production by employers, were actions that were assigned a formal equivalence. Even more to the point, legal strikes were those that 'had as their objective the establishment of equilibrium between the diverse factors of production, harmonising the rights of labour with those of capital' (XVIII). There were limits on these provisions. To avoid an illegal strike, public service workers had to give ten days notice to the Arbitration and Conciliation Council and no strike could involve violence against property or persons. The only legitimate reason for employers to suspend production was when they could prove to the Council that excess production was threatening price stability.

In making these provisions, the delegates to the Constituent Assembly articulated an important statement recognising the formation of collective identities of both workers and employers that assumed no necessary antipathy between them. Effectively, the right to organise employers' associations or unions, as well as the rights to strike and lockout, were premised on the argument that a balance of power was the natural social condition and conflicts would only arise when this balance had been upset, that is, in exceptional circumstances. Additionally, the concern with balance was addressed under the provision which permitted workers to claim a percentage of employers' earnings each year. Workers were thus encouraged to see their interests aligned with the profitability of the enterprise. Municipal councils would determine the percentage of these profit-sharing programmes along with minimum wage rates.

Labour law was seen to be largely a matter of state jurisdiction and would be administered under state level Arbitration and Conciliation Councils made up of an equal number of worker and employer representatives as well as one government official. These Councils were to be ultimately responsible for most aspects of labour law, including dispute settlements and the approval of municipally determined minimum wages. They would determine whether a strike or halt in production was legal and they would respond to individual complaints and conflicts over contracts. If employers did not comply with the decisions of the Arbitration and Conciliation Councils, the worker would be provided with three months compensatory wages, or in some cases, the right to return to work according to the terms of the individual's contract. This provision also held if a member of a worker's family was mistreated by the employer or one of his family members, compelling the worker to leave his job.

Evidently the Constitutionalists understood Article 123 as part of a process of state development that would emerge as the legal framework was developed. The rights of labour were set out under a general statement giving Federal and State level assemblies the responsibility to formulate relevant and future laws. As well, employers were meant to comply with laws on training and health and safety and were responsible to provide compensation for work related accidents, according to laws that would be written. Similarly, future consideration would be given to popular insurance funds in order to cover disability, old age and life, involuntary termination of work, accidents and other related matters, and to the institution of cooperative societies for the construction of affordable housing. As well, state and federal governments would denominate those goods that were part of workers' 'family patrimony' and thus inalienable. It was yet to be seen whether 'social provision' would be carried out in a way consistent with the Constitutional guarantees, but this legislation was to emerge within the regulatory framework of labour law.

Article 123 became an important ideological element in the construction of a the state in Revolutionary Mexico and there are key assumptions about working-class identities, family form, employers' responsibilities and the role of the state written into this Article. While assuming the gendered division of labour within the family, protective legislation served as the legal mechanism through which free wage labour was expected to emerge. Women workers were introduced into a structurally unequal position in the labour market as a result. Social reproduction was understood to be linked to the workplace, and within the domain of employers' responsibilities. The federal state gave jurisdictional supremacy to the local level of government in matters of labour law, while employers would be made responsible for most aspects of social provision.

Article 123 affirms workers' rights to form coalitions and strike but does not advance a class-based vision of Revolutionary Nationalism. Insofar as a collective working-class identity is recognised, it is to assign benefits to working-class men through their roles as heads of their families. This was the case primarily because the Constitution brought workers into the model as individuals defined in relation to their families, not in relation to existing labour organisations. Workers and employers were given equivalent rights to association and employer responsibilities came to be identified by a regulatory framework in which protective legislation and social provision are their central characteristics. The family as the foundational ideal of society was reinforced in other legislation introduced by Carranza. In particular, the 1917 Law of Family Relations modernised patriarchal relations inscribed in colonial law by introducing limited reforms. However, husbands were still obliged to support their wives and husbands would decide where the family would live. The management of the household remained the legal responsibility of the wife (Varley 2000, 242). As argued by Ana María Alonso (1995), patriarchy was not undermined by liberal reforms. Rather, it was taken out of the realm of violence and rationalised, legitimised and re-inscribed in law. Even in the 1915 law permitting divorce, there is a correspondence between the role of the father in the family and the paternalistic state arbitrating between parties in cases where women fought for divorce: 'In spite of the nominal equality of wives and husbands, then, the parallels between state authority and male authority within the family re-emerged, albeit in paternalistic guise' (Varley 2000, 254).

At the outset, it appeared that the state itself would act as guarantor in the consolidation of capitalist relations of production. The new Revolutionary government was in no position to control foreign investors, despite the nationalist guarantees of land ownership and subsoil rights. The federal state would eventually enforce this organic, corporate view of society within Mexico in tripartite institutions and in authoritarian control of trade unions. Yet the immediate post-Revolutionary period compelled state actors to closely attend to the role of employers in the task of reconstruction. Economic development would depend, not only on the extent to which the newly emerging state would oversee the balance of social forces, but on its ability to extend the discourse of national interest beyond the ideology of the

Constitution and into an institutional framework and a productive structure as well (Roman 1976, 143–4).

In Mexico, the assertion of employer's responsibilities for schools, hospitals, and municipal infrastructure was not unusual in the context of single-industry towns in northern states where foreign investors had long been a dominant presence. There was no reason to suppose that new industrialists would find an affirmation of such historical practices a challenge to local power relations. With the extension of private resources into these areas, the costs of reproduction were not socialised, but were recognised as serving a productive function. If employers agreed to take on responsibilities for social provision, it was clear that the state would not. This permitted employers a rather large amount of discretion over the speed of fulfilment and scope of their responsibilities.

Article 123 incorporated the nation building priorities of a small class of liberal constitutionalists in the spirit of early twentieth-century capitalism (Roman 1976). After the Revolution, the conditions for free market in land and labour were still being established and the labour provisions, together with other key constitutional Articles formed the ideological basis for the Revolutionary state. Together these principles declared that 'the land belongs to those who work it', 'the worker has the right to strike', 'the subsoil wealth belongs to the nation' and 'public services should be nationalised' (Beteta, Wilkie and Wilkie 1969, 31–2; see also Wilkie and Michaels 1969, 13–14). The Constitution however, protected workers, peasants and indigenous people, as well as employers and the investments of national capitalists. In fact, the inclusion of popular classes in the ideology of the Revolution was the outcome of both their resistance and the Constitutionalists search for stability in the wake of their incomplete victory. The labour provisions of the Constitution were primarily the outcome of the politics of Revolutionary *caudillismo*. It is to this conflicted history that we now turn.

'Caudillismo' and the Mexican Revolution

As the twentieth century began, the Mexican economy was highly integrated into the classic international division of labour. The Mexican state became an active promoter of this export-orientation under Porfirio Díaz who, in the name of Liberalism, maintained a dictatorship between 1876 and 1911 (Cockcroft 1968, 4–5). Under the *Porfiriato,* a sizeable railway network had been constructed and mine and plantation owners became highly integrated into the international economy (Furtado 1976, 50). International trade was expanded and diversified. Mexico became an exporter of industrial metals as well as precious metals. Traditional exports were augmented by the production of new primary products.[3] Between 1893 and 1907, exports increased by six while imports grew by three and one-half times (Camín and Meyer 1993, 2; see also Furtado 1976). As investments in infrastructure grew, Mexico became increasingly open to the international economy (Guerra 1988, 336).

---

3   The production of henequen, wood and hides was followed by coffee, cattle cotton, chickpeas, sugar, vanilla and chicle (Hansen 1971, 18).

During the *Porfiriato*, Mexico acquired an international reputation as a site for stable investment, especially in the areas of mining, commerce, utilities and industry. Historian Frank Brandenburg notes:

> Americans seized the cement industry. The French monopolized large department stores. The Germans controlled the hardware business. The Spanish took over foodstores and together with the French, controlled the textile industry. The Canadians, aided by Americans and Englishmen, concentrated on electric power, trolley lines, and water companies. The Belgians, Americans, and English invested heavily in the railroads. And what ultimately shook the roots of revolutionary ideology was the American and British exploitation of minerals, especially oil. (Brandenburg 1969, 20)

Mexico's credit rating was excellent and foreign investment moved freely. Between 1884 and 1911, foreign investment increased from 110 million pesos to 3,400 million pesos (Guerra 1988). Between 1876 and 1910, foreign investors expanded the railway network from 640 km to 19,980 km. They were aided with government subsidies and granted concessions for mines and land along the railways (Guerra 1988).

Large landowners supported the liberal world order which provided open markets for commodity goods. These commodity exporters were not opposed to free trade, but they were not, however, concerned with universal suffrage or expanding the basis of citizenship. Uninterested in ceding to the general population the freedom to pursue advantages that hierarchy had already afforded them, propertied classes endeavoured to suppress all opposition. Under these circumstances, liberalism offered no utopian vision to *mestizo* peasants and indigenous peoples. Neither were any of the political freedoms championed by liberal reformers and working-class movements in Europe extended to the small industrial working class (Carr 1976). While national capital contributed to the technological development of the mines, as well as the growth of the agro-food, textile and steel industries and the banking sector, the population suffered because agricultural production for internal consumption stagnated (Guerra 1988).

It was only by means of mobilisation that a small and well-organised section of the popular classes of Mexican society was able make its demands for social rights a matter of national concern. The southern revolutionary army led by Emiliano Zapata led a sustained battle for indigenous and peasant demands for land elaborated under the *Plan de Ayala* in 1910. But it was the miners at the Cananea copper mines that proudly claim to have initiated the Revolution. Unprotected from the boom and bust economy of the mining industry, hundreds of Mexican miners were laid off from Cananea and from many other mines in 1906–1907. Miners faced horrendous working conditions as well as mine disasters claiming the lives of many men. The injustices were topped off by the fact that the company paid higher wages and benefits to American workers (Ruíz 1976, 8). Joblessness faced miners in all regions. While the mining industry was facing a crisis due to the international prices of copper, over-capacity in the textile industry also created much unemployment at the same time. The Cananea workers' strike, along with the of the textile workers of Rio Blanco, and the Railway workers, opened up space for popular mobilisation beginning in 1906 which continued beyond the defeat of Porfirio Díaz in 1911 (Guerra 1988).

The Revolution began when, in October 1910, Francisco Madero issued his *Plan de San Luis Potosí* and called for a general uprising in support of liberal political freedoms. With support from local armies across the country, Madero led a popular insurrection that defeated the federal army in a matter of months. In May 1911, Díaz resigned as President, was sent into exile with Madero assuming the Presidency after elections in the autumn. As a result of the profound social polarisation that arose during the *Porfiriato*, the restrained Revolutionary program which Madero brought to the Presidency was to cause his undoing. Not only did the government have to contend with the forces of counter-revolution and restoration, but it was unable, or unwilling, to respond to the generalised dissatisfaction with the patterns of land tenure on the part of the peasants. Nor did it have much to say about the labour relations that depended upon de facto indentured labour in the mines, textile factories and agricultural estates. Madero soon found himself fighting new rebellions and relied upon General Victoriano Huerta to quell the conflict (Muñón 1982).

It was not, however, this internal struggle over the course of the Revolution, but the active intervention of the United States, that ended the first interval in the Mexican Revolution. On 22 February 1913, President Madero was assassinated by order of General Huerta, with the explicit support of the United States Ambassador to Mexico, Henry Lane Wilson (Camín and Meyer 1993, 34–5). The United States government and other foreign interests, as well as the most reactionary forces within the country supported the coup d'état (Tuñón 1982). The new administration of Woodrow Wilson that took office in the United States less than a month after Madero was shot, however, was unconvinced that Huerta would be able to deliver stability.

The second interval in the Mexican Revolution surged into motion with Venustiano Carranza's declaration that he would avenge the death of his fellow *Coahuilense* by mounting a campaign against Huerta's illegitimate regime. Carranza issued the *Plan de Guadalupe* in March 1913. The *Plan de Guadalupe* rejected Huerta's regime and those state governors who had accepted him. The *Plan* affirmed Carranza's leadership of the Constitutional Army and gave him executive powers to call elections. The call from the State of Coahuila was supported by the armies of Generals Pablo Gonzalez of Nuevo Leon, Àlvaro Obregón of Sonora and Francisco Villa of Chihuahua. These forces, although relatively autonomous entities, saw themselves as part of a larger effort to return Mexico to a legitimate Constitutional order. In the south, indigenous peasant forces continued their struggles for land reform. Over the course of 18 months, these armies fought back against Huerta's forces and caused their surrender in August 1914, but not before the United States had once again intervened in the affairs of its southern neighbour. As the country plunged into a massive effort to oust the military government, relations between the US and Mexican administrations deteriorated quickly. The United States government was soon looking for a new solution to the 'Mexican Situation'. The US Marine Corps assaulted the port of Veracruz on 21 April 21 1914 and stayed for six months. The intervention was not supported by the Constitutionalists or the *Zapatistas* and over the months of occupation, the administration of Woodrow Wilson was opposed by the Revolutionary forces.

The third Revolutionary interval may be characterised as the struggle of popular forces to define the politics of the Revolution. It began as the Constitutionalists prepared to take power in Mexico City in July 1914. The divisions between the Revolutionary forces became untenable. Carranza's self-imposition as First Chief of the Constitutionalist Forces was disputed by Villa, and the *Zapatistas* adamantly refused to accept that a restatement of the liberal guarantees of the 1857 Constitution would be the only result of the Revolution. It became clear that some sort of negotiation would have to resolve the issues that divided the victorious armies in order to prevent the imminent eruption of civil war. After negotiation, a final attempt at a peaceful settlement between the anti-Huerta forces was organised for the Convention of Aguascalientes during October and November 1914.

The attempt failed. The Convention split apart and Carranza's Constitutionalist forces departed the meeting. The *Zapatistas* and the *Villistas*, now known as the *Convencionistas*, forged a provisional alliance based on the principals of the *Plan de Ayala*, Zapata's program for agrarian reform and *ejidal* rights. The subsequent, and indeed substantive, discussion of the Convention addressed issues of political and social reform including land reform, resources and monopolies, suffrage and fair elections, trade union rights, education and the Church.

In these discussions, argues Richard Roman, the *Zapatistas* appeared as radical agrarian anarchists, who favoured state intervention to equalise power of workers and capitalists. The *Villistas*, in the company of other northern armies, demonstrated strongly conservative and elitist tendencies within their ranks. They spoke against mass electoral participation, in favour of private property and supported similar positions in the debates on the rights to trade union association, strike and boycott. Roman argues that Villa did not tend towards anti-imperialist statements because he was dependent on cattle trade and arm purchases from the United States, but neither did the *Zapatista* delegates made any mention of their opposition to foreign economic domination (Roman 1976). At the Convention at Aguascalientes, it was agreed that the large landholdings ought to be divided up according to the right of peasants to own land. The Convention opposed resource and industrial monopolies. It supported universal male suffrage, the right of trade union recognition and the right to strike. It rejected the Church's role in education (Roman 1976). Thus prepared with a governing program, the Convention travelled to Mexico City with the advancing armies.[4] At first, it appeared that the Carranza would not be able to defeat the opposition from the *Villista* and *Zapatista* forces as they arrived in Mexico City in the first week of December 1914. The *Carranzistas* retreated to Veracruz.

The fourth Revolutionary interval began as links between a newly emerging state and civil society were forged by pitting workers against peasants. As he prepared to retake Mexico City from internal exile, Carranza attempted to construct alliance with the war-stricken sectors of civil society. He had not been successful at gaining popular support solely through military victories. In an attempt to gather mass support for the Constitutionalist cause, Carranza's forces conceived of an economic and social program which included limited agrarian and labour law reform. As part of this program, General Obregón was asked to call upon the *Casa del Obrero Mundial* (COM) to organise workers into 'Red Battalions' to defeat the opposing forces.

---

4   For more information on the different phases of the Convention, see Roman (1976, 5–7, 24–5, 36).

For this loyalty, they were guaranteed the right to organise within Constitutionalist territories (Niemeyer 1974). The COM was the largest labour organisation of the time but it was a loosely organised anarcho-syndicalist association. By signing an agreement with the representatives of the Constitutionalist forces on 17 February 1915 it abandoned its anarchism and independence (Freyre Rubio 1983, 65). With the aid of the Red Battalions, the Constitutionalist forces succeeded in fighting back the *Villistas* and *Zapatistas*, and Carranza assumed power by mid-1915.

The bloodiest period in the Revolution took place during 1915. From mid-1915 onwards, Carranza and Obregón exerted punishing blows on the retreating armies until the autumn when Villa remained in control of only relatively small area of his native Chihuahua. The *Zapatistas*, who had continued their program of land reform in their occupied territories during most of 1915, were brutally defeated at the hands of Carranza's forces in Morelos within 12 months. The early summer of 1916 saw the execution of 132 men, 112 women and 42 children as a lesson given by the victors to Tlaltizapan, the home town of the *Zapatistas* (Camín and Meyer 1993, 61).

The formation of the Red Battalions in the service of Carranza's campaign against Zapata represented a determined strategy to foment divisions between workers and peasants. The peasant armies who occupied Mexico City were no match for the urban industrial workers who were 'in their own home' (Hellman 1983, 19). Yet it was not long until the alliance between the state and labour was proved illusory. The Red Battalions were dissolved by Carranza in January of 1916 and Carranza's brutal anti-worker sentiments became evident during the 'Big Strike of 1916'.

This strike was sparked by the demands of the Labour Federation of Mexico City (*Federación Sindical del Distrito Federal*) for payment of all wages in gold or in hard currency, due to the fact that the Constitutionalist bills in circulation since the beginning of Carranza's term were not held in any confidence. Having been refused, the workers went on strike under the leadership of the Electrical workers union. The union cut all electricity to the Federal District and neighbouring states on July 31. At this point the labour leadership was called to an audience with Carranza. The First Chief threatened them with the 1862 *Law Against Traitors* and the leadership was arrested on the spot. Carranza issued a decree on August 1st against all those who incited, supported, counselled, took part in, approved, defended, discussed or attended meetings about the suspension of labours. These offences were all punishable by death.[5] The anti-Carranza reaction was so swift in its condemnation of these measures that the leaders did not face the death penalty, but were subjected to lengthy prison sentences instead.

Back in Chihuahua by March of 1916, the *Villista* forces raided Columbus, New Mexico in retaliation for the US recognition of Carranza's government. Immediately, Woodrow Wilson responded. During the spring of 1916, Mexico was invaded by a force of 12,000 National Guards who came in search of Villa. The members of the National Guard had moved into Chihuahua by mid-May to the San Miguel Ranch,

---

5   For the full text of Carranza's decree, see Moreno (1967).

200 miles south of El Paso.[6] The US forces remained in Mexico for nearly one year.

In the autumn of 1916, the *Casa del Obrero Mundial* was shut down by the government (Lerner and Ralsky 1976, 46). By this point, it appeared that the creation of a stable resolution was not in the offing. No social consensus prevailed. Rather, there was a dramatic polarisation of social forces, as well as the exclusion of popular forces from the Carranza government. The Constitutional question was still outstanding and Carranza sought legitimacy for his authoritarianism by means of the Constitutional project. It was in the unexpected resolution of that issue that sustenance for the new Revolutionary state was found.

The Constituent Congress of 1916–1917

The Constituent Congress has retained it place in Mexican history precisely because it did effect a substantive expansion of the liberal guarantees in the Constitution of 1857. The Constitution of 1917 became an expression of the Revolutionary Nationalist project in the areas of labour rights, national ownership of resources, land tenure, education and church–state relations. It is the story of constitution-making which gives us insight in to the role of *caudillismo* which went beyond the conflict between strong leaders on the battlefield. In this process of Constitution-making, *caudillismo* meant the exclusion of the defeated *caudillos*, negotiations and alliance-building between the President and leaders of other sectors; an ideological effort to overcome class conflict by 'Mexicanising' and 'modernising' structures of production; and the institutionalisation of social conservatism and gendered ideas about the family.

On 12 September 1916, General Carranza called for a Constituent Congress which would be held at the end of the year in order to reform three Articles of the 1857 Constitution which referred to individual liberties, and affirm his own *Plan de Guadalupe* (see Moreno 1967, 21). Given Carranza's record during the Revolution, there were few reasons to suppose the Constituent Congress would be able to address the broad social and economic issues facing the country at the beginning of 1917. Carranza continued to hold onto his position of authority through his military power and control over Mexico City and the centre of the country. Despite his self-designation as a defender of the Constitution, on more than one occasion, Carranza contravened it. He did so again by calling for Constitutional reform before holding elections.

The oppositional *Convencionistas*, with their transitional program of government, were excluded from participation at these Constitutional talks. Labour leaders were excluded as well. The peasant and rural popular forces were defeated by divisions fomented between worker and peasant organisations, and the workers had been marginalised in turn. Carranza lacked popular support and had continued to

---

6   The attack against the Villista forces was conducted by heavily armed men in three Dodge touring cars. General George S. Patton Jr. led the first motorised attack in US history and announced: 'We couldn't have done it with horses. The motorcar is the modern warhorse' (as cited in Gelderman 1981; see also Wilkie and Michaels 1969, 35).

crush opposition in areas where dissent might do the most damage Delegates to the Congress would be selected by those 'who had proved with actual deeds, their adherence to the Constitutionalist cause' (Niemeyer 1951, 35–7; see also Roman 1976, 62). Neither was there to be any representatives from those geographical areas controlled by Villa or Zapata. With no support from the organised labour movement, there was little prospect that significant gains would be made on Constitutional reform. On 1 December 1916 when the Congress began, it did not appear that the Constituent Congress would provide much of a basis for any lasting Revolutionary social compromise.

Given these antecedents, it is surprising that the *Carrancistas* were moved beyond their initial limited constitutional program. In fact, they were pushed by a well-articulated modernising view within the Assembly despite Carranza's efforts to produce a quiescent Assembly. In the course of this debate, the *Carrancistas* recognised that any presidential contender would not be able to rely solely on the defence of legality and constitutionalism, underwritten by military power and violence. The country was in too much economic and social turmoil for that. In response to the challenge, the *Carrancistas* resuscitated a version of their 'Legal Project on Labour Contracts' and submitted it to Congress as 'Article 123: Of Labour and Social Provision'.

Article 123 grew out of that period in the Revolution when Carranza faced exile in Veracruz. As outlined above, the *Carrancistas* had successfully negotiated an alliance with the workers in the Casa Obrera Mundial (COM) by offering limited labour rights in exchange for their support in forming Red Battalions to fight the peasants.[7] After the defeat of the *Zapatistas* at the hands of the Red Battalions, law professor José Natividad Macías was sent to the United States to observe working conditions, visit plants and conduct interviews with both labour and management. While there, he collected documentation on US labour legislation and studied the legislation of England, France and Belgium and prepared a labour code that was never officially proclaimed (see Niemeyer 1974, 113–14). When Carranza ran into opposition at the Congress, the intellectuals in his group were convinced the modest proposals in the Veracruz labour code of 1915 could be presented to the Assembly. Through a process of negotiation, these proposals were quickly reworked into Article 123 during December of 1916 by a small committee of the Congress and accepted by the Assembly.

Article 123 and World Order

Article 123 did not emerge out of the national dynamics of the Mexican Revolution only but was influenced by the international context as well. As Hector Aguilar Camín and Lorenzo Meyer argue, the first elected president of the Revolution had been assassinated because he was perceived to be unable to protect US foreign investment (Camín and Meyer 1993, 34–5). The fact is that the United States occupied Mexico on two occasions during the course of the Revolution and there was a serious debate in the United States about the merits of mounting a full-scale intervention during the

---

7   The *Casa Obrera Mundial* (COM) was formed in 1912 (see Carr 1976, 47).

Revolution. US troops remained in Mexico during the Constituent Congress. This had the effect of reinforcing nationalism within the Constitutional project.

There was a second and very important international dimension to Constitution building in Mexico that arose out of the most modern and optimistic assumptions of industrialists at the turn of the century. When the Constitutionalists studied production and labour relations in the United States and Europe, they engaged with the experiments in modern labour relations in other more industrialised countries. In the United States, in the early years of the twentieth century a discourse of progressive capitalism offered support for the argument that the power relations between labour and capital could be balanced if both recognised their mutual interests in the success of the enterprise. The productive industrial enterprise was seen to depend, in part, on the family and on women's domestic labour. In many respects, Article 123 embodied the progressive assumptions of a productive system that was being implemented in the factories of the United States.

One of the most important advocates of these ideas was none other than Henry Ford. During the period 1914–1920, the 'world's first billionaire' promoted profit-sharing with his employees. He built schools, offered bonuses, organised credit for workers' housing and took an interventionist and paternalistic interest in workers' families and community. This was done within the context of a highly productive system that was streamlined, efficient, profitable and modern. Of course that experience was watched closely by international observers.

In January 1914, Henry Ford decreed the five-dollar-eight-hour day, to the astonishment of many of his contemporaries, and came to be known as a great social reformer. Overnight, Henry Ford distinguished himself for more than the rapid production of 'Tin Lizzies'. The Ford Motor Company explicitly substituted profit sharing for demands around industrial democracy promoted by the labour movement. As Ford said:

> The average employee in the average industry is not ready for participation in the management. He is ready for participation in the profits as I have suggested. An industry, at this stage of our development, must be more or less of a friendly autocracy... Every industry that ever got any where at all has been a little monarchy, the leadership belonging to the leader simply because he can lead. That happens even in a democracy. Indeed, real democracy gives leadership its greatest opportunity. (Stidger 1923, 194–5)

Thus, Henry Ford was able to confront worker resistance to the intensification of labour and bureaucratic management that was manifested in high levels of absenteeism and turn-over, while undermining labour militancy.[8]

Under the new five-dollar-day, workers' wages were not actually increased. Workers were entitled to receive a percentage of company profits in addition to their wages, at the rate of about $2.50 per day but this entitlement depended upon their passing a series of tests set by the new Sociological Department. The Department was responsible for sending investigators into the workers' homes to ensure that the worker was supporting and living with his family, and that unmarried workers

---

8   For an excellent analysis of the emergence of Ford's industrial system during the Highland Park years, see Meyer (1981).

were supporting dependents and living moral lives. Workers were prohibited from smoking and drinking, both on and off shift. Their wives were given 'helpful hints' on frugal homemaking and were explicitly prohibited from taking on borders. Ford is quoted as saying:

> There are thousands of men out there in the shop who are not living as they should. Their homes are crowded and unsanitary. Wives are going out to work because their husbands are unable to earn enough to support the family. They fill up their homes with roomers and boarders in order to help swell the income. It's all wrong- all wrong. It's especially bad for the children. They are neglected from necessity. Now, these people are not living in this manner as a matter of choice. Give them a decent income and they will live decently and will be glad to do so. (Marquis 1923, 152–3; see also Nevins and Hill 1954, 580)

Women and male clerical workers were prohibited from entering into the profit-sharing plan.

Ford is credited with having built complete villages with houses, schools, chapel, firehouse, hospital and commissary in the regions where the company held mines, factories or rubber plantations. It would be a gross exaggeration to suggest that the Ford Motor Company was so benevolent as to provide all workers with housing, for Ford's philanthropy was piecemeal and charitable at best. Neither was it evident that Ford considered these activities an *a priori* responsibility of government. In fact, it is more likely to find him quoted in favour of the privatisation of schools, fire departments and prisons. His belief in private initiative, productive capital and innovation was consummate and his individualism made him bitterly opposed to any collectivities, especially unions that would question his own role in the expansion of such an order.

When asked by the *Chicago Tribune* whether the Ford Motor Company would pay the wages of its workers called up from the Reserves, a Ford official indicated that not only would the soldiers not be paid but they would also lose their jobs if they went to fight in Mexico. The next day, the *Chicago Tribune* called Henry Ford an anarchist and suggested:

> Mr. Ford proves that he does not believe in service to the nation in the fashion a soldier must serve it. If his factory were on the southern and not the northern border, we presume he would feel the same way. We do not know precisely what he would do if a Villa band decided that the Ford strong boxes were worth opening and that it would be pleasant to see the Ford factories burn. It is evidence that it is possible for a millionaire just south of the Canadian border to be indifferent to what happens just north of the Mexican border'...If Ford allows this rule of his shops to stand he will reveal himself not as merely an ignorant idealist but as an anarchistic enemy of the nation which protects him in his wealth... The proper place for so deluded a human being is a region where no government exists except such as he furnishes, where no protection is afforded except such as he affords, where nothing stands between him and the rules of life except such defenses as he puts there. Such a place, we think, might be found anywhere in the state of Chihuahua, Mexico. Anywhere in Mexico would be a good location for the Ford factories. (Gelderman 1981, 184–5)

Ford sued for libel, asking for one million dollars in damages. He won the case and was awarded six cents by the Jury.

In many respects, Henry Ford came to signify the most optimistic elements of American liberalism at the beginning of the twentieth century. He was an internationalist in the tradition of those industrialists who argued that the US would secure international stability only through export of a productive system not by diplomatic means, nor by war. He advocated free trade and industrial development in Mexico:

> We mustn't go down there with a rifle. We must go down there with the plow, the shovel and the shop. If we could put the Mexican peon to work, treating him fairly and showing him the advantage which is sure to come from working fairly and treating his employers fairly the Mexican problem would disappear from the continent as steam fades from the windowpane. There would be no more talk of revolution. Villa would become a foreman, if he has brains. (Gelderman 1981, 184–5)

In 1925, when Henry Ford opened the first Ford plant in Mexico, the President of the Republic guaranteed 'he would have no problem with labour unions' (Smith 1972, 258; see also Ruíz 1976, 3).

There was one important difference between the Mexican and US views on these issues. In the United States, these progressive capitalist ideas did not include the right to form unions or to strike. In Mexico, they did, but these rights were curtailed by the corresponding right of employers to form organisations and rely on the state to maintain social order. In granting these provisions Constitutional status, the Mexicans went farther than their northern counterparts. That is not surprising, however, given that the Constitution was the central legitimating tool of the governing generals. So too was it in keeping with the long tradition in Latin America of constitutionalism.

Through the internationalisation of ideas, *caudillismo* gained legitimacy for reconstruction through a vision of labour relations which would include an organic corporate understanding of society based on a natural gender division of labour; a moral code for workers as family members; the subordination of trade unions in an unequal structure of representation; an active role for employers in social reproduction; profit-sharing and an incentive for workers and employers to share interests in the company; foreign investment; as well as state intervention to maintain industrial peace and ensure labour militancy would not challenge employers' rights.

Rather than incorporate the well-articulated demands of the defeated social forces which reflected the actual productive and social characteristics of the country, the victors accepted the promise held out by the modernisers in the United States. Because of their defeat, and within the terms of *caudillismo*, neither the southern peasant led by Emiliano Zapata, nor the northern forces under the command of Francisco Villa were able to impose the terms of the settlement. Because of their challenge, there would be no simple transition to a hegemonic order. Indeed, the main achievement of the Revolution was due to the massive engagement of Mexican society in the period between 1910 and 1920, with the result that the idea of struggle remained in collective memory throughout the century. As Adolfo Gilly argues, the Constitution became the testament to the mass struggle, but it was not the most important aspect (Gilly 2005, 238). In Gilly's view, the impact of the Revolution was felt most deeply, not at the level of leadership, but by the Mexican people themselves: 'Feeling themselves to be the subject, no longer the mere object of history, they stored up a wealth of experience and consciousness that altered the whole country as it is *lived* by its inhabitants' (Gilly 2005, 339). As a formal declaration of a Revolutionary state, Article 123 of the Constitution was meant to be the centrepiece of the new productive regime. Whether or not it would ever be reflected in law or practice was a question that would be at the centre of future political struggle.

'Caudillismo', the President and the Labour Movement in the 1920s

In the immediate post-Revolutionary period which began in 1920, it was not the idealism of the Constitution, but the centralisation of power within the office of President which characterised state-labour relations. Immediately after the Revolution, the labour movement was in no position to challenge the government directly and the *Carrancista* state governors continued to repress the labour movement within their jurisdictions. Although Carranza did not oppose the founding Congress of the *Confederación Regional Obrera Mexicana* (CROM) in 1918, its existence remained precarious during the years of his government (Barbosa Cano 1980).

After Carranza was assassinated in 1920, the northern *caudillos* established a virtual presidential dynasty. Successive members of the 'Sonora Group' were the real power behind the presidency until General Lázaro Cárdenas came to the presidency in 1934. Labour was seen as a potential ally of the nationalist opposition that had been marginalised by large capital and the landed interests of the Carranza government (Barboso Cano 1980, 13). When Álvaro Obregón became president in 1921, the government took the labour movement into its governing coalition. The pact also resulted in the formation of the *Partido Laborista Mexicana* (PLM), the party of Obregón and the powerful President Plutarco Calles throughout the 1920s (Carr 1976).

The CROM, a long way away from the anarcho-syndicalist tradition of earlier labour movements, adopted a highly pragmatic approach to politics. Rather than build a broadly based movement of mobilised members, the CROM sought to incorporate itself within the state (Bensusán 1989, 10). From its inception, the CROM advanced its position as the official voice of labour and its leaders sought to assume key positions and influence within newly emerging state institutions (Freyre Rubio 1983, 13). Luís Morones, formerly of the anarcho-syndicalist *Casa del Obrero Mundial*, was designated the first General Secretary of the CROM and became the government's Secretary of Industry, Trade and Labour and a member of the cabinet (Ochoa Campos 1976, 43). With the support of the government, the CROM claimed a membership of 50,000 in 1920 to over 1,200,000 by the end of Obregón's term in office in 1924. It is important to note however, even according to CROM's figures, as many as 40 per cent of these members were peasants (Carr 1976, 132).

In the office of the presidency, Obregón continued to reassure employers, as well as the US government that he would not favour the interests of labour over those of capital, but would work to establish a balance of social forces. As a result, the alliance between Obregón and the CROM was a troubled one (Carr 1976, 132–3). The CROM was further challenged by the resurgence of anarcho-sindicalism in the creation of the

Confederación General de Trabajadores (CGT) in 1921.[9] During the Plutarco Elías Calles presidency (1924–1928), the CROM became embroiled in a series of conflicts with the government, as well as the CGT, that fractured its base of support and left it considerably weakened.

Almost immediately after being re-elected as Calles successor, Obregón was assassinated in 1928. Many *Obregónistas* accused the CROM of responsibility for the assassination, and in an effort to calm the crisis, Calles ensured that one of Obregón's group was named to replace him as provisional president. In what is usually referred to as the *maximato*, Calles continued to work from behind the scenes until Lázaro Cárdenas became president in 1934. Calles worked to create the ruling *Partido Nacional Revolucionario* (PNR) in 1929. The PNR was a decentralised body that institutionalised the alliance of regional *caudillos*, and served to strengthen the authority of the presidency. As well, Calles was responsible for establishing the juridical-institutional framework of the federal labour law (*Ley Federal Del Trabajo*, LFT) of August 1931. With this labour law, Calles brought the family-oriented paternalism of Article 123 together with the authoritarianism of the presidential *caudillismo*.

The CROM, out of official favour since the assassination of Obregón, did not join the new party. As government protection decreased, so too did the strength of the CROM (Lerner and Ralsky 1976, 84–87). The disaffiliation from the CROM of the *Federación Sindical de Trabajadores del Distrito Federal* led by Fidel Velázquez and four other union leaders in 1929 was the first in a series of ruptures that continued to weaken the Confederation. As dissatisfaction grew within the CROM, movements for union disaffiliation were supported by other union centrals (Carr, 1991, 128; Roxborough 1984, 16–17). Once the reform movement within the CROM left the organisation under the leadership of Vicente Lombardo Toledano in 1933, the CROM was weakened to such an extent that had to cede its position as the exclusive voice of labour to competing labour confederations.[10]

With the rise and fall of the fortunes of the CROM, we see the significance of *caudillismo* in relations between the President and trade union centrals. Labour's place within the emerging historic bloc was tenuous, and always a subordinate one. By the time Cárdenas came to power, the CROM had been ousted. It had shown itself to be neither a legitimate voice of labour nor an effective means of controlling workers' demands. In the newly emerging Revolutionary Nationalist state, *caudillismo* characterised the relationship between the Presidency and the labour

---

9   The CGT was formed in February 1921; during its first congress in September of the same year, it decided to leave the Red International (Freyre Rubio 1983, 84).

10   From 26 October to 31 October 1933, the dissident groups organised a congress forming a new proletarian organisation, the *Confederación General de Obreros y Campesinos de México*. The CGOCM was formed by the *Confederación Regional Obrera Mexicana (CROM) depurada* (purified); the *Confederación General de Trabajadores* (CGT); la *Confederación Nacional de Electricistas*; *la Confederación sindicalista de Obreros y Campesinos del Estado de Puebla*; *la Federación Sindical del Estado de Querétaro;*and *la Federación Local de Trabajadores y la Federación Local de Trabajadores y la Federación Campesina del Distrito Federal* (Freyre Rubio 1983, 88).

movement. This relationship was institutionalised in the party system, but it was also constructed within the Federal Labour Law of 1931.

The Federal Labour Law and Representation

In the Federal Labour Law of 1931, there are three levels at which the masculine power of *caudillismo* was inscribed. These were elaborated in the 1) federal executive power over union recognition; 2) centralisation of representative functions within union executive bodies; 3) disciplining of the worker-father and the dependence of women and children on his 'social provision'. In this law we have a clear example of the way in which institutional power can be used by powerful groups of men to subordinate other groups of men and women. The impact on working-class politics was profound.

The Federal Executive Powers of Recognition

Labour law, which had been the responsibility of the states, was transferred to the Federal government in 1929 by means of a constitutional amendment of the power to proclaim a Federal Labour Law. One of the most important aspects of this jurisdictional shift meant that the regionally based tripartite Conciliation and Arbitration Boards became subject to federal authority. Almost immediately afterwards the Department of Labour was separated from the Secretary of Industry, Commerce and Labour (Freyre Rubio 1983, 107–9). The *Junta Federal de Conciliación y Arbitraje* (Federal Conciliation and Arbitration Board) was designated one of the central institutions of the labour relations regime which was subject to the power of the federal executive by the *Secretaría del Trabajo* (Department of Labour). While the national character of labour law conferred most responsibility for labour relations on the federal institutions, the structure of the Federal Board was mirrored at the state level through local Conciliation and Arbitration Boards.

This was designed as a highly centralised system. The presence of the federal executive power was felt in every dimension of labour regulation in Mexico and because of the way in which *caudillismo* was reflected in state-society relations, state governors extended presidential prerogatives through the control they exercised over the decisions of local boards (Fuentes 1994, 37–8). Unions were required to keep the labour authorities up to date on any changes in leadership or changes to their constitutions within ten days of their occurrence, with quarterly reports on membership and on other matters as requested (Fuentes 1994, 47).

The labour boards were comprised of three members meant to represent the interests of labour, capital and the state. If a union wished to apply for registration, it made its application at the labour board. If a union wished to hold a strike, it made an application in which it proved its objective to '[s]eek the equilibrium between the diverse factors of production, harmonising the rights of labour with those of capital' (LFT Artículo 450:I 1993, 97).

If the union leadership was changed in an election, or at any other time, the labour board was to be notified. The union had to receive a document stating that the Board had 'taken note' that the leadership has changed for it to become official. The Federal Labour Board became the epitome of a corporatist institution. The decisions reached there had a significant effect on the character of the labour relations regime, given that the majority of labour actions were mediated through this tripartite institution. Labour autonomy became highly restricted as a result.

To exist legally, a union had to obtain registration by the Labour authorities (Fuentes 1994, 42). The Federal Arbitration and Conciliation Board was made responsible for the approval or rejection of applications. As a result, the Board could make it nearly impossible for workers to organise. The law stated that an application for registration must, among other things, include the employee numbers, names and addresses of the leadership and all union members, as well as the names and address of the company. The Board could require, in addition, that the union have the company prepare or stamp the forms to verify that these workers were indeed employed by the company (Fuentes 1994, 45). Such demands were coercive, threatened members with instant dismissal and, in effect, curtailed the right to association.

In fact, the LFT of 1931 contained the most minimal requirements for authentic representation of workers' rights. A union or executive committee could be registered without any indication of support from the membership and there was nothing that would cause a General Secretary of a union to call a strike or desist from doing so, according to the wishes of the membership.[11] Union assemblies might never be held and it was possible for workers never to have met their union leadership.

A contract was negotiated only by the officially recognised union. If there were a number of unions in the workplace, then the one that had the majority would sign the collective agreement, provided it was officially recognised by the labour authorities. If there was a dispute over which union was entitled to negotiate the collective agreement, challengers went before the Labour Board for judgement on the matter. After an initial hearing, the process allowed for a membership vote to be taken in order to determine which union they wished to belong to and thus, who will hold the title to the collective agreement. Although there were official limits on how long this process should take, there were actual delays of two years or more. These votes were not taken in secret. For plebiscites such as these, the Labour Board named the place and date of the vote. Usually they took place in the workplace. Only those workers who attended the meeting could vote and only those who were valid employees, except for those fired after the appeal was made, could vote (Fuentes 1994, 78).

The right to strike was defined as a collective right in the Constitution, but the Federal Labour Law elaborated the way in which this right came to be exercised. The Federal Labour Law denied approval for a strike if, in the opinion of the labour authorities, the petition was not made according to proper procedures (Fuentes 1994, 110–11). 'Proper' applications were to be directed towards the company, describe the petition, warn and give notice as to when the strike would be. It had to justify the legal basis of the strike. If these requirements were not met to the Board's satisfaction, it called the strike 'non-existent' once it was underway.

---

11 These practices are in contravention of International Labour Organisation Convention 87 on 'Union Liberties' signed by Mexico on 4 July 1950 (see Fuentes 1994, 40–41).

A strike could be called non-existent if less than 50 per cent of the members were on strike or if workers were deemed not to have tried 'to seek the equilibrium between the factors of production.' Solidarity strikes could also be called non-existent. If the strike was declared non-existent, workers had to return to work within 24 hours, or else all collective agreements were considered broken (Fuentes 1994, 113–14). If the employer became bankrupt, all labour relations were ended, and this put an end to any strike occurring at the time (Fuentes 1994, 111–12).

Before a strike was held, labour authorities arranged an audience with the parties for purposes of conciliation. The union had to attend the hearing, but there were no sanctions against management if it did not. The law stated that the labour authorities could compel the company to respond to the demands of the workers. If the strike was considered 'existent', it could go on indefinitely and the union was the only party that could ask for arbitration by the Board. At the petition of the union, a hearing was to be held within 48 hours at the Labour Board, to determine whether the union or management was responsible for the strike. If management was the cause, then it was obliged to comply with the petitions of the workers and pay lost wages (Fuentes 1994, 116–17).

By means of the Federal Labour Law, the executive of the federal government remained in control over union representation. As a highly centralised political system built on the hierarchy of groups of men developing alliances and exerting power over other men and women, *caudillismo* was institutionalised in the law and infused the regulation of labour relations in Mexico.

Centralisation of Power in Union Executives

The centralisation of representative functions within union executive bodies was set down in the Federal Labour Law. This had the effect of reproducing *caudillismo* within the union leadership, consolidating the power of union leadership over its members, and effectively centralising power within the organisation through the union's own constitution. For instance, the right to association was guaranteed in subsection XVI of Article 123, but the Federal Labour Law diminished that collective right and permitted the transfer of all legal powers of representation to one person. Article 376 of the LFT established that 'the representation of the union will be exercised through its General Secretary or whoever is designated by the leadership (Fuentes 1994, 41). This could mean, for example, that the General Secretary could designate a labour lawyer to stand instead of the union executive.

Moreover, the Federal Labour law did not require unions to prepare financial reports for their members, nor was the employer required to offer any account of the monies given to the union leadership (Fuentes 1994, 39). Union dues were automatically deducted from workers' paycheques by the employer and given over to the union. As stated in its union constitution, Ford workers paid one per cent of their basic salary in union dues. With this arrangement, the union had the security of numbers as well as a stable financial base, but this too, was a contradictory provision of labour law. While it ensured the union had resources to carry out its work, the National Union would customarily gather the resources and, at its discretion, disburse money to the locals, rather than the other way around. Money was also allocated through the official union hierarchy to the governing party (Sindicato Nacional de Trabajadores de Ford Motor Company 1989).

One principal claim of labour law was that workers were entitled to continuous improvement in their conditions of work. It was explicitly stated that a collective agreement that diminishes workers' rights or is less advantageous than the previous agreement, may not be negotiated (Fuentes 1994, 75). Yet almost no union included provisions allowing workers to vote on the revision or signing of the collective agreements. Neither was there any requirement that votes be taken secretly and very few unions have ever had union constitutions with that provision.[12] In the Federal Labour Law, the task of labour representation was moved into the offices of the union bureaucracy. As a result, *caudillismo* was reproduced within the labour institutions themselves.

Under the Federal Labour Law, the union was responsible for providing the employer with the names of workers from which the employer would make their hiring. Relatives of current employees were given priority and trade unions regarded this right to an 'inclusion clause' in the collective agreement, as one which protected their integrity as a working-class organisation. The collective agreement at Ford, for example, stated that 'the union will provide job applications to all applicants recommended by whoever works in the company', while the Ford workers union Constitution indicated that applicants who were sons of union members would be given priority (see Meza Ponce 1984, 36). Upon reaching the age of 16, these young men would work on simple tasks in all parts of the plant during school holidays, under the assumption that this would prepare them for their future and eventual permanent contract. With this provision, fathers could offer their sons a 'patrimony'. In the words of one worker, 'Because I am not rich, the best that I can give my son is a good job.' Further,

> It is not just that sons are like their fathers, or 'from such a staff such a splinter.' Above all else, it is that the company's mechanisms of control will be strengthened by the control that the father exercises over his son. The father advises his son or nephew on how to behave and the latter, in order not to deceive him and not wanting to 'tarnish' the recommendation, behaves appropriately. In this way he integrates himself into the Ford Family and to the factory system. The father puts his best foot forward so that his son can enter and the son responds with his labour for his father and the company. (Meza Ponce 1984, 36; Translated by the author)

Both fathers and sons were disciplined by their shared relation to the employer and their need to remain employed. The power of the union executive and bureaucracy was used to quell dissent among union members even before workers became engaged in the hiring process.

Worker-father and Social Provision

The third way in which *caudillismo* came to characterise representation in the Federal Labour Law was in the construction of the 'individual worker' as the 'worker-

---

12 The *Instituto Mexicano de Seguro Social* (IMSS) is a rare exception and even then, ratification is taken by indirect vote. Union delegates vote on the collective agreements (Fuentes 1994, 75–7).

father' disciplined by his subordinate position *vis-à-vis* more powerful men at the point of production. The labour law reinforced the male worker's responsibility for receiving a social wage which in another context might have been extended on the basis of citizenship. Insofar as the family became highly dependent upon the benefits extended to him, the worker-father had great incentive not to challenge the trade union leadership and its relationship with the employer and the state.

Since 'social provision' was understood to rest in the realm of labour relations, the employment status of working-class men had an impact upon women, children and the extended family. Essential social services were not extended on the basis of universal citizenship rights; access depended on whether the bread winner was employed in the public or private sector. The *Ley Federal Del Trabajo* (LFT) was the only labour law for all Mexico but because Constitutional Article 123 considered 'labour' and 'social provision' together, the LFT came to be associated with other laws including the national social security law, the national worker housing fund and health and safety laws.[13]

This construction of the worker-father increased the dependence of family members not considered 'workers', while exerting a disciplinary effect on those who were employed. Once a worker became unemployed, social benefits were lost and since there was no unemployment insurance, the loss of a job meant economic destitution for an entire family. Health care and housing rights were social rights based on the wage relationship. The lack of unemployment insurance in Mexico and the relatively good benefits derived from the social programs for a worker and family within the state corporatist mode therefore offered a powerful incentive for workers to remain employed.

The union played a role in determining whether or not workers had any job security. The union had the right to suspend workers from their jobs for a short period of time, or to suspend the union rights of a worker entirely. The power of the union leadership was strengthened both by their disciplinary powers and by the responsibilities of the worker-father. This point requires further elaboration. Under the federal labour law, an 'exclusion clause' could be negotiated in collective agreements. Again, following upon our earlier example, Ford workers losing their rights to union membership also lost their job, since all workers had to be union members. Workers could be expelled from the union only if two-thirds of the membership of a general assembly voted against the member and after the member had an opportunity to offer a defence. Nevertheless, each Ford workers' union Constitution included a list of conditions for which members could be automatically expelled. If a worker was expelled from the union for any reason, the company was required to fire that worker. In such cases, the employer was under no obligation to compensate the worker with a severance agreement.

The constitution of the National Union of Ford workers stated:

Members who commit the following misdeeds will be expelled from the Union, with the application of the Exclusion Clause:

---

13   The Federal Labour Law is comprised of 16 Chapters and over 1000 Articles. It is 460 pages long.

a) Contributing to the dissolution or the disorganisation of the Union.

b) Misuse of Union funds.

c) For free or paid espionage in the service of the Company.

d) For unfounded attacks on the prestige or the dignity of the union.

e) Working against strike movements, or activities undertaken by the Union.

f) Betraying the trust of workers after being designated to a Union Commission.

(Sindicato Nacional de Trabajadores de Ford Motor Company 1989; Translated by the author)

Any one of these 'misdeeds' certainly would be antithetical to the principals of trade unionism, but the ability of the union to ensure the firing of any union member through the application of the exclusion clause was usually based on highly politicised factors. As a result, the exclusion clause was a very effective instrument, whether it was used or simply threatened, against oppositional movements within unions.

Taken together, then, the inclusion and exclusion clauses were mediated through the patriarchal relations of the family and the social relations that constituted a male workforce at the core of the industrial model. They were part of a larger social structure in which labour relations were intertwined with the gendered relations of *caudillismo*. One implied the other and remained at the heart of the Revolutionary Nationalist state.

Gendered Norms in the Federal Labour Law

Throughout the mid and late part of the twentieth century, the Federal Labour Law continued to be a contradictory site of contestation. To the extent that we may speak of social compromise after Cardenas' *sexenio*, it is in large part because of the success of the ruling groups in constructing a more general and shared set of norms based in Revolutionary principles. This framework meant that the dominant parties could agree that the Constitution embodied the general goals of the Revolution and the nation in general. It protected the country from foreign domination. It reaffirmed the family as the basic social unit. It elaborated a wide range of rights that would be realised over time. The debate among social forces took place within this framework. Labour Law, rather than Constitutional Article 123, kept the 'balance' by preventing an autonomous and representative labour movement from emerging.

The right to association was accepted by both labour and management, within the discourse of 'equilibrium'. The provisions for 'inclusion' and 'exclusion' gave unions a significant role to play in labour relations. As well, the collective interests of workers appeared to served by giving unions control over hiring lists and union activities. Unions played an important role in the construction of masculine power within the union and in the working-class family.

Contributing to the argument that the Mexican state was overseeing the construction of a just Revolutionary order were the strict sanctions that the LFT was meant to level against workers who were mistreated or fired unjustly by their employers. Workers were entitled to a significant percentage of annual profits and severance agreements were generous. Both labour and employers were permitted to shut down operations under certain conditions, so employers could not easily discredit this provision by arguing that the right to strike disadvantaged them in particular. Workers, however, fiercely defended their right to shut down operations entirely during a strike. So too did workers defend their individual rights to the labour standards set down in the LFT. Here again, we may recognise the persistent assumption of the importance of the Revolutionary worker-father in relation to his family. Social reproduction was shared by the state and the employer. Ostensibly, workers were paid by the day according to the needs of their families and conditions of the regional economy. Employers were responsible to pay them on their day of rest as well as on the days they worked. As well, part of the social compromise depended upon the state's taking responsibility for other costs of reproduction, including subsidised housing.

Furthermore, because important guarantees in the LFT, such as the right to sectoral bargaining, were left unfulfilled there was a certain amount of legitimacy to the claim that the law itself was not so bad. Either it was un-enforced, would be enforced at some point in the future or was corrupted by the impunity of powerful men. As a result, the unfulfilled promises of the Federal Labour Law became constant rallying points for labour struggles. The expectation that social rights had a place in Mexican society was an idea that persisted in popular consciousness. Even in the official discourse of the most conservative Presidencies, the rights of the peasant, working and capitalist classes as they were regulated through the Constitution were a constant point of reference. The fact that the state had not lived up to its full responsibility to preserve and extend social rights was a matter which was acknowledged within the rubric of the Revolution that was ever becoming, ever present, and ever 'perfecting'.

Every labour mobilisation engaged with the institutional arrangements of Mexican corporatism and trade unions constantly moved within the legal and judicial terrain. The history of twentieth-century trade unionism in Mexico was conditioned by the specific way in which labour law was written and applied. As a legal framework, the Federal Labour Law was central to the history of contestation which, for almost 40 years, established the limits of stability in Mexico.

Cárdenas and the Corporatist Compromise

Caudillismo was consolidated in the labour movement as state development continued. Very soon after it was proclaimed, the Federal Labour Law (LFT) became entwined with the institutions of corporatist representation established by the government of Lázaro Cárdenas. After the LFT was promulgated, there continued to be a divergence between those labour rights declared in official discourse and legislation and the actual enjoyment of those rights by the working classes. With no legitimate body to represent the state interests to workers, union militancy was on the rise. The years following from the Constitutional Congress had been tumultuous ones marked by presidential assassinations and resignations, a civil war, negotiations over reparations to US interests harmed in the Revolution, a succession of presidencies thwarted by the manipulation of former president Plutarco Calles, and a world depression.[14] Labour discontent was

---

14 For a detailed discussion of these events, see Camín and Meyer (1993).

only one reason for the instability Cárdenas faced as he took power away from Calles in 1934.

At the heart of the social compromise that Lázaro Cárdenas forged was the promise that the working class was entitled to certain social guarantees and would receive them if it continued to lend its support to the state through the official labour organisations. Despite the increasing level of Revolutionary institutionalisation, this promise ensured that *caudillismo* would remain at the heart of the relationship between the President and the labour movement. It was also a promise made to the peasants, but their position within the social compromise was much more marginalised, and they felt the effects of state authoritarianism much more directly. But for labour, the promise of *caudillismo* made sense of the divergence between the rights proclaimed in the Constitution and the uneven extension of social rights during the early years of the Revolution. The relationship was institutionalised through forms of corporatist representation in the Revolutionary Nationalist state.

Under the presidency of Lázaro Cárdenas, the *Confederacion de Trabajadores de México* (CTM) was created in February 1936 as the institutional link between the working class and the *Partido Revolucionario Mexicano* (PRM) (Hellman 1983, 39). Many diverse labour organisations were brought together in Cárdenas' consolidation of the state during the 1930s. The CROM was much weakened by this point, but remained outside of the CTM. Unions that had disaffiliated from the CROM in protest over the continuing power of ex-president Calles formed the *Confederación General Obrera y Campesina de México* (CGOCM) in 1933. As the largest labour confederation in opposition to the CROM, the CGOCM disbanded itself at its second congress in 1936 to affiliate with the CTM. During 1936, the *Federación Nacional de Trabajadores del Estado* (FNTE) was formed and affiliated with the CTM. At the same time, Fidel Velázquez brought the *Federación de Trabajadores del Distrito Federal* into the new organisation. Velázquez soon became General Secretary of the CTM and remained in that position until his death in 1997. Along with the *Confederación Nacional Campesina* (CNC) and the *Confederación Nacional de Organizaciones Populares* (CNOP), grouping a variety of business, trade and professional organisations and, for a time, the military, the CTM was intended to build and maintain broad support for the ruling party (Hellman 1983).

Cárdenas dissolved the *Partido Nacional Revolucionario* (PNR) and formed a new party named the *Partido Revolucionario Mexicano* (PRM) in December 1937. Further institutional reordering ensued when, at the end of October 1938, the Secretary of the Interior called a Congress to remove state workers from the CTM and form the *Federación Sindical de los Trabajadores al Servicio del Estado* (FSTSE). Immediately afterwards a governmental decree compelled all state workers to join this Federation (Freyre Rubio 1983, 107–9). These changes gave the state increased control in defining the terms of labour regulation.

A further reorganisation of the party took place in 1946 when it became the *Partido Revolucionario Institucional* (PRI). Membership in the PRI was made mandatory for all CTM trade unionists. In exchange for its position at the head of the subordinated groups in society, the CTM was expected to deliver its membership in support of the ruling party. Over time this support became ritualised in May Day parades during which workers were compelled to march past the president or the governor at the presidential palace or state legislatures. Any worker failing to do so would be fined at least one day's pay and sometimes more. But, as we shall see below, this formal expression of support was the public expression of a much more profound power structure. Although it has been argued that the reorganisation of the ruling party along sectoral lines moved the party farther from a regionally based *caudillismo*, into a party with a broadly based mass organisation (Álvarez 1987, 48; see also Córdova 1990), the Revolutionary Nationalist institutions remained infused with *caudillismo* as the hegemonic masculinity.[15]

Women's Representation in Corporatism

In the 1920s, women's organisations included the *Consejo Feminista de México, Las Mujeres Libres* and the *Union Cooperativa 'Mujeres de la Raza'*, Women fought for legal equality with men, reforms to the divorce law, an end to fighting, and the vote. Other women's organisations were actively concerned with issues of child welfare, temperance and social reconstruction (Macías 1982). The reform of the Civil Code in 1927 did establish limited property rights for women, as well as juridical equality in some areas but still ensured that husbands could deny wives the right to work if it would affect their domestic responsibilities (Olcott 2005, 19). The women's movement gained strength in the early 1930s with a series of Congresses of Women Workers and Peasants calling for the vote for women. The women's movement was divided along familiar class lines and political tendencies which ranged from seeking the recognition of individual rights, to a more direct challenge to capitalism.

The Great Depression was very difficult for Mexican workers. In 1931, 1933 and 1934, Congresses of women workers and peasants from all political perspectives were organised to discuss the situation of women workers. The first Congress called for minimum wages and an eight-hour day. It called for women to be granted equal rights with men to acquire land under agrarian reform and that the government provide rural services. It further called for women to have the right to vote. The call for suffrage united women across political divisions, but by the time the Third National Congress of Women Workers and Peasants concluded, it was evident there would be no agreement between liberal and communist positions (Macías 1982).

During the Cárdenas *sexenio*, however, women's organisations united in the *Frente Único Pro Derechos de la Mujer* (FUPDM) in 1935. This organisation of intellectuals, professionals, teachers, Revolutionary veterans, women from unions and political parties counted 50,000 women and 800 organisations in its membership (Macías 1982, 127). Among the wide range of issues addressed by the women's united front, women demanded to be permitted employment in jobs such as the docks and the salt mines, traditionally considered men's work. They were opposed by the CTM (Olcott

---

15   In time, *charrismo* came to refer to the specific form that *caudillismo* took in the official labour institutions. *Charrismo* is a term that stems from the anti-communist official union leadership of the late 1940s. During this period, the government directly imposed new leaders in the railroad, petroleum and mine and metal workers unions. One of these, Jesús Díaz de León was known as *El Charro* because he dressed in the typical cowboy fashion. *Charro* now refers to the official union bureaucrats representing the state (La Botz 1992, 66).

2005, 117). By 1937, in response to the increasing militancy of women's organising, Cárdenas agreed to introduce legislation to modify Article 34 of the Constitution which would redefine citizens as those men *and women*, over 18 if married and over 21 if not, having the quality of being Mexican and living an honest life (Olcott 2005, 11). In exchange, the FUPDM integrated itself with the ruling party and the corporatist state structures. Between 1937 and 1938, the legislation was passed in all federal and state legislatures but in the end was not promulgated, nor published in the *Diario Oficial*. As a result the new definition of citizen did not become law. At this point in time, the ruling *Partido Revolucionario Mexicano* was gearing up for elections of the official candidate, Manuel Ávila Camacho. Within the ruling party, the argument for keeping women from voting was based on the fear that women would disproportionately vote for the conservative candidates supported by the Catholic Church (Tuñón 1987, 186). Mexican women were not, however, uniformly Catholic and women were involved in the movements led by both communists and anarchists in both rural and urban areas. They were active in teachers' unions and textile unions, but the leadership of the unions continued be led by men and the ideal of the male bread-winner was held on to by the trade union leadership (Olcott 2005, 117, 133). Through a long process of alliance building which served to undermine women's interests, *caudillismo* was used to propose a political alternative to democracy which subordinated women's fight for democracy to the officially-defined Revolutionary project.

It was not until after Miguel Alemán took power in the presidency in 1946 that the government looked for a broader base of legitimacy by deciding to grant women suffrage. Congress approved a reform of the Constitution permitting women to vote and be elected at the municipal level because, according to Alemán, 'the municipal level is that which has most contact with the interests of the family and that which is concerned most with the needs of the household and children' (see Tuñón 1987, 187). During the subsequent campaign for president of Ruíz Cortines, the candidate promised to introduce a Constitutional reform to give women the vote if the *Alianza de Mujeres de México* could gather 500,000 signatures from women in favour of the initiative. The campaign was successful and Ruíz Cortines took power in 1952. On 17 October 1953, women gained the rights of citizens to vote and to be elected to public office (Tuñón 1987, 189).

Throughout these years the PRI, ruled continuously and the institutions of the Party became inseparable from those of the state. Despite the inclusion of popular sectors, these institutional links tended to mean that economic development more closely reflected the interests of employers, rather than workers or other subordinated social forces. During this period, the Mexican state was enormously successful in surmounting the political challenges arising from the opposition. Electoral politics were not the site for contestation between social forces. The PRI extended *de facto* control over the party system and the power of the Presidency ensured the transition of the leadership of the nation from one administration to another. It was an authoritarian system in which dissent was, on one hand, incorporated through the discourse, practices and institutions of the state and, on the other, repressed when it became too threatening.

The antagonistic relations between social forces in Mexican society were not resolved in corporatism. Rather, the implications of this reorganisation of the ruling party reached deeply into state-society relations, insofar as it provided for the formation of mass organisations as the base of state power. In Mexican corporatism, as Arnaldo Córdova describes so clearly, 'that which exists is that which is organised; that which does not exist, is that which is not organised' (Córdova 1990, 389; Translated by author). It is not individual citizens, but organisations that are the political subjects in corporatism. Córdova argued that the PRI was the only national political actor not because Mexico has a one-party system, which it does not, but because the PRI was the only party based upon mass organisations (Córdova 1990, 390). Córdova's analysis offers an important insight into the importance of the CTM in structuring working-class politics in relation to the state, not only institutionally, but on questions of legitimacy and efficacy in relations with the state and employers (Córdova 1990, 397).

State Corporatism: A Masculinised Productive Mode

By the mid-twentieth century, the employers' role in social provision had given way to more clearly defined social relations regulated by the state, but the importance of the working-class family in the structure of production persisted. The institutions of labour law organised the terrain of labour struggle in which the gendered division of labour was strictly enforced. Women were excluded from the most favoured production mode in which the established male worker and the family wage were championed by the state. Here, I discuss the material basis of this mode by describing the origins of automobile production, which was chosen as a key industry within state corporatism.

The economic roots of state corporatism in Mexico are to be found in the Great Depression. During these years, mining production fell by 50 per cent and oil production by almost 20 per cent. These industries did not have many linkages to the rest of the domestic economy and the economic impact of the generalised downturn was not as severe as in those economies more open to international capital flows (Camín and Meyer 1993, 106). Yet the economy suffered and President Cárdenas' nationalist economic development strategies were supported by the dominant social classes. The nationalisation of the oil industry provided much of the economic basis and ideological legitimacy for the state-led developmental direction that Revolutionary Nationalism took in mid-century.

Although auto assembly had been established in Mexico as early as 1925, manufacturing did not emerge in the industry automatically or easily. The market for vehicles was small and the infrastructure needed to support their use slow to expand. In this early stage of production, vehicle parts were imported and assembled in small workplaces within the Federal District.[16] Here Mexican companies assembled automobiles for the internal market, usually under license from a foreign producer. There was no corresponding auto parts industry and technological advances were few. Official unionisation rates were close to 100 per cent in these years.

---

16 This is the first of three phases (or 'productive nuclei') and their central characteristics, as analysed by Arnulfo Arteaga (1985).

Between 1940 and 1960, the Mexican economy experienced what many external observers have called the 'Mexican Miracle'. In Mexico, this period is referred to as *desarollo establizador* (stabilised development). In these years the annual GNP growth averaged 6.3 per cent and growth in the industrial sector averaged 7.7 per cent (Bennett and Sharpe 1984, 200). The state corporatist mode underpinning economic growth depended upon an internal market among the upper and middle income groups supplied by a domestic manufacturing sector in consumer goods, both durable and non-durable goods. This may be described as an import-substitution industrialisation (ISI) strategy.

Much of this economic growth depended upon the intervention of the state. In 1947, the PRI government issued a decree limiting automotive imports to a ratio of each auto company's level of production. Tariffs on auto parts were reduced relative to those on assembled vehicles and companies were required to adhere to national content levels in vehicle production (Aguilar García 1982, 20). This policy developed the basis for import-substitution in the industry and increased the number of assembly plants in the country.

With the intention of deepening the effect of import-substitution policies, the government of President Adolfo López Mateos (1958–1964) focused on the development of the auto industry. López Mateos expected that the auto industry could become the catalyst furthering the development of the model into consumer non-durables and production did become well established. Auto manufacturing was expected to expand the possibilities for forward and backward linkages, increase employment and decrease foreign exchange losses (Bennett and Sharpe 1984, 202). While foreign investment would be necessary for such a project, the dominant view held that the state would be able to initiate a process of 'Mexicanisation' in the industry (Bennett and Sharpe 1984, 201). As a result, state policies supported the development of a national capitalist class.

This form of development in Mexico's productive capacity was supported by changes at the level of world order. As the strongest of the post-war economies and a leader in the politics of post-war reconstruction, the United States fostered the development of *Pax Americana* as a hegemonic world order. Immediately after the Second World War, US corporations tended to export their products to emerging markets, but as the war-torn economies recovered in the late 1950s and through the 1960s, US corporations, along with their Japanese and European counterparts, turned increasingly to direct foreign investments. The US automotive industry was built in tandem with the internationalisation of production brought about by the rise of foreign direct investment and the emergence of multinational corporations in the late 1950s and into the 1960s. This network of US firms that had extended throughout the world during the postwar period was based on the idea, central to hegemony, that the most efficient form of industrial production was that of Fordism.

By 1960, there were 17 auto assemblers and 41 car models available in Mexico. This contributed to an irrational productive structure given the size of the domestic market. A series of decrees and regulations between November 1960 and May 1961 led to the withdrawal of some producers from the market. During this period, 22 models of vehicles were taken out of production (Meza Ponce 1984, 28). In 1960, in an effort to increase efficiencies in the industry, the Inter-ministerial Committee for Planning and

Development of the Automobile Industry, led by the state development bank, *Nacional Financiera* (NAFIN) made a series of recommendations for a new automotive policy.[17] It recommended that companies be required to incorporate 60 per cent local content in the finished vehicles. It suggested that the number of companies in the market be limited so as to increase the economies of scale and it recommended that companies standardise parts and limit the number of models in the market in order to enable autoparts companies to organise longer production runs. The report also recommended that all companies have majority Mexican ownership.

The 1962 Automobile Manufacturing Decree did impose a 60 per cent local content requirement for assembly operations and it encouraged the development of the Mexican auto parts industry by limiting the vertical integration of auto producers. No assembler was allowed to manufacture parts except for engines and those parts produced before 1962. Consequently, production increased in the parts sector. After 1964, the importation of assembled engines was prohibited unless companies could indicate their plans for local production (Aguilar García 1982, 22). Foreign capital was not permitted to exceed 40 per cent in the parts industry (Bennett and Sharpe 1985, 127). Still, the Decree did not require the standardisation of parts, nor did it limit the number of companies producing in the market. Under the 1962 Decree, Ford and General Motors were the two foreign-owned companies to be approved for licence, followed by Nissan in 1964. Other companies approved to manufacture, included *DINA*, *Fábricas Auto-Mex, Impulsora Mexicana Automotriz, Promexa, Reo, Representaciones Delta* and *VAM*. These were entirely Mexican owned. Given the government's decision not to limit the number of producers, all of these companies could not survive the inefficiencies that were created (Bennett and Sharpe 1985, 148).

Mexican-owned assemblers did not fare well under the Decree, partly because they did not have the same access to credit and technology and their import costs were higher than their foreign competitors (Bennett and Sharpe 1985, 127). Soon afterwards, three of the Mexican-owned companies shut down and three others sold most of their equity to their foreign affiliates, leaving five foreign-owned assemblers (Ford, General Motors, Chrysler, Volkswagen, Nissan) and two state-owned companies (DINA, VAM). *Promexa* sold to Volkswagen in 1964. VAM sold 40 per cent of its equity American Motors, and the Mexican state held the rest. The Mexican family that owned *Auto-Mex* sold one-third of its equity to Chrysler. DINA remained a wholly state-owned company (Bennett and Sharpe 1985, 117–27).

Economic growth came at high costs to those subordinated within less favoured production modes such as the household and peasant production. Despite the guarantees of the Revolutionary Constitution, land reform had been minimal and welfare spending limited. Peasants did not benefit equally from the growth of the economy and a cheap food policy supported urban industrial development through the state institutions that controlled the distribution of agricultural products. As with other experiences of import-substitution industrialisation in Latin America, income distribution remained skewed and the market for consumer durables was only narrowly extended into the industrial working class. Educational spending was only 1.4 per cent of GNP in the

---

17 For a full discussion of the bargaining process between the state and transnational capital regarding the 1962 Auto Decree, see Bennett and Sharpe (1984).

late 1950s (Hansen 1971, 85–6; see also Bennett and Sharpe 1984, 28–9). By 1970, out of a population of 50 million, only 12.2 million or 24 per cent of the population was covered by social security.[18]

In 1950, 82 per cent of the male population over the age of ten years was economically active, as compared to 12 per cent of the female population. At this time, the census showed that there were 8.3 million workers in total. By 1960, there were 11.3 million workers. By this point, 75 per cent of men over the age of ten were economically active, compared to 16 per cent of women.[19] In 1960, 59 per cent of the active male workforce and 13 per cent of women workers were located in agriculture. Women workers were overwhelmingly in services (46 per cent) where only 8 per cent of male workers were located. Fourteen per cent of male workers and 16 per cent of women worked in manufacturing. Women factory workers were in textiles, food and 'other' categories, while men worked in all of these and metallurgy and machinery as well. Sixteen per cent of women workers worked in retail trade, where 7 per cent of men worked. Very few women and only 1.4 per cent of men worked in the mines. Almost 4 per cent of men worked in transportation industries, and 1.2 per cent of women workers worked there. Four per cent of male workers were in construction (Morelos 1973, 416).

The anti-inflationary policy of *Desarrollo Estabilizador* (Stabilised Development) ensured that taxes would not be increased, so as not to discourage private investment. Internal credit was not sufficient to meet the government's expenses, however, and it sought international credit and foreign investment. Because of profit repatriation, this strategy increased the pressure on the current account. Between 1960–1970, 2,059 million $US in new foreign investments and reinvestment had been made in Mexico, while 2,991 million $US in earnings and other payments was taken out of the country (Sepúlveda and Chumacero 1973, 75; see also Tello 1990, 39). To finance the current account deficit, the government increased its external debt. Moreover, the government's 'Mexicanised' industrial production strategy was unable to limit the chronic balance of payments problems that had become endemic by the late 1960s. Especially in the auto industry, rising import levels pushed forward a debate over appropriate state responses (Bennett and Sharpe 1985; Aguilar García 1982, 23).

Labour and State Corporatism

Ford Motor Co. de México was the first of the transnational auto producers to arrive in Mexico. The company arrived in the neighbourhood of San Lázaro, Mexico City in 1925. In this first installation, 295 workers built five Model T autos each day in

18 Government figures report that social security coverage increased from 24 to 36 per cent of the population between 1970–1976 (Tello 1990, 186).

19 Official figures indicate the decrease in the percentage of economically active men over the age of 10 in 1960 is largely due to the decrease in child labour. In 1950, 26 per cent of male children between the ages of 10 and 14 were economically active. This figure decreased to 15 per cent in 1960. The change is not as dramatic for girls. In 1950 only 6 per cent of girls between the ages of 10 and 14 were economically active. This figure dropped to 5 per cent in 1960 (Morelos 1973).

the 'Completely Knocked Down' (CKD) assembly production. Ford Motor Company was welcomed to post-revolutionary Mexico with guarantees from President Plutarco Elías Calles that it would have no labour problems to contend with (Ruíz 1978, 147). Indeed, Ford workers were not unionised until 1932 despite evidence of dissension in the workforce and an unsuccessful 1929 work stoppage. Although Mexican Ford workers had been eight years without a union, they were organised earlier than their US counterparts, who did not become members of the United Auto Workers until 1941. Mexican Ford workers were initially affiliated with the prominent but declining CROM.[20] They later transferred to the CGT but found themselves in a jurisdictional dispute in the late 1930s. At the *Junta Local de Conciliación y Arbitraje*, the question of affiliation was resolved in favour of the CTM (Roxborough 1984, 77).

Although the presence of the Ford Motor Company was significant, there was no real correspondence between auto production at Ford and the broader character of the Mexican economy in these years. It is impossible to speak of this mode as 'Fordist' if mass markets, high incomes for workers and standardised production processes are the central indicators. In the early years, the characteristic link between patterns of production and consumption was that the Mexican market was small and served by a limited number of craft-based producers.

By the late 1930s, however, production was expanding. General Motors was founded in Mexico in 1935. In 1937, 48 workers formed a union and affiliated with the *Federación Sindical del Distrito Federal* (Aguilar García 1982, 45). After holding an assembly in 1947 to discuss the question of affiliation and the possibility of forming a national autoworkers union, the union at General Motors decided to affiliate with the *Confederación Única de Trabajadores* (CUT) that had been formed in the same year. In 1952, the CUT joined with other centrals to form the Revolutionary Confederation of Workers and Peasants (CROC). The General Motors, Federal District union continued this affiliation throughout the century (Aguilar García 1982, 47).

The first strike at General Motors occurred in 1965 when the company attempted to move workers to a new plant in Toluca. Previously, the company won the right to sign collective agreements in new plants with new unions and with centrals other that of the CROC. In its relations with the CTM, General Motors acquired a more advantageous collective agreement at the Toluca plant than those in the old plant in Mexico City. As a result, General Motors workers were divided into two unions, with two different centrals (Aguilar García 1982, 47–8).

In 1938, *Fábricas Automex* was established to assemble Chrysler vehicles. A union was formed in the same year. In 1964 the union became part of a nation union of *Automex* workers and affiliated with the CTM. In the next year, the union was transformed again, into a national autoworkers union named the *Sindicato Nacional de Trabajadores de la Industria Automotriz Integrada, Similares y Conexos de la República Mexicana* (CTM).

---

20 The *Unión de Obreros y Empleados de la Industria Automovilística y Similares del Distrito Federal* affiliated with the *Federación Sindical de Obreros del Distrito Federal* (FSODF) at the regional level and thus with the national *Confederación Regional de Obreros Mexicanos* (CROM) (Roxborough 1984, 76).

Volkswagen was one of the plants built outside of Mexico City in the relocation of production during the second stage of the development of the Mexican auto industry. In 1954, the company *Promexa* was established to assemble Volkswagens in Mexico. A local union was established in the same year and affiliated with the *Confederación General de Trabajadores* (CGT). In 1964, in an attempt to extend their influence within the sector, the workers formed a national union, *Sindicato Nacional de Trabajadores de la Industria Metalúrgica, Mecánica de Precisión, Similares y Conexos de la República Mexicana* and also affiliated to the CGT. In 1966, the company was bought by Volkswagen. Soon after, Volkswagen moved the plant from Xalostoc to Puebla and in collaboration with the CTM, facilitated the formation of a local CTM union (Aguilar García 1982, 50). The union at Volkswagen left the CTM in 1972. After the elections of 1975, the victorious official slate suspended the union rights of their campaign opponents (Aguilar García 1982, 57–8).

In 1946 the assembler *Willys Mexicana* was established in the Federal District and later transformed into *Vehículos Automotóres Mexicanos* (VAM). The union was formed at the end of the 1940s, and by the end of the 1950s was affiliated with the *Federación Sindical de Trabajadores del Distrito Federal* and the CTM at the national level. In 1966 the union affiliated with the *Federación Sindical de Toluca* (CTM).

Diesel Nacional was established in 1951 and the union was organised in 1954. The *Sindicato de Trabajadores de Diesel Nacional* affiliated with the CTM. After five years of internal divisions, the union left the CTM and joined the CROC. During 1961 and 1962, two strikes were called and both were declared 'non-existent'. The union remained divided between CTM forces and opposing groups and a coalition executive could not function.

From this brief overview we see that even in periods of relative stability, contestation persists. Although working-class men in the auto industry may be considered the epitome of the relatively protected, well-paid worker with stable employment, they continued to be subordinated, not only by their employers, but by the state through the official labour movement. As a result, we must not suppose that the 'Mexican Miracle' was a golden age for workers. The auto workers were not the first to form themselves into a movement in an effort to contest the official trade unions. This was the achieved by the teachers, the miners and, most forcefully, by the railway workers, who ushered in a period of political 'effervescence at the national level' that began in the late 1950s and lasted until the late 1970s (Domínguez 1993). During the late 1950s, the *Movimiento Sindical Ferrocarril* (MSF) was violently defeated within the Railway workers union, and it was over a decade before another would take up its issues in such a forceful way again.

In response to the obvious cracks that were appearing in the official labour Confederation's ability impose authoritarian solutions onto the contradictions of the period, an institutional reorganisation took place within the official labour movement in the mid-1960s. Since its foundation in 1936, and after the end of Cárdenas's rule in 1940, the CTM held an important position as interlocutor with the state. In 1966, a central labour body, the *Congreso de Trabajo* (CT), was formed to preside over the organisation of all officially sanctioned labour confederations. The CTM was a founding member. The *Confederacíon Revolucionaria de Obreros y Campesinos*

(CROC) joined the CT, as did the CROM, the CGT and the *Confederación Obrera Revolucionaria* (COR). The CT also grouped together federations such as the *Federación de Sindicatos de Empresas de Bienes y Servicios* (FSTSE). Some national industrial unions such as the mine and metal workers (STMMRM), the petroleum workers union (STPRM), and the railroad workers (STFRM) were also directly affiliated.

The CTM did not simply represent the interests of its membership within corporatist forms of representation. It inherited and then embodied the paternalistic and authoritarian dimensions of gendered power institutionalised in the Federal Labour law. The CTM restricted autonomy and independence within the labour movement as part of a system of representation in which the dominant classes exerted control over the working class through the state, as well as in the social relations of production. Given the lack of accountability within the labour relations regime, labour law acted with the corporatist organisation of state structure to prevent the development of a strong relationship between the working class and its leadership within the labour movement

Gender and the Limits of Stabilised Development

From the Revolution to the late 1960s, the gendered character of Revolutionary Nationalism was established in terms of ideology, political practice, institutions and economic conditions. The Constitution established the ideal, organic relationship between the family, classes and the state, while *caudillismo* defined the practices of the 'legitimate' leader. Labour law institutionalised the ideology of the worker-father in relation his family and subordinated him to his political and trade union leadership. The model of industrialisation subordinated working-class women as well. It demanded the extraction of value from peasant and indigenous men and women for use in the newly industrialising regions. By the late 1960s, however, the PRI leadership explained away the class inequalities underlying Revolutionary Nationalism as economic limitations and brooked no dissent. They began looking for opportunities which were presented as the United States economy faced its own internal contradictions. Meanwhile, working-class men and women suffered the lack of democracy, autonomy and independence of their organisations.

By the late 1960s, President Díaz Ordaz was compelled to respond to Mexico's deteriorating economic situation, but restructuring was conditioned by dynamics at the level of world order as well. This dynamic became apparent with the continued decline in United States competitiveness relative to Japanese and Western European industrial economies. Over time, corporations took advantage of uneven development within the United States and moved some branches of production to the southern states, leaving behind what came to be considered a 'rustbowl' in the former industrial heartland (Bluestone and Harrison 1982). As we see in the auto industry, US producers broadened the geographical basis for economic restructuring and began to look beyond national boundaries to source component parts. Corporations took advantage of the provisions of new trade regulations between the United States and Mexico by setting up low-wage, labour intensive production zones along the northern border.

In the 1960s, Mexico became initiated into an increasingly internationalised production dynamic according to what Frobel, Heinrichs and Kreye called the 'new international division of labour' (Frobel, Heinrichs and Kreye 1980). As distinct from the classical international division of labour in which colonised regions exported raw materials to the industrialised north, by the late 1960s, corporations were beginning to relocate certain parts of the production process to countries in the global south for export back to the industrial centre for final assembly. This transformation was brought about by the creation of a world market in labour, new transportation and communication technologies, and a fragmented production process (Frobel, Heinrichs and Kreye 1978). It was not long before observers began to analyse the fact that these newly industrialised workers were disproportionately women (Benería and Roldán 1987; Mies 1986; Nash and Fernández-Kelly 1983; Safa 1986, 58–71; Sen and Grown 1987).

Chapter 3

Nissan Workers, *Caudillismo* and Social Unionism

The years from 1968 to 1982 marked the first stage of a long organic crisis which was significant for the extent to which it shattered commonly held Revolutionary Nationalist assumptions. In this first moment of crisis state actors tried to re-establish the corporatist social compromise in opposition to the demands of subordinate groups for far-reaching social transformation. Instead of challenging the class relations underlying the deterioration of the old economic model, the Mexican government opted to subordinate a new feminised, productive mode to the demands of the highly industrialised, masculinised economic core, while reinforcing the role of the worker-father in social provision.

In this period, movements for trade union independence challenged the corporatist basis of trade union representation, as well as the state's legitimacy as guarantor of Revolutionary ideals. Independence movements aimed to disaffiliate from official labour bodies, as other significant sectors of Mexican society began to demonstrate publicly that the 'Party of the Revolution' no longer represented them. The failure of the dominant classes to create a consensus was manifested in the massacre of students in 1968. In was in this context that unionised workers in the Nissan plant struggled to create a new independent union that would respond to the issues they faced in the plant and in the wider community.

Nissan Workers' Struggle for Democracy

In the auto industry, oppositional movements within official trade unions were an important part of what has been called the 'national effervescence' of labour and other social movements (Domínguez 1993). The crisis of representation within official labour organisations was demonstrated by rank and file opposition, as well as the serious discontent among employers who resented the CTM's privileges within corporatism (Middlebrook 1995, 228). In the auto assembly sector, independent movements both propelled and were propelled by the state's strategic 'democratic opening'. The Nissan workers' movement for democracy is an important story in the history of independent trade unionism in Mexico because it describes a battle between two very different paths towards 'independence' in this period of crisis. It also provides us an opportunity to consider the way in which *caudillismo* extended beyond the official trade union leadership and emerged as an issue in the movement for independence.

During the 1970s, Nissan workers were involved in a series of conflicts covering a broad range of issues. They worked for better wages and benefits and challenged speed-up on the line. They advanced new forms of shop floor representation. They broke with the official trade union confederation and confronted the politicisation of the local labour board. At times they developed alliances with the urban popular movement in Cuernavaca and with other unions in the state of Morelos, and at other times they withdrew. They developed relationships with two independent labour federations and were embroiled in a long internal conflict over competing alliances. Despite all of this activity, however, the most vital features of independent trade unionism had receded by the end of the decade. In this chapter, we will examine the struggle for independent trade unionism at Nissan and the way in which *caudillismo* was used against rank and file members to define what kinds of working-class politics would replace corporatist control.

Measured in terms of numbers of affiliates, the most successful independent federation in the auto sector was the *Unidad Obrera Independiente* (UOI) led by a lawyer, Juan Ortega Arenas. The UOI shared some of the ideas about modernisation held in the Echeverría government and used this advantage over its rival independent federation. The UOI succeeded in organising movements for disaffiliation from the CTM in the Volkswagen plant in Puebla during 1972 along with the state-owned *Diesel Nacional* (DINA) and Renault. A number of large national auto parts companies also affiliated with the new federation (Montiel 1991, 158). By 1976, the UOI had more auto workers affiliated to it, than did the CTM.[1] As I will show in the discussion below, the form of labour representation advocated by the UOI was contradictory. It offered a radical critique of corporatism, but it was also economistic and ultimately isolationist.

The other 'tendency' or faction among Nissan workers was represented by the *Frente Auténtico del Trabajo* (FAT), an independent labour federation oriented towards a more communitarian form of trade unionism we might refer to as 'social unionism' (Gindin 1995, 266–8). The FAT was originally affiliated with *the Confederación Latinamericana de Trabajadores* (CLAT), a Christian Democratic labour federation in Latin America, but distanced itself from this international labour organisation in the 1960s in opposition to the close ties between the CLAT and the Vatican. From that moment on, the FAT saw itself as a wholly secular trade union federation (Domínguez 1992). In Cuernavaca, the FAT sought to strengthen organisational links between workers in the region. It supported a union school, cross-sectoral solidarity movements and solidarity between men and women workers. Their efforts in support of community-based organising among the urban poor and was quite unlike the isolationist approach of the UOI.

---

1   Aguilar García reports that in 1976 the UOI represented 19,250 workers and employees at *Diesel Nacional, Volkswagen de México* and *Nissan Mexicana*. In contrast, the CTM organised workers in Chrysler of Mexico, Ford Motor and General Motors of Toluca for a total of 12,350 members in the auto assembly sector. The CROC counted 5,000 members from General Motors, DF and *Trailers de Monterrey*. The COM organised 2,000 workers at VAM (Agiuilar García 1982, 62).

During the 1970s, opponents of corporatism argued over whether trade unions ought to limit themselves to economic demands, or be part of broader movements for social transformation. The leadership of the *Unidad Obrera Independiente* (UOI) promoted the idea that independence from corporate state structures should be accompanied by a focus on clearly recognisable workplace issues defined on the 'labour terrain'. The leadership of the *Frente Auténtico del Trabajo* (FAT) promoted a type of independent labour activism that dealt with workplace issues and also fostered broader relations with other unions in the state of Morelos and the city of Cuernavaca. This was labour activism that crossed into 'political terrain'. Both federations built up competing bases of support within the union at Nissan.

Breaking from the CTM[2]

Nissan founded its Mexican subsidiary in 1961 and began production of cars and small trucks on land which now forms the *Ciudad Industrial del Valle de Cuernavaca* (CIVAC), the industrial park built on the outskirts of Cuernavaca, Morelos. In June 1965, *Nissan Mexicana* came to an agreement with the *Federación de Trabajadores de Morelos* (FTM-CTM) the official labour federation of the state of Morelos. This agreement gave the CTM the right to hold the 'title' of the collective agreement. Only afterwards, were the workers were engaged by the company (Bazán 1980, 338). The Nissan workers' union, the *Sindicato General de Trabajadores de Nissan Mexicana del Estado de Morelos*, was formed early in 1966. Scarely three years later, oppositional currents began to voice their discontent with the CTM leadership, contesting the executive committee elections in February of 1969 and April 1970. The Local Arbitration and Conciliation Board refused to allow the opposition to take office.[3] Discontent continued to build.

Tensions arose for many reasons. Workers wanted increased job security given that 40 per cent of the workforce was temporary. Workers were obliged to work overtime, and they had very few benefits (Bazán 1980, 338). Working conditions in the plant were poor (Domínguez 1993). Union leader Raymundo Jaimes remembers there was no real union strength to shape the terms of production:

First we pushed the vehicles. Then they introduced mechanical chains. Then everything was mechanised... In one area they asked for 80 units, then the next day it was 100. It was a heavy load. We had the lowest wages, then Ford. Volkswagen earned more. There was no mechanism in the sense of having a national union. Not in autos. (Jaimes 1993; Translated by the author)

---

2   In this section I rely heavily on interviews with Alfredo Domínguez, FAT (1993); Juan Ortega Arenas, UOI (1993a, 1993b); Raymundo Jaimes, ex-General Secretary, Sindicato Independiente de Trabajadores de Nissan Mexicana, SITNM (1993). As well, I have incorporated the perspectives of Gerardo Thijssen, Ecclesiastical Base Communities (1993); Gerardo López, Nissan (1993); and Francisco Chávez Samano, General Secretary, SITNM (1993).

3   In 1969, an elected union executive was not recognised by the local Conciliation and Arbitration board. Dissent within the union challenged the Secretary General, Alfonso Avella and the CTM (Aguilar García 1982, 53).

The food in the cafeteria often made workers sick and the women who worked in the cafeteria suffered deplorable working conditions as well (Domínguez 1993). Most important for the Nissan workers was the fact that their CTM union contact was very disconnected from workplace issues. He had no office at the plant, but worked from the CTM regional offices and he remained quite distant from the workers (Middlebrook 1995, 234).

In 1971 an oppositional slate was organised to contest the local elections that had been controlled by the CTM. Nissan management made it clear that it preferred the official labour body to the opposition. Nevertheless the opposition, with Raymundo Jaimes as General Secretary, was elected with high levels of rank and file support. Jaimes remained part of the Executive Committee until 1973 (Roxborough 1984, 99). It was under his leadership that the Nissan union disaffiliated from the CTM.

Social Unionism in Morelos

The CTM bureaucracy in the predominantly rural state of Morelos was weak and inexperienced. Some argue this may have presented opportunities for the newly independent union which were unavailable to independence movements in regions with longer industrial and union histories (Roxborough 1984, 99). Only with the creation of the industrial park, CIVAC in 1963 did regional industrial production surpass that of sugar cane production (Roxborough 1984, 100). Throughout the 1960s and 1970s Morelos was a state in transition. By 1979, industrial production contributed to 51.1 per cent of production in the state of Morelos. Industry employed 17.6 per cent of the labour force. Agriculture contributed to 8.9 per cent of state production and employed 43.4 per cent of the labour force. 28.6 per cent of industrial production derived from the auto industry in 1979; 22.4 per cent from the long established textile industry and 7.3 per cent was based in the production of chemicals and pharmaceuticals (Martínez Cruz 1983, 35).

It is not the case, however, that because of their agrarian history the people of Morelos were without collective political experience. Indeed, Morelos already had a long history of popular organising before the wave of new industrialisation in the 1960s and 1970s. Morelos was the seat of *Zapatista* power during the Revolution and the textile workers of Morelos were among the most militant during the labour insurgency in the last years of the *Porfiriato*. It was true that a series of unpopular decisions worked against the official union confederation at the regional level in the early 1970s. When, for example, the FTM-CTM demanded all workers help finance a new sports complex by contributing one day's pay, they created a great deal of resentment in the labour movement. As far as local dynamic are concerned, it was a combination of weakness on the part of the FTM-CTM, rapid economic change, as well as internal movements for democracy at Nissan and militancy in the wider community that combined to challenge official unionism in the region.

One of the most significant reasons the independence movement at Nissan gained strong community support was due to the active presence in the Valley of Cuernavaca of the *Frente Auténtico del Trabajo* (FAT). The FAT saw its role as a promoter of a broadly based labour movement, independent of the official trade union movement, political parties or other forces, autonomous, and democratic in its practices (Domínguez 1993). In the view of the FAT, any such movement would present a fundamental challenge to the political and economic structures from which power was derived in Mexico. As the FAT's General Secretary, Alfredo Domínguez expressed it at that time:

> The FAT's position is a position which questions all of society and the capitalist system. We do not conceive of the union movement only within the daily tasks it must take on. The union movement has to re-evaluate its whole structure and functioning. It has to move towards building the organised power of workers, taking into consideration every area: trade unionism, urban issues, cooperatives, consumer issues, women workers, young workers, rural areas…. [S]ometimes the FAT appears to be more of a political organisation than a union. Some people do not understand that we have to carry on developing a new way of thinking in the labour movement. We must understand that the union movement, constituted from workers and the people, has a much larger reach. This implies structural change. Any other way makes no sense for a renewed union movement. (Domínguez 1972, 34; Translated by the author)

From its birth in 1960, the FAT became active in the independent labour movement. It did not affiliate with the *Congreso del Trabajo*. Instead, the FAT promoted local organising and leadership training to develop its institutional base. As Raymundo Jaimes remembers, 'In 1970 the FAT lawyers came to us as advisors. We liked their form of working'. He became involved with them in organising and education: 'In 1970 there was a training course in Venezuela with the CLAT through the FAT. I was invited to go. I had only primary education and this course opened up my life' (Jaimes 1993; Translated by the author).

One of the most significant initiatives of the FAT was their involvement in the *Centro de Formación Sindical en el Estado de Morelos* (CEFOSEM), a small union school which brought together union educators, as well as leaders from other community groups. CEFOSEM had been organised to train union activists and the school first worked clandestinely with small groups of leaders of democratic movements preparing to challenge elections in the factories. It became one of the first efforts to coordinate activities between democratic sections of CTM unions and the independent unions (Thijssen 1993).

Some of the CEFOSEM activists came from the *comunidades de bases eclesiásticas* (Christian-based communities) which were part of a wider movement within the Catholic Church across Latin America that challenged social inequalities, and critiqued the traditional alliances of the institutional church in favour of a 'preferential option for the poor'.[4] These communities were begun in Morelos by two French priests who had originally developed this work in Chile. Meeting first

---

4   In their 1968 conference in Medellín, the *Consejo Episcopal Latinoamericano* (CELAM) (Latin American Conference of Bishops) encouraged the formation of Christian base communities as a means by which the Church could realise its commitment to solidarity with the poor and the denunciation of injustice. During the 1970s, the more conservative bishops accepted Catholic social action as an alternative to Marxism and left political organising, but as a whole CELAM's commitment to a 'preferential option for the poor' was affirmed at their subsequent conference in Puebla in 1979 (CELAM 2007).

in houses, the communities slowly developed their spiritual, political and social analysis from the perspective of the poor and their oppression. In Morelos, the base communities and the popular movements had strong ties by the mid-1970s. Gerardo Thijssen, a long-time facilitator in the communities, attributed their continued success to the way in which individuals who were marginalised in society at large came to see their value in relation to their own community.[5] Further, he argued that over time, this reflection led to an understanding of the common problems shared between members of the popular classes:

> Many workers have been directly related to communities since they live in communities and they work in a factory. In the meetings of the communities, they spoke a lot about human service, Christian love, help to the sick etcetera. They people went about discovering that to give food to the hungry or helping the sick goes on endlessly. The poor continue to be poor. Then the people go about learning to think structurally, which is to say that they see the relation between oppression and those who maintain the poor in their poverty...In the 1970s, the way in which the people lived their commitment was especially to help the unions on strike. To help, by bringing food to those on strike, to hand out flyers, to take up collections, to spread information, and visiting, talking to the workers. What is their problem? Why are they on strike? Why choose this form? Etcetera. There was a lot of solidarity. (Thijssen 1993 Translated by the author)

In this context, the struggle of the Nissan workers to secure a representative union was by no means an isolated one.

Of importance too, was the role played by the Archbishop of Cuernavaca, Sergio Mendez Arceo. As an outspoken and radical theologian who supported workers' movements, the bishop lent legitimacy to social unionism within the Nissan union and in the region more generally. Gerardo Thijssen recounts the story of the conversion of the Archbishop to the workers' cause:

> In 1952 he became bishop. He arrived here as a very aristocratic bishop, a friend of the rich but he was converted to the poor. One time he met with a group of workers who came to see him. In these days, Don Sergio used to go to eat with the director of the *Fábrica Textiles Morelos*, one of the largest factories here. Each week he would eat there with the boss. So the workers, through the CEFOSEM school, declared a strike and went to talk with the bishop. The bishop said, 'Yes, go ahead. Struggle to get a better salary. But also, do your duties as workers because I know you are lazy and irresponsible. You break the machines.' 'Of course', said a worker, 'That's because each week you speak with the boss, but when do you speak with us? Each week you go to eat at the boss's house, but you never come to eat with us.' So he said, 'Okay, invite me.' Then he began to go and eat with the poor people and did not go back to eat with the boss... He began to solidarise himself with the workers to such an extent that he said that 'I am partial. I am not impartial. I am with the people. When there is a struggle, I am with the poor people, even if they make mistakes. I am not going to say that the people are always right, but even if they are

---

5   Thijssen estimates that in 1993 approximately 10,000 people participated in the CEBs in the state of Morelos and about 5,000 within Cuernavaca itself. Many local councilors come from the communities and almost all are active in various dimensions of local politics (Thijssen 1993).

wrong, I am with them, with the peasants, with the workers'. (Thijssen 1993; Translated by the author)

In the fall of 1971, Mendez Arceo gave a sermon in which he denounced the effect of industrialisation in the region and the impact on workers. In particular, he chastised the employers for having created the so-called 'black lists' of workers with the cooperation of union leaders, thus putting workers in danger and justifying firings at Rivetex, Textiles Morelos, Mosaicos Bizantinos, Artmex, Nissan, Dina, and Renault, among others. In response, Fidel Velazquez accused the bishop of violating Article 130 of the Constitution prohibiting the clergy from commenting on political issues. The CTM and the state politicians, relying on traditional corporatist practices to shore up support, convened a mass rally to denounce Mendez Arceo (Punto Crítico 1972, 28). Employers were asked to extend the 'invitation' to their employees. A letter from *Nissan Mexicana* sent to the Nissan union executive committee on 21October 1971 called workers to the meeting. The letter read:

> We are conveying to you the invitation issued by the Governor of the State of Morelos. The Governor requests that workers attend a meeting to protest the foreign elements that are disturbing the tranquillity of the nation. We are informed that the appointment is for next Sunday the 24 of October at 10:30 in the morning at the same place and in the same way as the march this past May 1st. (Nissan Mexicana 1971; Translated by the author)

Late in 1971, the executive committee was locked out by the company. Seven permanent workers were fired. The conflict was taken to the highly politicised local labour board (Roxborough 1984, 100). Other unions in Morelos demonstrated in solidarity with the union's call for the dismissal of the president of the labour board. The conflict was eventually resolved, but not before Fidel Velázquez, leader of the CTM, raised the ire of the executive by claiming responsibility for the successful conclusion of the conflict.

The executive committee had presented their complaint through the official arbitration process and in an audience with the State Governor. As a result, reported the executive, the company had promised to reinstate the workers, respect their union rights, and repay the holiday pay which had been lost. The union agreed that the workers would return to work as normal. At that point, Fidel Velazquez, long-time General-Secretary of the CTM, without speaking to the executive committee, claimed he had resolved the problem by telephone. The executive committee protested publicly that the CTM was not respecting union autonomy, and was violating the terms of the collective agreement by maintaining direct links with the company (Centro Nacional de Comunicación Social 1972a).

In March 1972, the union signed a collective agreement with Nissan. In a denunciation later that year, the executive described how the collective agreement was not being complied with:

> They do not allow the Commission on Hygiene and Safety to function; There is no drinkable water... so workers must drink bottles of soft drinks or dirty water; vacation days are paid whenever the company wants to pay them; they do not pay wages according to the classifications that the workers actually occupy; they do not respect the scale as it

should be reflected in wages, especially when there are changes in positions etc. So, the contract is applied however the representatives of the company want to apply it, and not according to the agreement.

There is another important violation in the collective agreement which occurs when the representatives of the company constantly and systematically intervene in the internal life and the affairs of the union; this situation occurs in different ways, the most important being the meetings which employees outside the bargaining unit have with groups of union members, insisting that they depose the Executive Committee of the union for being 'communist' and when they threaten workers by saying that 'when Raymundo Jaimes's committee is no longer in power, then you will get the benefits you ask for.' So, in all these ways they repress the workers for having a 'subversive' committee. (Centro Nacional de comunicación Social 1972b; Translated by the author)

The committee also denounced the fact that the company continued to pay workers who had been temporarily suspended from the union for having violated union solidarity and causing division. The company said it was under a 'moral obligation to help the boys' and protect those who were disciplined by the general assembly and suspended from the union for a month.

While the independence movement at Nissan was gaining strength, other union movements seeking greater autonomy from the CTM were also organising in the largest unions of the region. The highly feminised textile and clothing industry had long been a central source of economic activity in the state of Morelos and in this sector as well as in smaller industrial factories, workers became highly mobilised during 1971 and 1972. In *Textiles de los Gallos*, *Hilados Morelos*, *Textiles Morelos* and *Rivetex*, both men and women workers saw their issues as shared ones. This sentiment caused a great deal of alarm amongst the employers and public officials as the actions took on a more coordinated form. The textile workers' union issued a leaflet that read:

Sindicato Nacional de Trabajadores de la Industria Textiles Morelos, Seccion 51 '1972 Año de Juarez'

'Peace is Respect for the Rights of Others' B. Juarez

The unified workers in the State of Morelos declare their profound support for the ideas of Benito Juarez and so demand that the rights of the Nissan workers be respected. Peace will only be achieved if justice is applied and not by means of repression, or the firing of workers.

Brother Worker of Nissan Mexicana, we are with you and with your workers' struggle! (Translated by the author)

At *Rivetex* in the fall of 1972, 400 women textile workers struck the company and proceeded to occupy the plant after their strike was deemed illegal. In an impressive act of solidarity, workers in all of the major centres in the Valley of Cuernavaca stopped working. At a regional level, the crisis was profound. As labour leader Alfredo Domínguez describes it, 'It was a whole conflict that put almost all the state into crisis, the unions, the society, the government, the official union leaders, everyone' (Domínguez 1993). Supported by working women's struggles such as this one, the Nissan workers decided to leave the CTM in the fall of 1972.

Manhood and the Making of a Union

The Nissan union became independent of the CTM but the experience of social unionism was not directly transferred into the new institution. The Nissan workers did not elect to join the FAT. Instead, they affiliated with the UOI. The UOI had already successfully led the Volkswagen union into its independent labour federation. Under the leadership of its coordinator, lawyer Juan Ortega Arenas, the UOI led a convincing campaign to build support. It was able to show how union dues had been decreased from two per cent to one per cent of wages. It could point out that, for the first time, each Volkswagen worker was given a copy of the collective agreement and his own union constitution. It could refer to the reformed union constitution and the creation of departmental representatives within the new independent union at Volkswagen. Workers could see that the UOI organised its own marches on May 1st and appeared to offer a real alternative to the official unions (Juárez 1993). All of these things were meaningful to workers who had not experienced effective representation within CTM structures.

Nissan workers held a general assembly in Cuernavaca in October of 1972. At this assembly, chaired by General Secretary Raymundo Jaimes, the Archbishop was present, as was a CTM representative. Alfredo Domínguez, General Secretary of the FAT and Juan Ortega Arenas, coordinator of the UOI, and leaders of the Volkswagen union were there as well. In his recollection of the day's events, Juan Ortega Arenas talks about his speech to the Assembly:

> So I made my intervention and after 30 minutes I said, '*Compañeros*, there isn't any more time to talk about this. We came to explain and now we are going. So you have to make a decision. Either continue with these gentlemen, servile, with your heads bowed down, *gachados* (on all fours), as impotent men, and with lack of respect for yourselves. Or you can take your own union into your hands and throw these people out. But that's your problem, it's not mine.' More people got up on stage and the big man became afraid. One of the brothers said, 'Listen friends, I want to ask the *compañeros* of Volkswagen and *compañero* Ortega not to leave. Right now let's make a resolution to send these other gentlemen to the devil. All of them all. Unanimously.' The big man, Domínguez, grabbed the microphone and he said, 'I do not agree with this.' Then people ran up to the stage and began to push him. The one from the CTM ran away. In less than 40 minutes, with the support of the people, we made dust of 5 years of domination. That's how we got into Nissan. (Ortega Arenas 1993a; Translated by the author)

In this recounting of the events leading to the independence vote by the General Assembly of Nissan workers, Juan Ortega Arenas demonstrates the power, at least in his memory of that moment, of hegemonic masculinity and the discourse of the *caudillo*.

All reports indicate that time and time again Ortega Arenas moved thousands of workers in assemblies with his superb skills as an orator. He understood the magnetism of the oral tradition and used it to his advantage at every opportunity.

Those who did not suffered his derision. 'Fidel Velázquez doesn't know anything, not how to speak or anything. He is an imbecile but he has the shoulder of the state behind him. That is his strength' (Ortega Arenas 1993a; Translated by the author). In this recounting of the evening the General Assembly voted to join the UOI, Ortega Arenas demonstrates how important it was to call male auto workers forward into action by appealing to their ideas about 'independence' and masculinity. Here, he demonstrates the kinds of interactions between men which were to typify his involvement with the union members from that point on. The Nissan workers may have been leaving the official union movement, but the gendered dimensions of authority continued to hold a central place in the independent union. This option de-legitimised the possibility these workers would join with the broader movement of women and men organised by the FAT.

In part, the idea that Ortega Arenas had the ability to turn workers into self-respecting men stemmed from the notion that the male subject develops along with the development of the productive forces. Because capitalism has perverted this process, he argues, it is the responsibility of those who can think abstractly and speak well to renew the movement. This was an idea he developed in his prolific writings:

> The world imperialist system, the present phase of capitalism, slowly converts the great mass of human beings into a group of undifferentiated beings, similar in their indefinition and without singularity or individuality, lacking consciousness, ragged, illiterate, able only to manage a computer, a plane, or an automobile like simple ants, with no goal for themselves beyond their mere survival, selfish and isolated, at the very most only existing in relation to their own family. It is the task of the advanced and thinking human being to act to develop human consciousness and rescue the capacity for reasoning in order to allow humanity to reach its capacity for *social action*. This is what makes possible changes in the capitalist system which is, at present, annihilating the essence of humanity. (Ortega Arenas 1992, 124–5; Translated by the author)

The rational man, he argued, emerges along with modernisation and technological development. The UOI, with its emphasis on productivity increases and labour culture, was the vehicle for such a transformation in the masculinised Mexican industrial working class (Osorio 1980, 88). According to Ortega Arenas:

> We are an organisation that first wants workers to have capacity as workers and then be able to talk of other things…. You must go along with them in making the first steps towards their development as workers…. It is just like with children. You have to respect their decisions. You can't convince them. You can't force things. You need to develop things with a lot of respect. You can't force things or it would be like the old Chinese man who went about pulling up rice stalks to try to make them grow. (Ortega Arenas 1993 a; Translated by the author)

Although the UOI emerged victorious in October 1972 when the General Assembly at Nissan voted to leave the CTM, there continued to be a great deal of support for the FAT within the union. In fact, the executive committee was led by Raymundo Jaimes who was closely aligned with the FAT during the transition away from the CTM which meant that the UOI did not have *carte blanche* to operate. For example, on 8 January 1973, a work stoppage led by Jaimes's executive committee was criticised by the UOI (Unidad Obrera Independiente 1975, 5). The union officially disaffiliated from the CTM in 1973, before joining the UOI the same year.[6] The fact that the Nissan workers' union was affiliated with the UOI throughout the decade did not mean the internal debate had been resolved. In fact, supporters of the FAT elected executive committees frequently throughout the decade and the question of whether the union should have a broader or narrower orientation continued to play out in conflictual ways.

Ortega Arenas wrote statements for approval by the executive committee and assemblies. In reference to the earlier strike at Nissan in 1973, Ortega Arenas denounced the 'adventurers' who provoked the work stoppage and the danger they put the independent union in. He blamed the FAT for supporting this opposition within the Nissan workers union, and called the FAT 'fascistic adventurers' and 'false socialists who are even more false than those who disguise themselves as "communists" and the little groups of boys who put on "revolutionary" masks, and call themselves vanguards, "red flags," and [make] many similar posters with the words "unity" group [and] "democratic" tendency of the electricians etc.' In April 1974, the UOI slate took the workers out for 20 days. When the opposing Executive Committee returned to power, the UOI denounced the FAT for having tried to 'destroy our jobs for the benefit of North American automotive companies. This is the aim of these gentlemen. For this reason do they travel to the "United States" and have meetings with their masters and then come back here to carry out their orders' (Unidad Obrera Independiente 1975, 6; Translated by the author).

As the fully formed male subject in the relationship, Ortega Arenas saw himself as central to the formation process by which less developed, potential male subjects would become full subjects, and be recognised as such. He divided men against one another to make his case:

> [O]ur role is to be an instrument of the Mexican people to offer them what we know: organisation, discipline, work systems etcetera… It is possible and we will see the end of (capitalist exploitation), but not with simple declarations or by clowning around. Not with 'Homosexuals for Socialism', or with 'This Little Fist, Can be Seen', but with the organisation of the whole people. When will this occur? When we no longer act as provocateurs, and do not look for sterile confrontations, when we let the process develop as it should, along with the development of the working class. (Osorio 1980, 88; Translated by the author)

Juan Ortega Arenas never extended the promise that workers would become *caudillos* themselves. They could, however, claim their manhood by disciplining themselves to their responsibilities as worker-fathers, and by submitting to the leadership of the union by the *caudillo* himself. He battled constantly with other leaders of independent unions and made every effort to undermine them by questioning their masculinity in light of a heterosexual, virile, and rational ideal.

---

6   The union formally disaffiliated the following year and subsequently joined the UOI (see Middlebrook 1991, 278).

Juan Ortega Arenas is not to be dismissed. His analysis of Mexican labour history was extensive and as a leader, he developed a deep critique of the power of official trade unionism. He produced, for example, a very good book which included examples of all the documents unions would need to in their engagement with the state and Federal Labour Law (Ortega Arenas 1984). In the words of oppositional leader Jaimes:

> The UOI wanted to control the executive committee and the general assemblies. The lawyer was very capable and he had power with the government, and had its cooperation. Juan Ortega Arenas controlled the executive. The union was independent of the CTM, but dependent on him. He knew how to manage us. (Jaimes 1993; Translated by the author)

Although Ortega Arenas prided himself on advancing a form of unionism which would correspond to employers' search for increased productivity, from the point of view of the company, the shift away from the CTM was very difficult. At least from one manager's view, in the CTM years, there was 'tranquillity and peace', but when the union left the CTM, there was a great deal of conflict (Lopez 1993). Indeed, there was a strike in each of 1972, 1973, 1974, 1976, 1977 and 1978 (Middlebrook 1995, 251). Gerardo Lopez a manager at Nissan explains that part of the conflict arose from cultural differences between the Japanese managers and Mexican workers. Lopez goes on to explain, that even more important, was the 'unknown' of the new relations with the independent union:

> The union movement in Mexico was not principally a representative movement of the workers but was an important political force which constructed a system – a system which Calles devised and perhaps Cardenas perfected afterwards.... In many respects the CTM played a more political role than anything. In no way was there real labour representation.... With the traditional system, the labour movement had understandings with capital... the form, the relation of respect, including the way of carrying things out. This was very important.... Let's say we're going to sign a collective agreement. I, beforehand, come to some agreement with the leader because I know that I cannot give an increase of more than 15 per cent. This is an understood agreement. The system itself used to permit this. There was no voice of the workers, but it was 15 per cent. This is very different than bringing in all manner of talks, conversations, bringing the workers in and negotiating in order to arrive at 15 per cent. It's very different from saying 'I negotiated 15 per cent and that's what you have.' The Japanese felt very confident in the system. I speak with the leader if I have a problem and it doesn't matter to me whether representation exists between the leader and the workers. I want to have a good relationship with the CTM. This is what created a series of conflicts and resentments. (Lopez 1993; Translated by the author)

The conflicts and resentments continued, from the company's perspective, when the question of representation was not resolved in the independent union:

> This labour advisor used to arrive, speak, negotiate and resolve. And that's it. In many respects he did not have an exchange with the workers and the workers resented him a lot. He was very authoritarian and he did not let them express their questions. The company itself used to complain because this man was very authoritarian. But he used to resolve things. So, sure he resolved things very badly since we constantly had strikes

in CIVAC.... What we have attempted to do now, with the Mexican administration, is to look for criterion like the representativeness of the leader and we now have negotiations, and dialogue which on occasion has been difficult for us. (Lopez 1993; Translated by the author)

Contesting the Terms of Production

Once the Nissan workers joined the UOI, Ortega Arenas instituted a new system of representation in which worker delegates would be elected at the departmental level within the factory. The union constitution was rewritten to ensure the executive would no longer be the only significant element within the union. Many observers have argued that the new union constitution devolved power from the executive committee and allowed for a greater participation of the rank-and-file in the union (Bazán 1980, 339). As Javier Aguilar García saw it, the new 'departmental delegates' were closer to shop floor issues than the union bureaucrats and had technical knowledge of the changing production process that the CTM did not have. Without knowledge of how work was actually organised and transformed, the CTM staff were lacking in arguments needed to propose new demands on working conditions and wages. The departmental delegate structure offered the possibility of new demands for increased control over the production process (Aguilar García 1982, 65). The delegates were elected. They were responsible for intervening in daily conflicts and calling departmental meetings to make decisions. Moreover, they were directly accountable to a relatively small group of workers and the new structure presented the possibility for conflicts to be resolved quickly. At times the delegates became an important force for opposition and debate within the union.

The constitution of the *Sindicato Independiente de Trabajadores de Nissan Mexicana* (SITNM) did give departmental delegates an important role in representing workers' interests to the union executive, and in the organisation of general and departmental assemblies. It cannot be assumed, however, that the delegates always and automatically increased the democratic participation of workers in the life of their union. They were not autonomous of the executive committee. They announced the decisions taken by the executive committee to workers in their unit. They acted as a conduit for discussion and information sharing between the executive committee and the members (Bazán 1980, 339). At times, the delegates acted as the 'eyes and ears' of the executive committee on the shop floor.

Moreover, in the new structure of representation, the role of the departmental delegates was not the most important one in the union. The legal advisor from the UOI was given an enormous amount of power. The constitution provided that the Secretary General could give the status of 'third party' to a representative who would act on behalf of the union and membership (Juárez 1993). This status was given to Ortega Arenas on numerous occasions. Although there was a negotiating committee made up of members from all departments of the plant, union members did not ratify the new collective agreement upon conclusion of contract negotiations. The newly independent union did not change this common practice.

The conflict between the two currents continued within the union but management favoured the UOI over the FAT (Delgado 1989, 85; Roxborough 1984). This factor strengthened the influence of Ortega Arenas and UOI in the new leadership (Aguilar García 1982, 56–7). An example may serve to illustrate this point. In 1977, during a period of high inflation, wage controls of 10 per cent were imposed by the federal government (Bazán 1980, 340). 'Normal' bargaining practices were revoked. At Nissan a strike over contract and salary issues was resolved within a day. Since bargaining issues were taken out of the union's hands, and due to simultaneous increases work intensity, the opposition was mobilised once again. Workers in three departments began a slow down in order to pressure the company for control over aspects of the production process and reductions in the speed of the line. Production was immediately decreased by 60 per cent. About half of the workforce allied itself with the *tortugistas* (turtles). This was not, however, a movement led by the executive committee or backed by the UOI. It was led by supporters of the FAT. The division within the union, among the supporters of Ortega Arenas and those of Jaimes, was intensified as the autumn progressed and eventually, the activists were defeated (Bazán 1980, 337–43). In the fall elections Jaimes's slate lost to Quirino Delgado, who was affiliated with the UOI, and the support for the movement was lost within the union. Throughout the autumn of 1977, union activists, including four departmental delegates and Jaimes, were fired.[7]

A study undertaken by academics and published by the *Secretaria del Trabajo y Prevision Social* and the *Instituto Nacional de Estudios del Trabajo* in 1976 was based on interviews with managers and a survey of workers at Nissan, CIVAC (Campero et al. 1976). According to management, Nissan workers had little previous industrial experience and found it very difficult to work in repetitive tasks and routinised work. Their impression was that workers were originally *campesinos* (peasants) who found it difficult to participate in the 'collective character of industrial work'. They thought it was not easy for peasants 'to become part of the whole; ordered and routinised in work stations' or to use sophisticated tools and industrial equipment. Managers assumed workers were acting like peasants when they would use their physical force to deal with problems at work until they were trained in the rhythm of the assembly line. They blamed injuries on young workers and workers who had come from the countryside for not using safety equipment to protect themselves against noise, contamination and danger. They further suggested that accidents were often the result of 'machismo' among young workers and professional pride among more experienced workers who would avoid health and safety precautions on the job (Campero et al. 1976, 38, 39, 59).

The study found that managers were wrong. In 1976, 60 per cent of Nissan workers had parents who were at one time or another, peasants and 70 per cent of the workers had lived in a rural environment at one time in their lives, but they were not peasants themselves. Most workers at Nissan came from either Guerrero or Morelos, but 70 per cent had no agricultural work experience at all. Rather, 68 per cent of the auto workers had worked previously in the service sector. They had higher than

---

7   The relatively low turnout for these elections may indicate that discontent was widespread in the plant. Membership had grown from less than 600 voting members in 1970 to 2,750 members in the plant in Cuernavaca in 1976, yet less than 1500 participated in the elections of 1977 (Aguilar García 1982, 64; Roxborough 1984, 99, 101).

average educational levels. Fifty per cent were between 17 and 26 years old and 60 per cent were married. In 1976, 67 per cent had less than five years' seniority (Campero et al. 1976, 93–7).

The research report indicated that 53 per cent of the workers wanted to leave the factory in the long run because they wanted work where they would have more autonomy. They wanted to develop skills and have better jobs where the pressure wasn't so high and they could work 'under their own authority' (Campero et al. 1976, 154). They stayed in order to ensure their children would have a good education, and in order to have social security and other benefits. Young workers who were most sought after by Nissan might be the only ones in a position to support their family. Working in the factory meant a chance to increase their stature in their family and community. As well as the fact that high rates of unemployment in the region meant that workers were under pressure to cooperate with management, workers gained almost no experience which would help them acquire work outside the factory.

This would suggest two very different perspectives on masculinities in the automotive industry. First of all, managers assumed conflict over the terms of industrial production was produced by workers who had not yet abandoned their peasant masculinity. Managers assumed workers would never be able to become part of a modern industrial work force by holding on to their 'machismo' and tendencies to resort to 'brute force'. For managers, the conflicts on the line were an aspect of workers' masculine identity, and not derived from the working conditions, organisation of production or workplace health and safety hazards. The workers themselves, however, did not identify as peasants. Their assumptions were that they were not going to work long in the factory, but they would ensure their family responsibilities could be met before they would seek work elsewhere. They were, in the mean time however, consciously trading their own 'authority' for the ability to take their place in the community as providers for their own and extended families. The masculinity of the 'worker-father' combined with the realities of the labour market actually motivated these relatively young men to accommodate themselves to life in the factory. Workers were not emasculated in the process. The promise of their life as independent trade unionists was that they did not have to submit fully to the discipline of the assembly line. So too did they challenge the authoritarianism of the official *and* independent trade union *caudillos* through collective action. As shown by the history of contestation during the 1970s, within the union and in the community, agency was a central characteristic of working-class masculine identity.

Contestation and Coalitions

Just as the Nissan union was influenced by regional political dynamics, so too did the union have an impact on labour relations beyond the walls of the plant. During the 1970s, the UOI held sway but the oppositional movement led by Raymundo Jaimes and supported by the FAT was still active. As we have seen, Jaimes was elected and deposed a number of times during this decade. During the years when this more radical current was in power, its presence supported the emergence of militant responses on the part of other trade unions in the region surrounding Cuernavaca and in the state of Morelos. When the current was defeated, social unionism was weakened in the region.

As the newly independent Nissan union continued to challenge the regional leadership of the CTM and the PRI through its activism at the level of the workplace, other unions were encouraged to disaffiliate as well. Movements for independence emerged in IACSA, a large auto parts plant, as well as in the union of university workers at *the Universidad Autónoma de Morelos*. As a result of the sustained pressure, the regional leader of the CTM had to resign (Aguilar García 1982, 60). In January 1973, the Nissan workers union accepted the cafeteria workers as members, but the company and the food workers section of the CTM opposed this move. The cafeteria workers were subsequently fired after the CTM excluded them from the Union. The Nissan production workers conducted a work stoppage in solidarity (Aguilar García 1982, 61). They were not reinstated. In this instance, the union was not able to maintain the solidarity between men and women workers.

As part of the same dynamic which built solidarity among trade unions, Nissan workers, led by the movement supporting the FAT, found support and developed relations with urban popular organisations. The union was active in Cuernavaca during the 1970s in a series of alliances between union and community groups long after it gained independence from the CTM. It actively organised around demands for water, transportation, housing, health care and security in the community.

Together, unions established regional organisations that were independent of the official labour structures as well. During the textile workers' strike at *Rivetex* during the fall of 1972, the Comité Coordinador (CoCo) was formed as a way to bring broader based support to the workers and to coordinate action amongst the independent unions. CoCo disappeared at the end of 1974 as a result of internal differences, including conflicts with the Nissan union leadership. The CoCo disappeared precisely at the time that the UOI slate in support of a more economistic plant-based unionism gained ascendance within the Nissan union. The importance of state opposition to union solidarity ought not to be underplayed. The authorities and employers moved against the CoCo's mobilisations. There were a series of union defeats and state reprisals against the movements in 1974 that made coordinated action very difficult to sustain. An independent march of 10,000 workers rivalling the official parade on 1 May 1974 was severely repressed. During this time hundreds were fired and strikes were broken at Rivetex, Upjohn and IACSA (Martínez Cruz 1983, 38). The success and failure of regional solidarity movements did not depend entirely on the capacity of the independent unions themselves to form alternate organisations, as there were larger national and international dynamics in play as well.

Following from the initial experience of coordination among independent trade unions, a more broadly based effort at coordination organised worker, peasant, student and popular sectors into the *Coalición Obrera Campesina Popular del Estado de Morelos* (COCPEM) in December 1975. It was precisely at this point that the leadership of the Nissan union turned again to those most closely aligned with the FAT, after the UOI slate was deposed in the General Assembly. The COCPEM was supported by the broad opposition in the region, and included activists from left-wing political parties, as well as communist, trotskyist and maoist organisations. In an effort by the government and employers to link the COCPEM with the *guerilleros* and the armed resistance, the police arrested members of the Nissan workers' executive committee. The union's *Secretario de Trabajos y Conflictos* (Secretary of labour and conflicts) left the country and went into exile (Martínez Cruz 1983, 38–9).

During the early part of 1976, Nissan workers went on strike for 46 days. At the same time, the movements of sugar workers, the Nissan union, textile and clothing unions converged in another attempt to contest the official May 1st parade. Again, repression followed the mobilisation and the coalition was dismantled. Jaimes was replaced as Secretary-General by the UOI slate after the strike ended and the leaders of most of the largest unions, including Nissan, decided to withdraw from the broader coalition in favour of a union-only *Frente Sindical del Valle de Cuernavaca* (FSC). Again, this dismantling coincided with the re-entry of the UOI into a leadership position within the Nissan union. The FSC tended to be more declarative than oriented towards mobilisations, and somewhat sectarian, but it organised support for the 1977 IACSA strike. This movement was eventually defeated by the authorities and the FSC disappeared soon afterwards (Martínez Cruz 1983, 40).

As the presence of the *Frente Sindical del Valle de Cuernavaca* (FSC) was waning, the textile workers struggle was emerging as a significant political force. The textile workers became the leaders of a new labour front, a *Coordinadora Sindical del Valle de Cuernavaca* (COSIVAC), formed at the end of 1979. In the late 1970s, the democratic movement of teachers was also becoming organised. This movement grouped together democratic locals of primary and secondary teachers in the state and called itself the *Consejo Central de Lucha del Magisterio Morelense* (CCLMM). The independent unions, including the university workers union, textile workers, fired Nissan workers and human rights organisations were joined by this dynamic and democratic teachers' movement in independent march on 1 May 1980. When the leadership of their democratic sections was not recognised by the official teachers' union, the 75 elected delegates of the CCLMM conducted a hunger strike in the central square of Cuernavaca in March 1981. Forty thousand people marched from the edge of Cuernavaca to the central square in solidarity with the teachers. On May Day 1982, the mobilisation in Cuernavaca turned to the national issues of the austerity policies of the government and the economic crisis in the country. This march was not permitted to enter into Cuernavaca's central square (Martínez Cruz 1983, 40–42).

Such expressions of solidarity are difficult to sustain but these are made even more difficult when they are actively opposed by large labour organisations. As noted above, the disappearance of the CoCo coincided exactly with the election of the slate supported by the UOI, while the re-emergence of an executive committee linked with the FAT in 1975 corresponded to the creation of the cross-sectoral alliance COCPEM. Not surprisingly, the demise of the alliance was accompanied by the return of the UOI slate to a leadership position within the union. Ortega Arenas was no idle observer. He constantly criticised other independence movements for having invited state repression. He denounced the militancy of the railway workers in 1959, as well as the leaders in struggles in *Medalla de Oro*, Cinsa y Cinfunsa,

General Electric, Pemex, Up-John, Lido, Hulera Industrial Leonesa, the electrical workers movement, and Spicer (Unidad Obrera Independiente 1991, 278). Insofar as the UOI could envisage coordinated trade union action, it participated in a narrowly constituted and short-lived union fronts, usually between UOI unions. The UOI was not simply uninterested in, but actively opposed to, the building of cross-sectoral and popular coalitions.

Ortega Arenas was clear and direct about these issues in his public speeches. In a very lengthy address at the *II Pleno Nacional Unidad Obrera Independiente de 1976* (Second National UOI Plenary), he argued that the working class was highly disorganised in Mexico. Consequently, he argued, it was the role of the UOI to 'organise and create consciousness among all the popular sectors'. He opposed as 'anti-worker' the official labour movement which calls itself revolutionary on placards, but tries to convince workers of the 'kindnesses of state capitalism'. As well, he denounced other independence movements as being 'opportunistic-sectarian currents' trying to convince workers to engage in provocative and suicidal activities' that ended in repression. He accused them of 'diversionistic acts that disorganise, divide, destroy and move the labour movement backwards' (Ortega Arenas 1976).

The UOI repeated its own divisive form of organising again at the beginning of the 1980s when, in the face of national economic crisis, the national movement of *paro cívicos* (community strikes) were being organised. As the national labour movement faced new austerity programs, the UOI initially supported the organisation of popular mobilisations involving small business, workers, peasants, urban popular organisations. In a massive national coalition, these groups organised to withdraw their support temporarily for the governing PRI in a series of coordinated actions across the country (Carr 1986). The UOI was one of the sponsoring organisations, but at a crucial point in building the movement, Ortega Arenas blocked the initiative, arguing that political organisations had co-opted the effort and were simply provoking state repression. In defence of his position Ortega Arenas argues:

> We are forever proposing unity of action but we do not engage in exhibitionism.... Not only are we not sectarian and propose broad fronts, we have proposed them all our lives. We have constructed a front with the Mexican bourgeoisie that exists right now.... Every day in the paper you will see the demands of the Mexican bourgeoisie for freedom of association. They are following our political line which we have given them in conferences. If we are capable of uniting with the small and medium bourgeoisie do you not think we are capable of uniting ourselves with workers? (Ortega Arenas 1993a; Translated by the author)

The movements against the UOI within Nissan gained strength from 1979 onwards. In 1981, a democratically elected executive committee led by Carlos Contreras was fired after the union opposed changes in line speed and working conditions. A new executive committee was registered but not supported by the majority of the membership. In an overt and fierce show of force, the union applied the exclusion clause and over 200 workers were fired (Martínez Cruz 1983, 40). With this move, the UOI lost all legitimacy within the rank and file and almost immediately the union left the UOI. Although national political and economic crisis certainly contributed to the weakening of the independence movements in general terms, the UOI also faced critical, and in the end, insurmountable crisis of representation within the Nissan union. The Nissan workers union left the UOI in 1981.[8]

Raymundo Jaimes offers this reflection on the experience that was brought to a close as the union left the UOI:

> In some ways there were advances... a greater sense of what class struggle is all about. But they got rid of all of us and it had to be started all over again. With López Portillo it was different, it was the reverse. There was an opening (under Echeverría) and then repression. Brutal repression.... In 1977 I left there. I was fired and others were fired. In 1981, there were 203 firings, all the most politicised people. It was a symptom that nothing had changed, in fact it became worse. Now the company controls the union. The movement of the UOI is dissipated. (Jaimes 1993; Translated by the author)

Thwarting Social Unionism

The UOI was roundly criticised by other independent labour leaders for the obvious contradictions in its political and ideological positions. It offered workers a radical discourse of opposition to capitalism, but immediately denounced other independent working-class organisations as traitors and enemies. It promoted a politics of division and isolation among the working class and sought justification in its radical ideology. It advocated economistic solutions to social problems and thus narrowed the strategic possibilities for its own organisation to command an important political presence during a critical moment in the history of working-class movements in Mexico.

The relative ease with which the UOI entered the auto plants was due in part to its explicit campaign against corporatist labour relations. Ortega Arenas argued that managers from Volkswagen, Nissan and DINA were willing to work with a labour central that explicitly advocated economic modernisation and a new and highly productive 'labour culture' in Mexico, outside of the CTM-PRI control. In retrospect, Ortega Arenas argued that these relatively new corporations wanted to work with the UOI because they were outside of the dominant sphere represented by the CTM in its relations with the Big Three auto producers. In his view, employers were receptive and supportive of the UOI's independence strategy because they themselves had been harmed by corruption and an unproductive labour relations regime. Both parties could agree that their interests would each be served if state control over labour relations were to be ended. The common argument turned on the importance of reviving a radically anti-statist variant of 'freedom of association' in Mexico.

If one considers, however, that DINA was a state-owned company, Volkswagen was the largest domestic producer and Nissan also had a substantial share of the domestic market, evidently these sections of capital were not marginalised in a national auto industry in which production was organised for internal consumption.

---

8   The company's pressure against the union did not end with the departure of the UOI. In 1983, a further 320 workers were fired (Martínez Cruz 1983, 42).

They were companies that operated within the older corporatist arrangements. Ortega Arenas's justification is incomplete as an explanation.

At its most basic level, the mutual interests of the UOI and the Echeverría government resided in their attempts to limit the power of the CTM. Echeverría argued that the government would create a 'democratic opening' in Mexican politics and society and so, it would seem, he attempted to recover some legitimacy for the state. By not overtly opposing the UOI, Echeverría gave tacit support to the independent labour federation. At the same time, other federations such as the *Frente Auténtico del Trabajo* (FAT) were not permitted to grow, and democratic tendencies within official unions, such as the *Tendéncia Democrática* of the Electrical workers, were severely repressed by the government. In playing off less contentious 'independent' movements with the CTM, Echeverría gained room for manoeuvre and increased legitimacy for his 'democratic opening'. In an early speech to the CTM in the Federal District, Echeverría asked, 'How are we going to speak of democracy in Mexico if, when a new executive is elected in a union, the process is not democratic?' Echeverría soon recanted, however, when faced with the opposition of the *charros* and their attempt to discredit the leadership of the most important independence movements (Punto Crítico 1972, 21).

Some argue that the emergence and relative success of the UOI reflected the weakness of the left in Mexico (Sánchez Díaz 1980, 212). Without strong and independent organisations, it is suggested the general dissatisfaction among workers took shape as relatively spontaneous movements. The UOI benefited from this state of affairs. As we have seen in this chapter, the UOI effectively neutralised the FAT in the case of Nissan. This defeat had ramifications in Cuernavaca and in the industrial heart of Mexico as well. The impetus for independent trade unionism and democratic union representation was channelled towards the companies' interests hedged within a 'marxian' discourse advocating the development of the productive forces. When the UOI chose to undermine union activities in the 'political terrain', a decisive opportunity for the sustained expression of alternatives to the corporatist model of representation was lost. In the words of Raymundo Jaimes:

> Those relations developed from a surge in popular consciousness. In the leadership of the urban popular movement, for example, were advanced people. But this did not last, it was a moment. The companies fired the activists and ended the movements, taking control of the movements. The management began to discuss who would become General Secretary. (Jaimes 1993; Translated by the author)

The UOI was successful because it developed a very sophisticated argument having to do with freedom of association and the development of the productive forces on the one hand, and, on the other, an affirmation of the limits of trade union action within the confines of what was permitted by the state.

One of the reasons often cited for the lack of labour strength in the auto sector is the failure to create a national union of autoworkers which could act in a coordinated way in the interests of its members. What is often over looked in this discussion is that national unions of autoworkers have existed according to the provisions of the

Federal Labour Law. The UOI created one such union in June 1978 with a reform of the constitution of the *Diesel Nacional* union.[9] Article One reads:

> Representing manual, technical and intellectual workers who work in all parts of the Mexican Republic in the automotive industry and related branches, the Union takes the name 'National Independent Union of Workers in the Automotive Industry and Related Branches'. (*Estatutos* 1991–1993, 00092; Translated by the author)

Since that time, the UOI, under the direction of its legal advisor, impeded the effective realisation of this national union, even to the extent that Ortega Arenas blocked the uniting of UOI unions in the auto sector into one union. UOI unions did, however, offer solidarity to one another (Middlebrook 1995, 252). The UOI rejected any suggestion of alliance with other movements for union independence.[10] The UOI was looked upon with a great deal of scepticism by other independent unions and the broader left. In the view of Alfredo Domínguez:

> This tendency did a lot of damage to the movement. They declared themselves so independent that they could not introduce themselves into other unions, because they were controlled. It was an experience of another type of corporatism. The union corporatism controlled by the state and by the official party, became controlled by a group of lawyers, self-named 'Coordinators' who controlled these unions.... They became independent thinking this was the alternative that the workers were looking for. Afterwards they realised that this was not a correct line since they moved from one form of official control to the control of the lawyers, which did not allow them liberty in their union activities. (Domínguez 1993; Translated by the author)

Despite a discourse of militancy, the UOI accepted the limits imposed by the state which led it, in the end, to a defence of the modernisation project advanced by the government (Zapata 1989, 189).

Nissan Workers in a National and International Context

The Nissan workers' struggle for independence from the CTM, internal democracy and autonomy from the state did not exist only at the level of the company and the region. It was also a manifestation of national level and international dynamics. Their movement corresponded with what we are identifying here as the first moment in the crisis which spanned two presidencies and implicated a third. This moment began in 1968 with the massacre of student activists and continued to 1982 when Mexico announced it could not meet its international debt obligations.

---

9   According to 1993 union constitution, the *Sindicato Nacional Independiente de Trabajadores de Diesel Nacional S.A* became the *Sindicato Nacional Independiente de Trabajadores de la Industria Automotriz, Similares y Conexos on the 6th of June 1978*. The official letter was signed by the subdirector of the Registry of Associations and issued its official approval of the change (*Estatutos del Sindicato Nacional Independiente de Trabajadores de la Industria Automotriz* 1991–1993, 00125).

10   All of the above are cited at length in Angulo, Ruiz, Solares, Tomás and Sánchez (1979).

The October 1968 massacre of unarmed students by the infantry in Tlatelolco at once revealed and provoked a profound crisis in Mexican society. After thousands of students were corralled and over three hundred killed in the *Plaza de los Tres Culturas* (Plaza of the Three Cultures), the idea of the Revolutionary social compromise was forever altered. This was the first time that state repression had been brought to the 'most sacred places' within the system (Niebla 1993, 62; see also Álvarez Garín 1993, 108). With this atrocity, those sectors of Mexican society that felt most entitled to Revolutionary guarantees were confronted with the authoritarianism that had been intrinsic to the stability of Mexican corporatism, but never visited upon them in such a direct way. For the students, however, the history of repression of workers and peasants was central to their movement. They saw themselves as opening up space for a much broader social transformation. The jailed student leaders, after having spent two years in Lecumberri prison, published their defence statements. Raúl Álvarez Garin who later went on to become a sitting member of the *Cámera de los Deputados*, the Mexican legislature indicated in his statement how acutely aware they were of how their ongoing protest challenged the government. On September 13, for example, the students let a silent march of 300,000 people in the capital city. 'It is clear that an action of this nature, conducted in silence, is only possible when there is in the citizens' consciousness a profound and absolute conviction in the righteousness of the struggle' (Álvarez Garin 1970, 64).

During the summer of 1968, the student movement opened up a space for reflection and action in which many popular forces participated:

In those days, we were living in a different climate in Mexico City. In spite of the fact that from the 26th of July repression did not cease for a moment, one could breathe in the air of liberty. The discontent and acts of resistance for so long time repressed, flowered every where and were exhibited publicly. People discussed freely, participated and saw the possibility of a changed future. The brigades went tirelessly to the factories, the markets and all public meeting places explaining the situation and calling on the people to participate directly in the struggle. In many unions and workplaces groups of opposition were organised which demanded that their leaders take positions in support of the students. Oil workers, electricians, railway workers and other small unions participated openly and as organisations in the marches and rallies. Resident doctors and interns from various hospitals in the city threw themselves into a solidarity strike and within the primary school teachers' union, movements for salary increases and solidarity with the students were generated. The press, for its part, had to give a more objective and impartial view of events. At the same time, international public opinion followed step by step what was going on in Mexico. In many countries, they organised acts of solidarity. In a very short period of time, the people took notice of many problems and acted however they could in their own sector. ... The movement presented itself before the government as the only opposition force capable of transforming the rigid system of political control of the masses. This was there in the way the people were becoming aware and gaining concrete experiences which signalled a possible path of action. A way for citizens to struggle was opening up, a way of holding public demonstrations, and criticising the government by naming the top officials, of directly challenging injustices and demanding respect for the opposition. In this way, the governmental control over unions was weakened, as well as popular organisations, press and the life of citizens. Eventually, organisations following this strategy could become independent and escape governmental control. The movement was opening this possibility, no more, no less. In no moment, and this was and is clear for any objective observer, did the triumph of the movement imply the overthrow of the government. Not in its demands, nor in its tactics, did it have an insurrectional character. (Álvarez Garin 1970, 57, 60; Translated by the author)

In his defence statement, Eduardo Valle recounted the links between the student and union movements:

> On the 15th of September, in a democratic spirit, we celebrated the feast of Independence, which for millions now held new meaning: the essence of militant struggle for liberty by the people. The bond between students and workers also was there. In the midst of the jubilation and the happiness, there we were united. Shoulder to shoulder, struggling for democracy and justice. This bond never will be broken, despite all the efforts of the government. It will never be broken, despite all the efforts of the enemies the people and of the students. (Valle Espinoza 1970, 31; Translated by the author)

The repression of the student movement in two weeks later at Tlatelolco caused wide sectors of society to question, not only the actions of the Díaz Ordaz regime and the violent way in which it moved to contain dissent, but the entire basis of Revolutionary Nationalism was re-examined in a period of intense social debate. No one would forget the events of 2 October.

La docena trágica, La docena militante

Mexican auto unions entered a new phase of militancy after 1968. In many respects, the tragic years (*la docena trágica*) of the 1970s were also militant years (*la docena militante*) for the labour movement as a whole. Unions in the automotive sector represented one of the manifestations of popular discontent within state corporatism, but not the only one. In general, the locus of dispute was the relationship between official labour bodies and the PRI, although the character of independent trade unionism during this period was heterogeneous. Some independent union federations, or 'white unions', were formed with the support of employers dissatisfied with their obligations to observe social rights under corporatism.[11] The Electrical workers' democratic movement formed parallel organisations within the official union. This union was nationalistic and Revolutionary in its origin and pushed for the fulfilment of guarantees long promised by the state. The Movement of Railway workers (MSF), for its part, battled with the Communist Party over whether it was more important to gain control over the local unions, or dedicate their efforts to broad based union organising under the leadership of the Party. Telephone and University workers mobilised to democratise the national union itself, and others in the civil service, such as health care workers, engaged in campaigns on a local by local basis. Where

---

11 Some independent unions of the northern states may exhibit autonomy from official trade union confederations, but are largely controlled by the employers. The federation of independent trade unions of Nuevo León, for example, represents an anti-corporatist current of thought amongst employers that found expression in the *Partido de Acción Nacional* (PAN), rather than in the governing PRI (Domínguez 1993).

it became evident that the movements would not be able to withdraw the union from the official centrals, other democratic movements concentrated on gaining local level elections or creating new structures within the union to confront the state over wage controls, lack of union democracy, the decline in real wages and authoritarianism. Competing political ideas within the movements, as well as institutional divisions between different sectors of the economy resulting from Mexican labour law contributed to this heterogeneity. Undoubtedly the pluralistic character of the debate was part of the 'effervescence' of the decade, there were, however, certain issues around which oppositional labour movements could agree. Foremost among these was the general sense that workers paid too high a cost for the partnership of the official labour bodies with the state.

After the democratic labour movements were crushed in the 1950s, the national industrial unions remained officially controlled by the CTM. These included the *Sindicato Nacional de Trabajadores Mineros, Metalurgicos y Similares de la República Mexicana* (SNTMMSRM) in the mine-metal sector; the *Sindicato de Trabajadores Petroleros de la Republica Mexican* (STPRM) in oil; the *Sindicato de Telefonistas de la República Mexicana* (STRM) in telecommunications; the *Sindicato de Trabajadores Ferrocarrileros de la República Mexicana* (STFRM) in the railway; the *Sindicato Mexicano de Electricistas* (SME) and the *Sindicato Unico de Trabajadores de Electricistas de la República Mexicana* (SUTERM) in the electrical sector (Bensusán 1990, 13). The corporatist social compromise was based on the protection of wages and job security in exchange for political support. 'Bilateral' rights of labour meant that the union would have to be consulted before employers could move workers within job categories and between shifts. As well, collective agreements limited the number of temporary workers and workers assigned to positions outside the bargaining unit. In most CTM workplaces, the union leadership had to be consulted on layoffs, new technologies, work reorganisation and sub-contracting (Bensusán 1990, 13; de la Garza and Bouzas 1999, 565–7). In corporatist forms of labour representation, workers themselves were permitted neither 'voice', nor 'vote'.

In February 1971, for example, the elections which brought Mariano Villanueva Molina to power in the railway workers union showed that the official forces made every effort to ensure the CTM remained in charge (Punto Crítico 1972, 26–7). The lack of democratic elections was so completely accepted as one of the unfortunate facts of labour politics that the President of the Republic apparently felt no hesitation in commenting upon it in his address to the meeting at which Villanueva took office. Echeverría declared:

> I know the protests have been given up and it was a democratic triumph. Certainly, the elections in which they triumphed were not perfect elections, as my own election was not perfect in many ways, but we are making improvements and we are about half way along the way towards the democratic process in our country. We have to accelerate the pace as the fatherland continues along its difficult path. (Punto Crítico 1972, 27; Translated by the author)

As one labour mobilisation followed another, it became apparent that a reorientation of state-society relations would be necessary to contain the political and the economic crisis.

Among the subordinated groups, issues of autonomy and democracy were raised together with demands opposing the policies of austerity imposed towards the end of the 1970s. Militancy was met with repression; in many cases, the large strikes were defeated. As real incomes fell and unemployment worsened over the decade, workers demanded effective representation from their union leadership. In moments when this was not forthcoming, internal conflicts within union locals emerged as conflicts in the labour boards or in regional organisations of labour centrals which challenged the institutional ordering of power between unions and the state. Insofar as movements for internal union democracy and autonomy from the state were generalised among many sectors of the labour movement, labour militancy took an unprecedented form in the 1970s. The wide variety of oppositional movements within trade unions opened up divisions within the alliance formerly consolidated inside of the governing *Partido Revolucionario Institucional* (PRI).

The lasting significance of these mobilisations lies in the shifting of the political terrain by conflict among social forces within the context of economic crisis that Mexico faced by the end of the Lopez Portillo presidency in 1982. In this sense, militant labour movements were protagonists within conditions of crisis. The severity of economic chaos and political turmoil indicated that the social compromise would not be easily reconstituted, if at all. Indeed, as the 1980s began, coercive responses seemed much more likely to resolve immediate difficulties for the state than consensual ones.

State Responses to Crisis: The Gendering of 'Shared Development'

As the head of the Ministry of the Interior in 1968, Luís Echeverría played a key role in the repression of the student movement and, as President from 1970–1976, was compelled to respond to the social and economic tensions threatening the stability of the regime (Hellman 1983, 189). Echeverría's reform program included nationalist economic development initiatives and a widening of the internal market by increased social spending. State strategies responded to the inability of state corporatism to overcome chronic balance of payments problems and external debt, but Echeverría's version of 'shared development', based on state-led growth strategies and income redistribution, gave way to austerity and a vigorous export-orientation introduced by Echeverría's successor, López Portillo towards the end of the 1970s.

'Maquiladoras'

The Mexican government bore the costs of the crisis in *Pax Americana* by continuing some of the policies set down by Echeverría's predecessor, Díaz Ordaz. This strategy solidified Mexico's entry into the new international gendered division of labour. In 1964, the US government ended the 20-year-old *Mexican Labor Program* under which Mexican *braceros* (male farmworkers) had been encouraged to work in the

US (Fernández-Kelly 1983, 209). As a result, thousands of workers were suddenly unemployed. The militancy of new peasant organisations and unemployment of up to 50 per cent in the border towns heightened pressure on the state to respond to the worsening situation and Díaz Ordaz oversaw the development of the Border Industrialisation Program (BIP) (Bustamante 1983, 232–3). The Program depended upon *maquiladoras* or 'in-bond plants' which were developed according to a twinning arrangement with factories on the US side of the border. The Mexican government argued that in order to attract light assembly industries to the region, Mexican laws restricting foreign ownership were lifted and domestic content levels were never imposed on these industries.

Many of these 'twinned' companies had already worked together in the import-substituting industries. Now, capital goods as well as raw materials and semi-processed goods were imported to the *maquiladoras* without Mexican tariffs, as long as 80 per cent of the finished goods were exported. Under US tariff codes 806.3 and 807, these finished goods went to the United States. The US tariff was applied only to the Mexican value-added, if US goods were used in production. Given the high level of imports and low wages, assembly work in the *maquilas* provided a relatively low value added. Consequently, companies paid low tariffs upon entry to the US market. With this arrangement, employers were also able to avoid the restrictions corporatist labour relations required.

The Border Industrialisation Programme never resolved the problem of male unemployment in northern Mexico, since employers sought out a female labour force. In the *maquila* region, employment for men continued to be scarce. Furthermore, employment was unstable, and workers were subject to plant closures.[12] As María Patricia Fernández-Kelly convincingly argued, employment in the *maquila* industries did not challenge women's subordinate position in Mexican society, even as the industry developed through the 1970s. In 1980, as Fernández-Kelly reported, 85 per cent of the *maquila* workforce was women between the ages of 17 and 25. This was unusual in the historical context of Latin American industrialisation. 70 per cent of these were single and sent more than half of their paycheques to their families. The young women lived with their parents and their wages were turned over to the family. Women who headed households provided the main source of income for their families, yet if they worked in the *maquilas*, their wages were inadequate to meet the family's needs. Fernández-Kelly found that most '*maquila* women' worked in either the electronics or apparel industries. Those recruited for the electronics industries were usually between the ages of 17–25, single, childless and had at least six years of education. Garment workers tended to be older women who were single mothers. Their educational level was lower than the workers in the electronic sector and their position in the labour market, weaker (Fernández-Kelly 1980, 15).

Maquilas were established in Mexico not only in response to the needs of US producers. Furthermore, although the *maquiladora* program appeared to respond to

---

12 Bustamante gives the example of the 30 industries that closed between 1974 and 1976, leaving 20,000 workers without work. Figures for the early 1970s indicate that only 2.4 per cent of migrants to the border regions found *maquiladora* work (Secretaría de Industria y Comercio 1974, 48–9, 96; see also Bustamante 1983, 248).

issues specific to the northern border region, it was also closely related to problems in the industrial core at the centre of the country. They offered a partial resolution to one of the central problems associated with import-substitution under state corporatism. In particular, the auto sector yielded a chronic balance of payments deficit (Arteaga, Carrillo and Micheli 1989, 6). By promoting the *maquiladora* program, the Mexican government attempted to gain in technology transfer, employment, foreign exchange, and income generation in the border region (Bustamante 1983, 242). If the export-oriented *maquiladora* industries could help replenish the national balance sheets strained by imports destined for the industrial centre, they would serve an important function.

In Mexico, the verb *maquilar* means 'to assemble', while the verb *maquinar* means 'to machine'; the first is a highly feminised production mode, the second highly masculinised. The similarity in the two verbs evokes the relationship which the two forms of industrial production have had over time. In a spatial sense the *maquilas,* in their border enclaves, were quite marginal to industrial production at the centre of the economy. However, the initiative was seen to have the potential to redress some of the structural problems within the industrial core. In this sense then, they were far from marginal.

Whether or not these new export-processing zones would meet the stated economic objectives, the *maquilas* also responded to the crisis of legitimacy faced by the dominant groups in Mexico. The new border industrialisation programme showed them to be actively seeking out 'forward looking' solutions to serious regional and national problems. In Mexico, the BIP met some of the ideological as well as material objectives that dominant groups sought as the limitations of import-substitution became widely apparent. Not only did dominant groups argue in favour of a solution to crisis that would not challenge the unequal social structure of the country, but this strategy depended upon the reproduction within the workplace of social practices subordinating women workers to the demands of the ongoing Revolutionary Project.

Industrial Policy

Along with the *maquiladora* programme, the federal government attempted to overcome the contradictions of state corporatism by nationalising key industries and expanding levels of national private ownership of industry. This national strategy was expressed in the 1972 *Decreto que fija las bases para el desarollo de la industria automotriz* (Decree to Establish the Bases for the Development of the Auto Industry) which outlined the government's objectives to increase employment and alter the structure of supply in the auto industry to reflect more accurately the purchasing power of the population (SECOFI 1972). The government sought to increase efficiencies and encourage the industry to develop its capacity as a net generator of foreign exchange. In this Auto Decree, support for majority national ownership in the parts industry was encouraged.

The new policy made it the responsibility of the manufacturers to overcome their own imports deficits by increasing exports and generating foreign exchange. Final assemblers were required to compensate for the value of their imports with a proportion of net foreign exchange generated by exports. At the same time, the Decree required auto manufacturers to permit national auto parts producers a share in production. Forty per cent of required foreign exchange was to be attained by the export of parts produced in the domestic auto parts industry (Bennett and Sharpe 1984, 175). The Decree limited the number of models produced by each company to seven. Any company making more than one basic gas engine would be required to export at least 60 per cent of the new engine. In exchange for compliance with these performance requirements, the Secretary of Finance and Public Credit would grant tax rebates of up to 100 per cent (SECOFI 1972, 6).

While the Decree was an important indicator of state strategy in this period, the active presence of the state in the auto sector did not achieve the results anticipated. During Echeverría's presidency, the auto industry demonstrated a higher than average growth index than all manufacturers and stayed ahead of the oil industry until 1976 (AMIA 1982, 9). Mexican automobile production increased 263.8 per cent between the years 1970–1981, but changes in production levels were closely linked with expansions and contractions in international markets (AMIA 1982, 9). Following the 1972 Decree, exports increased, yet the international recession of 1974–1975 and the resulting market contraction complicated the strategy. Furthermore, the goals of the Echeverría government conflicted with the strategies of foreign companies since, they argued, the Mexican market was not large enough to compel them to support exports from Mexico in a recessionary period (Bennett and Sharpe 1984, 186).

Together with the *maquiladora* programme and the regulation of the auto industry by Decree, state intervention was directed to the rescue of state corporatism in other highly masculinised industries. This strategy increased Mexican ownership in mines, mine-metal installations, steel, energy, petroleum and petrochemical industries. As well, the state promoted the development of large industrial centres around these industrial sites. The Mexican transportation industry was promoted in the vicinity of Ciudad Sahagún, Morelos for example. In this zone three companies *Diesel Nacional* (DINA), *Siderúrgica Nacional* and *Constructora Nacional de Carros de Ferrocarril* worked with another eight companies employing 17,000 workers to develop the industry.

The state-led development strategy included the regulation of foreign investment. Despite negative reactions from the US government, the 1973 *Ley para Promover la Inversión Mexicana y Regular la Inversión Extranjera* (Law to Promote Mexican Investment and Regulate Foreign Investment) was instituted in order 'to consolidate independence and avoid foreign interference in national decision-making.' It defined areas of exclusive jurisdiction for the state and national capital, instituted the principle of national ownership, restricted the sale of national companies to foreign investors and was overseen by the National Commission on Foreign Investment. According to Echeverría:

> There is no reason to grant special privileges or excessive stimuli. We need foreign participation to accelerate our growth process, but we are not disposed to accept it under conditions that place the heritage and the future of the nation at the mercy of interests that are not those of Mexico. (Echeverría, 1973: 205-6; Translated by the author)

Nevertheless, the legislation to regulate foreign investment could not address the severe crisis that the Mexican economy faced as a result of the deteriorating condition of the world economy.

Social Provision and the Renewed Role of the Worker-father

Along with the state-led economic development strategy that built upon the gendered dimensions of the new international division of labour, Echeverría attempted to rebuild the social compromise by expanding the internal market, redistributing income and extending the social security system. Assuming that demand would be met by the unused productive capacity of the national economy, the administration argued that state-led economic growth would not be inflationary (Cypher 1990, 89). These initiatives depended upon the gendered relations of the family and the social construction of the worker-father.

The idea of the social wage had always been present because of the Constitutional promises ascribed to 'Social Provision'. Echeverría's reforms re-asserted the industrial worker at the heart of his attempt to rebuild the social compromise in the 1970s. In Echeverría's words:

> Constitutional Article 123 is the principal foundation of all of our social policy and synthesises the Mexican philosophy towards development. It contains not only the essential norms of labour protection, but also the juridical instruments to attain the well being of the working class, the equilibrium of the factors of production and the more egalitarian distribution of what is produced. (Echeverría 1973, 216; Translated by the author)

Echeverría was explicit in his assertion of the relationship between collective identities as expressed in the Constitution and the rights that were derived from it:

> The social guarantees consigned to the Constitutional text, and in particular the dispositions of Article 123, are founded on the principle which considers man as a member of a social group and not as an abstract subject in juridical relations. The right to work, social security, and in a wider sense, all our systems of social well being are structured according to this conception. (Instituto Mexicano del Seguro Social 1993, 11; Translated by the author)

But we must remember that the 'social group' to which Article 123 referred was as much the family as it was class. Article 123 was the pillar of the social security regime in Mexico and beneficiaries were determined by their status as worker or the dependent of a worker. This, of course, was a principle that had serious implications for those who were not 'workers' including the unemployed, most women, children, the elderly, peasants, indigenous people, agricultural workers and workers in the informal sector.[13]

By 1970, only 10 million people were covered under social security; 40 per cent of these were residents of Mexico City, a region in which only 17 per cent of the

---

13 For an overview of the decline of the Social Solidarity programme during the latter part of Echeverría's term and its transformation during the presidency of López Portillo, see Spaulding (1982).

total population lived (Spaulding 1982, 142–3). The percentage of the population covered by social security doubled during Echeverría's term as president. Yet out of a population of 63 million, the social security program covered only 25 million people, or 39.7 per cent of the population in 1976 (Echeverría 1976, 54).

Under Echeverría, the 1943 *Ley del Seguro Social* was reformed to increase benefits to workers and their dependents and extend limited coverage to unprotected but economically active people, including homeworkers and agricultural workers (Echeverría 1973, 34; *Ley de l Seguro Social* 1993, 16–17). The reforms permitted beneficiaries to receive social security during strikes. Child care centres were set up for 'worker-mothers' and child benefits were reorganised under the *Instituto Mexicano para la Infancia y la Familia* (Mexican Institute for Children and the Family) which increased its presence in rural areas (Echeverría 1972, 123).

Later in his term, Echeverría revealed part of the gendered view of society underlying these initiatives:

> These results are the fruit of a new theory and a new practice of social solidarity, through which important transformative forces have been liberated; above all, feminine ones that up until a few years ago, had been frustrated in prejudice and in frivolous pastimes. (Echeverría 1976, 55; Translated by the author)

The integration of rural communities into the 'new practice of social solidarity' depended heavily on the volunteer labour of women, as well as the ideas of feminine virtue. The Sixth State of the Union address proclaimed during Echeverría's term indicated that one million peasant women and thousands of urban women had volunteered to participate in the National Coordinating Plan in 30,000 centres across the country.

While women were brought into the rural programs to facilitate the extension of social services in the most peripheral regions and among the most marginalised populations in the country, in the Valle de México, relatively privileged working-class men were still incorporated into the social security net through their union affiliations. Auto workers and their families received retirement and disability pensions, full medical care in clinics and hospitals, as well as recreational benefits at holiday centres. In the case of work related accidents, the state guaranteed life insurance of two months wages. Worker-mothers were entitled to six weeks paid leave before and after the birth.

According to the Mexican Constitution, large employers are responsible to provide housing for workers and their families, but this right was never guaranteed. Echeverría created a national housing fund for workers called the *Instituto del Fondo Nacional de la Vivienda para los Trabajadores* (INFONAVIT) which offered workers very low rates of annual interest and repayment schedules over 20 years. Employers were obliged to designate 5 per cent of nominal wages to the fund and the government would contribute enough to provide 100,000 new houses per year. The program was intended to increase employment in the construction industry and promote economic growth (Echeverría 1972, 125). Through the state-sponsored housing program, trade unions were responsible for having units built and allocated. As the number of housing units never equalled the number of workers willing to enrol in the program the allocation was often politicised. Loyal trade unionists had the best chance at receiving the housing benefit. A similar program, the *Fondo Nacional de Fomento y Garantía al Consumo de los Trabajadores* (FONACOT), was created to support savings and give workers access to a fund to buy consumer durable goods (Echeverría 1974, 75–6).

Echeverría attempted to win the support of intellectuals and students by increasing funding for education (Echeverría 1976, 57–69). Despite the governments efforts to re-establish legitimacy, in June of 1972, state violence was once used against the student movement during a demonstration in Mexico City (Echeverría 1972, 7). For the students, academics and university workers the 'university question' was not simply about chronic underfunding. They continued to fight for free and accessible universities, representative governing structures, democratic union-management relations, and academic freedom.

The government did not face opposition from subordinate groups only. From the beginning of his mandate, business leaders and their organisations fought a sustained battle against Echeverría's policies. They began to withdraw their investments and, over a prolonged period, refused to invest in the Mexican economy. There were severe shortages in basic goods because of lack of investment by businesses. Suspicions of hoarding abounded. Prices increased at outrageous rates and most labour organisations led sustained battles against the deterioration in real wages. Despite the government's economic development and social security policies, the legitimation crisis persisted throughout the 1970s.

Workers' reactions to the deterioration in wages during the 1970s prompted the Labour Congress (CT) to campaign for the creation in 1974 of the *Comité Nacional Mixto de Protección al Salario.* This joint commission, composed of union and government officials, developed a 1976 federal law protecting consumers against shortages, unsanctioned price increases and hoarding. The state was compelled to intervene in the sphere of direct wages as well. The day after the Congress of Labour (CT) called for a general strike for the first of October 1973, the President declared that workers' and employers' organisations would negotiate emergency wage increases.[14] Emergency wage increases were again decreed beginning September 1974. After a period of negotiations among labour and employer organisations, a general increase of 22 per cent was agreed upon, effective in 50,000 collective agreements (Echeverría 1974, 74–7).

In 1974, the Federal Labour Law was reformed to provide for an annual wage revision, instead of the traditional two year cycle. In the same reform, the profit-sharing provisions were changed to entitle workers to 8 per cent of pre-tax company profits payable each December (Echeverría 1975, 30). With this reform, there were now two lump sum payments due workers near the end of every year. The first

---

14 The agreement was to increase the minimum wage by 18 per cent in all regions; increase wages by 20 per cent for unionised workers earning more than one minimum wage; increase wages by 10–15 per cent for public and bank employees; and increase wages by 13 per cent for those earning more than 4,500 per month. With a subsequent increase in the minimum wage of between 12–15 per cent and 15 per cent in contract negotiations, workers' income levels was restored to that of the beginning of 1972 (Tello 1990, 71).

payment was the profit-share (*utilidades*), while the second was the Christmas bonus (*aguinaldo*) which was equivalent to 15 days of wages. The bonus was to be paid by 20 December each year and could be increased in contract negotiations (Fuentes 1994, 133).

While subordinated groups continued to mobilise around the limits to the reform program, the increasingly internationalised dominant groups came to resent the inflation and increased debt-load (Álvarez 1987, 23–8). During the Echeverría administration, the external public debt grew from US$ 4 billion to US$ 20 billion and balance of payments problems worsened (Álvarez 1987, 28). Landowners and large agro-industrialists were disaffected by the land reform (Hellman 1983, 215), while industrialists began to convert their currency to dollars, fearing a devaluation of the peso (Álvarez 1987, 28). By the end of Echeverría's term, the political crisis was profound.

International capital exerted its dominance within the economy by forcing a devaluation of the currency on August 31, 1976. A subsequent stabilisation agreement with the International Monetary Fund (IMF) re-oriented state policy towards the world economy (Álvarez 1987, 29). When Echeverría signed the stabilising agreement with the International Monetary Fund in 1976, it was clear that interventionist policies were to be abandoned in favour of a new phase of austerity. The previous social contract, which offered some concessions to labour, was undermined in this period of economic crisis. Where an expanding economy once offered labour increased wages and state services, the López Portillo years ushered in the first moves towards privatisation and cuts to government spending.[15]

By the end of Echeverría's mandate, with national capitalists and conservative forces in open conflict with the Presidency, the elements of the official labour movement calling for a return to economic nationalism, and with the prospect of a resurgence of armed battles in the countryside, it did appear that 'shared development' lived only at the level of official discourse. Echeverría's bid to return the state to legitimacy seemed to have failed miserably and the move towards further integration with the international economy was the strategy advocated by the next government as the way out of the crisis.

From Shared Development to Austerity and Export-led Growth

Throughout Echeverria's term, Mexico came under continuing pressure as a result of the weaknesses of *Pax Americana*. In the early years of the government's mandate, Echeverría's minister of finance tried to maintain financial stability by announcing that the government would not alter the traditional practice permitting free convertibility of the peso, nor change the convention that pegged the peso to the US dollar at a rate of 12.5 (Tello 1990, 47–50). On August 15 1971, however, the United States announced that it would no longer tie its currency to the gold standard and would raise tariffs by 10 per cent on many imported goods. In response, the Mexican government instituted a tight monetary policy and restricted its own

---

15 Punto Crítico, *Problemas y perspectivas*, 20–22.

spending.[16] It soon became evident that this strategy was politically unsustainable since there were far too many unresolved social inequities for the government keep this monetarist option alive. By the second year of its mandate, the Lopez Portillo government reported increased economic growth, a renewed commitment to public investments and increased social expenditures.[17] Mexico's troubles continued in the wake of the worst economic crisis faced by industrialised countries in the post-war period. The recession of 1974–75 had severe effects on marginalised countries, including Mexico. In 1974, for example, prices for imported goods increased on average of 40 per cent, while export prices increased only 27 per cent. Not only did the country face deteriorations in the terms of trade, but the markets for exported goods stagnated as well (Tello 1990, 119).

In the 1970s, state strategy depended upon the strengthening of the industrial infrastructure through targeted expenditures, along with the strengthening of the national capitalist class through targeted production plans and controls over foreign investment. As it became apparent that state policies favouring state corporatism were failing, the government of José López Portillo (1976–1982) ushered in a national austerity program as a response to the demands of the dominant classes in Mexico and in accordance with the three year IMF stabilisation program. Price controls were eliminated on many goods and social services were cut. Concerned with the reestablishment of business confidence, López Portillo secured investments from the private sector and wage controls from the unions. The discourse of modernisation continued to be set in terms of the Revolution but state policies marked a departure from previous practices (Álvarez 1987, 35). Intending to re-establish confidence and administer the crisis with authority, López Portillo followed the devaluations of 1976 with wage cuts and wage freezes in 1977–1978 (Punto Crítico 1980, 55–8). The paternalistic aspect of presidential *caudillismo* receded as the authoritarian response to crisis gained ascendency under López Portillo. Such was the price of stabilisation.

With the transition to the new administration, economic policy became increasingly outward-oriented. The 1977 Auto Industry Decree attempted to increase the industry's performance with respect to balance of payments equilibrium by rationalising the use of foreign exchange and favouring expanded exports. The Decree noted the deleterious effects that currency rates were having on the level of 'national integration' in the industry. An overvalued peso made it more expensive for producers to use nationally produced parts. At the same time, the Decree retained the objectives relating to other areas of national priority that would focus on the industry's national development. These included its concern to generate employment, take advantage of the internal market, develop an auto parts industry through import-

---

16 Echeverría reported that the government had reduced the general level of spending in his first year in order to contain an internationally generated cycle of inflation (Echeverría 1972, 105–6).

17 According to the President's address, authorised federal spending for all of 1972 was forecast to be 30 per cent higher than the previous year and would increase by the same amount during the rest of the term (Echeverría 1972, 111–12).

substitution and the national integration of the industry, support national companies, rationalise production and increase productivity levels (SECOFI 1977, 3).

The new Decree stipulated that the *Secretaría de Patrimonio y Fomento Industrial* (SECOFI) would assign an annual foreign exchange budget for auto producers based on an initial authorised quota and net exports (SECOFI 1977, 3). This quota would be calculated according to each company's previous balances of foreign exchange, the proportion of Mexican capital in the company and the national content levels of the vehicles. The quota was a highly formalised means of regulating the use of foreign exchange. Final assemblers were required to generate at least 50 per cent of net foreign exchange for their budgets, with the export of components manufactured by companies in the auto parts industry with programs approved by the Secretary. The remaining 50 per cent could be obtained by export of vehicles and in-plant auto part manufacturing, or from parts producers without approved programs. Component parts manufactured by *maquiladora* companies (under paragraph three, article 321 of Customs Code of the United States of Mexico), could only account for up to 20 per cent of net foreign exchange required.

Minimum national integration levels were set at 50 per cent for automobiles, 65 per cent for trucks, 70 per cent for tractor-trailers and buses and 65 per cent for agricultural tractors. It was recommended that companies increase these levels by 5 per cent in 1978 and each year following to 1981. As before, the Inter-Secretarial Commission on the Auto Industry published a list of obligatory national components. The assemblers were prohibited from manufacturing components produced by national parts producers, but the Secretary provided more leeway for applications when, in its judgement, it would be beneficial for the economy. As a result of the new Decree, companies were required to export, not only according to the importation of parts for assembled vehicles, but in compensation for the imported components from parts suppliers as well. Half of the exports would have to come from the parts suppliers. In addition, they had to balance foreign remittances, such as shipping and insurance costs through exports (Bennett and Sharpe 1985, 238).

The 1977 Decree was proclaimed in a year of severe economic crisis, but vehicle production increased dramatically in the following four years. From 1977–1981, vehicle production increased 97 per cent and automobile production increased at an average rate of 19 per cent per year. Exports, however, did not increase proportionally and in fact, the auto trade deficit with the United States tripled between 1977 and 1979 (Bennett and Sharpe 1985, 238). An initial wave of major investments in new export-oriented plants and equipment were made in the years 1978–1979 for production dates set in 1982–1983. Employment increased by 72 per cent to 37,830 workers and employees in the terminal industry. National integration increased significantly in the two categories which includes the smallest cars and the largest trucks while increasing only marginally in all other categories.[18]

As oil prices rose dramatically on the world market, the Mexican state turned toward the exploitation of new found oil reserves during the oil boom during the

---

18 The level of 'national integration' of the industry refers to the percentage national content integrated in the final product. It is calculated according to the cost-parts formula referred to the Decree of June 20, 1977 (SECOFI 1977, 4).

years 1978–1981. During this time, oil exports remitted as much as 75 per cent of all foreign earnings (Cypher 1990, 108), and the GDP increased at an average rate of 8.4 per cent in real terms (Cypher 1990, 104). This was an extraordinary rate of growth but the development of resources did not overcome the problems in the Mexican political economy. In fact, the way in which the state and dominant classes organised the development of the oil reserves brought the country to utter chaos.

New public spending was required to develop the reserves. The state, anticipating the continuation of high oil prices and low interest rates, invested heavily. As a percentage of total public long-term debt, the state-owned petroleum monopoly PEMEX's share rose from 12 per cent in 1975 to 21 per cent in 1979 and to 37.8 per cent in 1981 (Cypher 1990, 109). PEMEX received 25 per cent of the public budget in 1976. This percentage was increased to 45 per cent in 1980. López Portillo borrowed to the point of increasing the public debt by 102 per cent between 1980 and 1982 (Cypher 1990, 118).

Furthermore, this export-led development strategy also required the increase in imports of capital goods for petroleum development. Although the 1979 Development Plan suggested that domestic industry would develop capital goods, neither backward or forwards linkages resulted. López Portillo refused to limit imports (Cypher 1990, 117). The balance of payments problems worsened as a result of the import of capital goods, but also because of the import of consumer goods during the economic expansion. Imports grew from 5.9 billion $US in 1977 to 23.1 billion $US in 1981 (Bennett and Sharpe 1985, 230). Manufacturing exports became too expensive for external markets due to inflation and the overvalued peso. Oil exports were increased, in order to deal with the trade deficit, but this contributed to the cycle of increasing imports and borrowing. Consequently inflation and export problems worsened (Bennett and Sharpe 1985, 230).

The crisis approached as oil prices fell 11 per cent in 1981 and US monetary policy increased international interest rates. Capital flight increased to 15 billion $US in 1981 and the peso was devalued by 20 per cent in 1981 and by a further 78 per cent in February 1982. Much of the government's borrowed foreign exchange went to supporting the currency, but, in the most cynical of practices, massive amounts of private capital were converted to dollars and then reconverted to pesos after devaluation (Cypher 1990, 117–18). The state offered domestic industrialists low energy prices in the hopes that they would increase investment, but investors preferred speculation and capital flight to long-term investments, despite the extent to which the state had gone in meeting their demands.

On 1 August 1982, Mexico announced that it could no longer meet payments on its international government debt. Its bankruptcy threatened the international financial system and caused chaos within Mexico. By 15 August, the government had reached an agreement with the United States to sell the US Strategic Reserve an unspecified amount of oil over the next five years at $10 below the OPEC price which was then set at $34 (Teichman 1988, 132). The US also demanded that Mexico quickly come to an agreement with the International Monetary Fund (IMF). In exchange, Mexico received a loan for $1 billion from the United States. Two weeks later, in response to growing popular opposition and the upcoming transition to a new presidency, López Portillo announced that the banks would be nationalised. The bank nationalisation indicated that the Mexican state was vulnerable to the opposition of popular forces. The dominant classes intended to ensure such displays of autonomy would be closely circumscribed (Cypher 1990, 126). The antagonistic relations between the state and dominant classes were inscribed in the subsequent agreement with the IMF.

During the Echeverría and López Portillo years, the state moved between strategies of negotiation and repression. Equitable growth was not a priority (Punto Crítico 1980, 19–20). For the Mexican government to effect a modernisation of the economy, it would have to confront entrenched and powerful interests that had been established in mid-century. In part, this meant that the highly protected owners of national industries would have to be compelled to invest in their companies to increase productivity levels. As well, it meant that the official trade union bureaucracy would have to be modernised as well (Álvarez 1987, 19). As Alejandro Álvarez argues, the government's relations with unions in the 1970s must be seen in light of the legitimation crisis of the state, the corporatist system of domination over the trade unions, and the union bureaucracy (Álvarez 1987, 21). Echeverría did not try to end corporatism in the trade union movement, but his plans for modernisation depended upon his success in compelling the union bureaucrats to follow his lead. Otherwise, Álvarez argues, the antiquated trade union structures would not have been able to withstand the discontent that had arisen within the subordinated classes. As a result, the government's labour policy was two-faced, 'if one side legitimised union dissidence, the other repressive side crushed, without compassion, all opposition to the union bureaucracy' (Álvarez 1987, 22). With the outward turn under López Portillo, Mexican workers faced the disciplinary dynamic of the international market as well as intense repression by the state. The costs of dissent were evident to any trade unionist who was engaged in collective efforts to change the terms of representation and of production. With the failure of paternalism and the turn towards authoritarianism, it was abundantly clear in the early 1980s that a simple reconstruction of a social compromise was not in the offing.

Chapter 4

The *Maquilisation* of Ford de México

Without independence from the state, the freedom to develop autonomous ways of confronting their employer, or democratic forms of internal representation, unionised men in Mexico were bound to experience the crisis-ridden years of the 1980s as a convergence of over-lapping power relations. Was it the state or the employer's interest which was served by wage freezes? Was it the employer or the official union bureaucracy who benefited when democratic union committees were deposed? Was it the union bureaucracy or the courts which were responsible for permitting the denigration of labour rights? Was there a political solution to be found when industrial restructuring and *maquilisation* could not be fought by free collective bargaining? Was it international capital or national capital which benefited most from the debt crisis and the flight of capital from the country? The aim here is to explore how working-class men at Ford Motor Company strategised when faced with these questions, and reflect on how they fought back against the authoritarianism of the state and their employer as it was externalised and expressed through the institutional power of *caudillismo* and the CTM.

In this story, it is not *caudillismo* as embodied in the individual strong leader that we are considering. Rather, here we address the more complicated way in which institutional *caudillismo* was exerted and then challenged by a movement of working-class men. In the 1980s, patriarchy became a battle-ground where democratic movements of workers fought with the trade union bureaucracy and the state over the right to have a voice in the restructuring of production. As the worker-father tried to defend his rights as elaborated in the Constitution and the Labour Law, the official trade unions also resorted to legal, as well as extra-legal means which were themselves highly gendered. With brutality and impunity did they attack the workers' resistance to what the employers had set in motion. But this was not only a battle between men. It was also a battle premised on the construction of women workers in a much subordinated role. In place of the honourable 'worker-father', it was the highly-flexible, '*maquila*-woman' who came to be the preferred working-class subject of the restructured economy.

Ford Workers' Union

Ford workers became unionised in 1932, seven years after Ford was established in Mexico. The *Unión de Obreros y Empleados de la Industria Automotriz y Similares del Distrito Federal (FSODF)* and affiliated with the *Confederación Regional Obrera Mexicana* (CROM) They participated in the first assembly of the CTM, but affiliated with the CGT in 1936 and with the CTM in 1938. The corporatist social compromise was maintained at the Ford plants for many years and depended up on the plant delegate, who was a representative from the CTM, but neither a Ford worker nor a person who had held union office. He handled conflicts, as well as labour-management relations in all three plants until his death in 1975 (Middlebrook 1995, 233). In this period, the 'fordist' character of labour relations meant that the union was involved in negotiating some of the terms of production, including line speed, the length of the working day and the movement of workers from one position to another within the plant as established in the collective agreement.

To many workers, the 'involvement' of the union meant a discussion between the union official and managers, rather than any broader rank-and-file participation. Instead of discussing workload with workers at Cuautitlán, for example, the plant delegate would inform worker of the results of the discussion:

> [The Union official] would come and inform the representatives at the plant: that there would be this increase, and afterwards, the would pass by to see us and everyone to see what problems there were, but in reality, he never resolved a single one. Neither was there ever a strike. What there was, was an agreement between the company and [the official].
> (Talavera y Muñoz 1993, 6; Translated by the author)

In 1975 the CTM responded to the general opposition in the auto sector by restructuring its presence there. It organised the Ford workers into one union with a section for each plant and encouraged workers to participate in the elections (Aguilar García 1982, 76). Ford workers were able to attain a certain amount of union democracy without leaving the CTM and a democratic slate gained control of the executive at Cuautitlán in February 1976. A few months later, the democratic slate won in Tlalnepantla but the old guard stayed in place in La Villa (Aguilar García 1982, 56). The first strike at Ford in 50 years took place in July 1976 (Aguilar García 1982, 60). The question of separating from the CTM was raised but the opposition worked instead to disrupt the power of the CTM bureaucrat who had run the union and deal instead with the national executive committee of the CTM (Aguilar García 1982, 100). There were very few strikes at Ford; however, a strike in 1978 resulted in the creation of a joint training committee of both management and the union. Late in October 1980 there was a very successful strike which resulted in a salary increase of 27.5 per cent. In February 1983, another strike took place over wages and the dismissal of 1,800 workers (Trejo Delarbe 1990, 194).

By the late 1980s, the Cuautitlán collective agreement had institutionalised the role of the local union, as well as the CTM officials, to participate in the day-to-day organisation of production. Arnulfo Arteaga García analysed the main ways in which the 1985–1987 contract established the union's involvement in decisions around the assignment of workers to their positions, as well as wages and benefits: The company agreed to hire extra workers to cover absent workers; temporary workers would to be paid two days wages for every week should their contract be shortened; there were seniority-based regulations on promotions; any change in position had to be registered and any temporary reclassification to a higher position came with a corresponding increase in wages and benefits; during the 90-day probationary period in a new job in a higher classification, workers were entitled to the increase in wages and benefits, as well as training, after which time the wage and benefit increase would become permanent; when the employer needed to change workers from one place to another temporarily, the union and management were both responsible to ensure the rights of the workers in the new department, as well as the worker who was being moved, were not affected; workers were entitled to 495 days of wages for life insurance after one year, which reached 1,415 days wages when a worker had 44–47 years seniority.

Candidates for employment had to be examined by the company's medical doctor. If the candidate did not pass, the union could request the report in writing and submit it to an official medical institution which would then be binding; any candidate who was not accepted by the employer, could have their name submitted again by the union. If the employer and the union could not agree that a worker was qualified to a vacant position, together they would conduct tests relating only to the requirements of the new position; the employer would cover the transportation costs of a worker who was obliged to work between 11pm and 6 am; shift changes were routinised; weekend overtime was paid an extra 75 per cent: statutory holidays would be compensated at an extra 14 per cent of the weekend bonus. Finally, the agreement stated:

> The employer recognises the right of workers to work in a balanced way during the work day, which is understood as the rate at which an average worker works. It is the responsibility of the employer to avoid work over load derived from absenteeism; equipment failure or other irregularities which are not the responsibility of the worker. (Arteaga García 1990a, 71–4; Translated by the author)

These were the benefits accorded those who consented to *caudillismo*: relatively high wages, job protection, benefits and an active, if contradictory, presence of the union in the workplace. It was the basis for the corporatist social compromise. It was the proving ground for competing industrial masculinities, and the reason for the uneasy alliance between the collective-as-worker-father and the *caudillo*-as-union leader.

The Restructuring of Ford in the 1980s

The Ford Motor Company undertook to restructure its Mexican operations in the wake of the recession and economic crisis of the early 1980s. After the one-millionth car, an LTD, rolled down the assembly line, Ford closed down the La Villa assembly plant in 1982, except for two departments which closed in 1984. The Tlalnepantla foundry and machine shop was closed as well, leaving its highly skilled workers unemployed. The bulk of new investments were directed towards 'greenfield' investments in the northern states. Ford began production at its new engine plant in Chihuahua, Chihuahua in 1983. With an initial investment of 500 million $US, the new engine plant had the capacity to produce 440,000 units annually. In 1986, Ford began production at its new joint venture with Mazda in Hermosillo, Sonora. Initially, this new plant had the capacity to produce 130,000 Mercury Tracers each year, but new investments increased the productive capacity to 170,000 by 1990 and introduced Ford Escorts into the production line. Together these investments in Hermosillo represented 800 million $US (Arteaga García 1990a, 66–7). The Hermosillo and Chihuahua plants became the most automated plants in the country and were opened under conditions of maximum flexibility.

Before the new northern plants were opened, *Ford de México* signed collective agreements with the *Comité Ejecutivo Nacional* (CEN) (National Executive Committee) of the *Sindicato Nacional de Trabajadores de Ford Motor Company* (National Union of Ford workers) affiliated to the *Confederación de Trabajadores de México* (CTM). The union now represented workers organised into local unions at Ford-Cuautitlán, in the State of Mexico, Ford-Hermosillo, Sonora and Ford-Chihuahua, Chihuahua. Although workers in all three plants were represented by the same union through the national executive committee, they all had different contracts with different negotiating dates.

The fact that higher wages were paid to workers in the older plant in the State of Mexico was cause for labour discontent in the newer northern operations. Even in comparison with other auto plants, the average wage in the Cuautitlán plant was 12 per cent higher than the oldest plants in the auto industry that were built in the 1950s or before. These figures did not include amounts workers received for benefits, which included: punctuality bonuses, holidays, Christmas bonus, savings plan, meal tickets, profit sharing, and social security. When these benefits were added up, Ford-Chihuahua workers received the equivalent of 146 days wage per year in benefits, while the equivalent value for all other assembly plants, except the General Motors-DF was 89.1 days of wages. At General Motors-DF, one of the oldest plants in the country, workers were entitled to 149.4 days of wages in benefits each year. In comparison with the three different categories of assembly plants, the Cuautitlán workers earned 19.4 per cent more than the oldest, 32.5 per cent more than the middle and 62.4 per cent more than the youngest group of auto assembly plants. In comparison to other Ford workers, they earned 121.5 per cent more than the average worker at Chihuahua and 168.6 per cent more on average than a worker at the Hermosillo plant (Arteaga, 1990a, 69). In part, the strong collective agreement at Ford Cuautitlán reflected the age of the labour force. These were established workers who had years of seniority built up within the model of rights acquired by the worker-father.

Only the collective agreement in Cuautitlán stood in the way of a completely flexible production system in Ford's Mexican operations. Consequently, from the perspective of the Ford Motor Company, it was imperative that a new collective agreement be written for the Cuautitlán plant (Arteaga 1990b, 148). Employers wanted to reassert their rights to have complete control over production. A Ford worker described how this tension played out:

> There were a lot of conflicts with the supervisors. Even more when I had to confront one of these problems…, I said: 'You don't know anything. You're a little engineer that the company contracted with but I myself had to teach you.' And it was true. I taught them the whole process and the worst of it was that once they learned, they really screwed us. (Talavera and Muñoz 1993, 6; Translated by author)

Ford's restructuring plan involved the dismantling of the labour relations regime that had been constructed within corporatism and the old social compromise. It was not the case that the CTM became irrelevant in the new flexible environment. Where once it controlled workers who gave their consent in exchange for relatively high wages and benefits, the CTM came to exert control over workers without granting any benefits; except the privilege of remaining employed. In response, the democratic movements within the official unions had to contend with not just the relocation of production, but the intensification of work, the worsening terms of representation, as well as the national austerity policies of the government.

Strike, Closing and Severance: Cuautitlán in 1987

The existence of a strong contract at Ford Cuautitlán was the central issue to emerge in a protracted conflict between management and the local union during the 1987 negotiations (Arteaga 1990b, 141–74). The conflict at Cuautitlán began when, during the summer of 1987, the Mexican government decreed automatic emergency minimum wage increases for non-unionised workers. Miguel de la Madrid also decreed that any increases in unionised workplaces would be negotiated by employers and workers. With the National Union Executive pressing for the increases of 53 per cent, the Ford-Cuautitlán workers went out on strike on 21 July. Workers at Ford Hermosillo and Ford Chihuahua were granted a significant increase but went out on strike in solidarity with the Cuautitlán workers. With the strike moving into its second month, the company gave notice that it was about to close the Cuautitlán plant and terminate the contracts of all workers there. The workers were prepared to reduce their demands, but the apparently intractable position of the National Executive Committee justified the closure. What appeared to be a conflict over wages was an effort to improve flexibility in the collective agreement. Many observers concluded this conflict was provoked by the national CTM leadership and the company to move the situation to a critical impasse (Arteaga, 1990b, 153–4).

The strike had already been a long one and the general feeling among the workers was that they should accept the severance pay. Even though there was opposition to this position, the workers fell back into their own past practices:

> Unfortunately, when they coughed up this kind of money for the severances we were due, we fell for it. We all felt we should try to organise some kind of union response, but, from the point of view of the Ford workers, we were the best paid in the region, in the industry and in the country, and nobody wanted to get themselves into problems. Everybody used to say 'Am I going to risk my salary, my benefits and my seniority, no, no, no, no.... Better we fall in line and look for other means.' Never, never did we have a struggle and more than anything, what hit us were the very high percentages they would pay for the severance. So that's the route the people took. (Talavera and Muñoz 1993, 33; Translated by the author)

The Secretary General of the National Executive Committee was publicly in favour of the outcome and signed an agreement on 19 September, whereupon the company began the process of dismissing all 3,200 workers. Interestingly, the Federal

Arbitration and Conciliation board rejected the agreement, arguing that it did not guarantee the rights of workers. Still, the agreement provided more money than most workers had ever received and they accepted the settlement, even while knowing that they would have no job to return to (Arteaga 1990b, 153).

Although all workers received severance packages when the company closed its doors, the financial instability of the October 1987 stock market crash led to a period of economic insecurity throughout the autumn. Incredulous, the fired workers watched as the money that was to provide some future protection brought the instability of the international economy to their doorsteps:

> When we received the severance pay we thought we would invest it. At that time the interest rate paid by the bank was 160 per cent annually. As well, the banks came to the doors of the plant offering us advice on how to invest our resources that in total were millions of pesos. They offered us credit cards and I don't know what all... But, what happened? Twenty or 30 days after having received the severance pay, ... there was a devaluation of the peso of nearly 60 per cent. As well, the stock market crashed and many of the brothers attracted by the high interest rates had invested there.... So, many people that made investments, when all of this happened, well, they were out on the street. (Talavera and Muñoz, 1993, 33–4; Translated by the author)

Contracts and Working Conditions in the 'New Ford'

Although the severances had been paid out, Fidel Velázquez, General Secretary of the CTM and John Ogdin, Director of Ford, held talks throughout the autumn on the conditions of a new contract which would precede the re-opening Ford Cuautitlán. In the meantime, the Secretary General of the National Union of Ford workers was removed from his position by Fidel Velázquez who replaced him with Héctor Uriarte as interim leader. Within weeks, the company opened the Cuautitlán operations again, and rehired many of its old employees under a completely new contract. On November 9, the plant resumed operations with 2,500 re-hired employees. As a result the negotiations between the CTM and Ford which led to the reopening of the plant also opened up a new phase in labour relations.

The new collective agreements mandated a steep reduction in job classifications. After the conflict at Ford Cuautitlán, skill levels were reduced from 32 to 6, and job classifications from 303 to 160 (Carillo 1990b, 92). This brought it closer to the new Ford Hermosillo plant which was opened with only one classification. At Ford Cuautitlán, seniority rights were taken away and replaced by management prerogatives in individual cases regarding remuneration and job changes Arteaga, Carillo and Micheli, 1989, 13). The 'bilateral' relationship of unions and management was replaced with one rewarding individual workers' performance and productivity. This suggests a crucial difference from what was previously the case. In the new plants, the company asserted complete rights to establish levels of productivity and efficiency. Productivity levels were once negotiated by the union at Cuautitlán. As in Hermosillo, management claimed the right to impose whatever programs it deemed necessary in the area of productivity, quality and training (Carillo 1990b, 103).

By firing the workers and reopening the plant under a new collective agreement, management was able to break with the character of labour relations as they had developed since 1964 when the plant was first opened. The National Union gave up rights acquired over years of struggle in the industrial centre of the country by signing these collective agreements, and undermined the strongest collective agreement in the auto industry. As a result, the Ford-Cuautitlán collective agreement immediately went from being the best contract with respect to labour rights in the automobile industry in the country, to being the worst. Arteaga notes three important changes in the conditions facing workers upon their return to the factory. First of all, wages and benefits were substantially reduced. Secondly, there was a definite shift away from the concept of *bilateralidad*, that is, a diminishing of the local union's legitimate role in determining working conditions in the plant. Finally, the local committee lost autonomy in its relationship with the national union (Arteaga 1990b, 155). The collective agreement at Ford-Cuautitlán now conformed to the flexible character of production that had been introduced in the north of Mexico.

When the workers returned to Ford, they were told that a 'New Ford' now existed, with a new contract and new working conditions (Arteaga 1990a, 64–74). All acquired years of seniority were lost to the workers who were re-contracted. The new collective agreement indicated that management could move workers wherever they were required, without having to provide for the financial security of workers who were transferred. Management was permitted to expand the role of temporary workers in the plant and overtime benefits were reduced. Where movement up the job ladder was once based on seniority rights, management acquired the right to move workers both up and down the ladder, according to constant evaluations of 'competence, efficiency, conduct, attendance, punctuality and discipline.' The union lost the right to dispute management's decisions against workers who wished to move to vacant jobs. In this way, the new collective agreement diminished the union's role in conflict resolution and emphasised the responsibility of the individual worker to uphold quality and productivity standards. The new contract also increased the subordination of the local union to the control of the national leadership. Rather than leaving hiring decisions up to the local leadership, for example, the approval of the Secretary General of the National Union was required before workers were contracted by the company (Arteaga 1990a, 71–4).

So that all workers would keep up with the faster pace on the line, only uninjured workers were hired back. The buses that brought workers to the plant were instructed to arrive 30 minutes before the shift started, and once the shift started, there were no breaks.

We couldn't go to the bathroom to urinate and honestly, so that we wouldn't lose time, they put urinals on the other side of the line. From our work station, we could see them, but to be able to go, you had to stock up your work on the line for an hour working like hell and shout to the others, 'hey bastards, I'm going to piss' and everyone had to make way for you, because you had to do two operations which meant one hour fucked to be able to go and piss and when you got back, your operation was behind and then you had to run like hell for the next half hour to be able to catch up to the level of production. (Talavera and Muñoz 1993, 20; Translated by the author)

The organisation of the meal was changed so that the line would be stopped for one 30-minute period only, instead of the previous system in which each department had its own scheduled break. The longer line-ups resulted in a reduced eating period and the fact that workers were forbidden to sit down during the eight hour shifts caused a considerable amount of frustration.

> The people on the second shift have to be here at two pm, and gentlemen, from this moment on, it is forbidden to sit down, and if for any reason, the line stops, as the cleaning of your area is now your task, because now there will be no cleaners, the cleaning department is gone, the workers in the cafeteria are gone, the gardeners are gone, and the labour is now contracted-out because these are now services that are bought, since these departments don't have any reason to be here anymore. This is what they told us in that talk.... Ok, so in principle, we accepted it, but for the old habits, when we came to work and we sat down a minute, the supervisor used to come by and say, 'You know what, get up. Get to work.' But the line is down. 'Prepare materials.' They are already prepared. 'Okay, get yourself a broom and get sweeping.' It was forbidden to sit down and as a result, the productivity was increased enormously. So much so that just before the conflict we were producing 480 units each day with around 3,800 workers and the truth is that not even when we were 5,000 workers did we produce that many units, and that was with three shifts. (Talavera and Muñoz 1993, 37–8; Translated by the author)

Conditions in the plant had deteriorated with respect to workers' daily experience and high stress levels became evident early on. A worker describes the effect on the men in the plant:

> It's real agony. I remember one *compañero* who at the hottest hour of the day, around 1 in the afternoon, exhausted from the beating, was throwing tools, already going about enraged, a rage that the company takes advantage of and since everyone is furious, everyone enraged, everyone wants to tell them to go to hell, to tear them to pieces, and so the company uses all this fury to get us to work harder, because then they raise the speed on the production line. All of the sudden we find ourselves working quicker, quicker, until everyone on the line begins to hiss and boo, sshh, sshh, sshh, everyone punching the boxes and already at the limit, at the edge of hysteria, because we couldn't take the beating. (Talavera and Muñoz 1993, 19; Translated by the author)

To this, he adds:

> The anguish of living on the line was daily and on Sunday afternoons, I would disconnect from the world because on Monday I had to go back to work, it was the anguish of the stress of only thinking that I would be running back and forth for eight hours, in which you can't sit down, in which you can't drink water, can't even go to piss. (Talavera and Muñoz 1993, 20; Translated by the author)

Ford was able to alter the working conditions in the plant by unilaterally asserting its control over the production process but, as a result, the stability of labour relations under the old conditions disappeared. The company imposed the conditions it desired with respect to its flexibility program on the workers, but it could not compel workers to welcome it. In the words of an ex-Ford worker:

All this obviously increased productivity and with it, an exaggerated work-over load. In principal, over-time was eliminated; we were very accustomed to working over-time, but with the new company this was the slogan they used, over-time is eliminated for everything, productivity is increased to the limit and with the most miserable salaries you've ever seen. That's when people began to realise where they were leading us. Then people began to protest, to complain, to show it in low quality, in blocking up the production line, in producing defective materials, people began to do things to show their non-conformity. (Talavera and Muñoz 1993, 39; Translated by the author)

The company responded to the dissent on two levels. First, with increased authoritarianism, it began selective firings and was able to do so easily since all workers were still on temporary contracts. Second, in a more paternalistic way, the company instituted weekly meetings of *círculos activos* (circles of assets) in the plant in order to impress upon workers, their self-interest in improving the plant's competitiveness. A worker recounts the impact of the quality programme:

Before, we used to say: 'What I am selling is my labour power, and if the operation ends up badly, it is because the material is bad, things are going badly because the environment doesn't allow things to be produced well, it's not my problem.' But now, with the new philosophy, we are the ones at fault. That is the difference. So, a worker does his job and puts on the stamp of auto-certification, but it is his own conscience that becomes the police and it is telling you, 'Know what? Either you fix the operation, or take off the stamp,' and so this new philosophy is taking us back to medieval times because there is a supreme being watching you, that is watching us, and even worse, its our own conscience that we have inside of us. And this is what we talk about every Wednesday in the [quality] circles. (Talavera and Muñoz 1993, 27; Translated by the author)

Despite management assertions that the new Ford would be based on more egalitarian relations of production, this was not borne out in the workday. In effect, any 'flattening' of labour relations which occurred devolved more responsibilities to workers without increasing their level of control over the process. Workers in the '*Movimiento Democratico*' (democratic movement) reported that management's search for flexibility increased the tension in workers' relations with each other. According to one worker:

The 'Guiding Principles' are no more than a series of rules that regulate this whole philosophy, which is 'the client is the most important and here all of us are clients and all are suppliers,' because the *compañero* behind me is my supplier and I am his client. So, the *compañero* has to bring me the panel on time, because I cannot do his work, because if I don't provide [my piece] on time, how can the client be satisfied? But, moreover, I am the supplier for the *compañero* ahead, and if I don't finish my job then how can he put on the windshield? So, we are all clients and all suppliers where we say to our supplier, 'Hey, how come you're sending me bad work? What's going on?' So, now it is not the boss, the supervisor, or the manager who comes to tell you- 'Listen, you bastard, why did you do this badly?' No, it's the worker himself down the line who tells you '*Compañero*, there's a rod loose,' because he is my client. (Talavera and Muñoz 1993, 27; Translated by the author)

Here we have an example of the serious problems involved in the shift to lean production.

One of the new contradictions of flexible labour relations arises from the fact that a worker knows the person beside him is a '*compañero*' (a companion, a friend, the one with whom he shares bread), as well as a 'client' who holds him responsible for the quality of the product given. With this shift in discourse came a message from management about the increased weight of responsibility that individual workers were expected to bear. The way in which this undermined a sense of common experience among workers was well expressed by a Cuautitlán worker:

> [T]he philosophy is pure hypocrisy, because the employer tells us that they are going to give us better working conditions, but they pass on the mistakes of their productive planning to the worker. So now, the company is not responsible if something goes wrong. Now the guilty one is the worker, because he did his work badly and they can't accept that a unit could be produced badly for any number of reasons. 'What do you mean the tools are bad? The original material is bad? Impossible.' They wouldn't't admit that there wasn't enough time to do the job or that the *compañero* wasn't in the proper physical or mental state to do the job.. They speak of a new philosophy, of new guiding principles and moral values, that sound very nice but this all has to do with getting rid of the collectivity of the worker. They try to make it become an individual model instead. This is what they want us to get into our heads: 'Who do you think wins if you defend the rights of everyone? You look after yourself.' (Talavera and Muñoz 1993, 30; Translated by the author)

In this sense, work reorganisation at the Ford plant involved a distinct move towards individualisation, despite the extent to which the ideology of teamwork pervaded the discourse. As we see in the Cuautitlán case, workers took on more and more responsibility during the workday without a corresponding increase in decision-making power. Indeed, labour's collective rights over the production process were dramatically reduced.

Transformations in Representation and the Struggle to Democratise the National Union

Although Fidel Velázquez appointed a new National Executive Committee for the national union of Ford workers, the local union leadership at Cuautitlán was chosen in a democratic election after the plant reopened. This Local Executive Committee (LEC) mounted a campaign to challenge the unrepresentative character of the National Union. With the March 1989 contract negotiations approaching, the LEC convened a general assembly at which the workers elected representatives from each of the different plants in Cuautitlán to participate in the negotiations.

Ordinarily, collective agreements were negotiated by members of the National Executive Committee only. By forming a negotiating committee, the local leadership issued a direct challenge to the national leadership of the union, as well as to the company. Neither the employer nor the National Executive recognised the locally elected negotiating committee. The company argued that the negotiating committee was to be formed by members of the union. In contract language, 'members of the union', according to Ford, had to include the National Executive Committee. When this dispute was brought to the labour courts, it was the employer's definition that was upheld (Arteaga 1990b, 158n30).

The conflict between the local and national committees became irreconcilable as the local executive at Cuautitlán continued to press its demands for democratic representation. The local union held an Assembly on 17 June 1989 at which time it declared its intention to promote the direct election of a new National Committee at the upcoming Union Congress of delegates from the three Ford Plants. A week later the entire LEC was fired (Abogado, 1992). Workers responded by shutting down the plant.

Freed from the need to deal with the complaints from Cuautitlán, the Congress of Ford unions went ahead in July 1989 under the control of the national union and the CTM. In the lead up to the Congress, Héctor Uriarte, the General Secretary of the National Union, presented workers with an advance on their portion of the profit share, normally allocated at the end of December. Although the advance had been distributed outside of the legal provisions for the distribution of profits, Uriarte's 'gift' legitimised his continuation as Secretary General of the national executive committee, and gave the company a method of reducing dissent during a highly conflictual moment (Arteaga 1990b, 161 n32).

During the Congress, the Assembly approved modifications to the statutes governing the activities and role of the union. These had significant implications for representation at the local level. One of the most significant changes altered the definition of union member. Previously, members of the union were defined as 'those workers who offered their services to the Ford Motor Company in the auto industry, in present installations or any that would be established in the Mexican Republic' (Sindicato Nacional de Trabajadores de Ford Motor Company 1977, Art.51). In the July 1989 revision, a sentence was added which blurred the definition of 'union member'. Along with *miembro* (member), the union added the category of *socio* to its own constitution. 'Socio' may be translated as 'associate' in the language of lean production. The modified statute indicated that associates could be either temporary or permanent. This entrenched the union's acceptance of temporary workers and created a two-tiered structure of more and less entitled members of the union.

Other reformed statutes make the meaning of this change more apparent. For instance, previous delegates to the National Union Congress were elected on the basis of one per 100 workers. The reformed statutes declared that the number of delegates would be based on one per one hundred permanent workers in the plant (Sindicato Nacional de Trabajadores de Ford Motor Company 1977, Art.86). If the number of temporary workers increased, then there would be fewer delegates elected to the National Union Congress. Furthermore, quorum would now be based upon 50 per cent plus one of permanent workers (Art.93). Again, with the ratio of temporary to permanent workers increasing, this would make it more difficult to reach quorum. Similarly only permanent workers could be elected to union leadership positions (Art.109).

Historically, the CTM had opposed alterations in the contractual obligation of employers to turn temporary positions into permanent ones and to maintain a low percentage of temporary workers in the workforce. The union now accepted management's rights to impose conditions fostering insecurity among workers. If the union's own constitution indicated that different meanings could be ascribed to the category of 'member', this weakened the local committee's argument over who was entitled to sit as a 'member' of the contract Negotiating Committee, and to represent workers in negotiations. It was not a coincidence that these reforms to the union's constitution were made in the middle of a battle over the undemocratic character of representation within the Ford workers' union.

The CTM attempted to regain more control over representation through the use of sanctions and mechanisms of exclusion. Article 97 was rewritten to reaffirm the right of the National Union to control the activities of the Local Executives and their activities. The new article asserted that Assemblies would be 'presided over by a National Secretary, if one was in attendance'. Given that the 'president of debates' was charged with 'directing the discussion' and 'preserving the order' of such meetings, this was indeed a powerful incursion into the life of the local union.

The 1989 Conflict at Cuautitlán and the Search for a Negotiated Resolution

While most of the fired local executive at Cuautitlán accepted their severance pay, some the members of the committee refused and began a campaign to demand their reinstatement. They organised a 'Dignity Camp' outside the plant gates from which they distributed flyers and a weekly newspaper to the Cuautitlán workers. Two members maintained a hunger strike for 35 days at the Angel of Independence, a large monument in a public intersection directly outside Ford's main offices in Mexico DF. One night, they and their supporters were beaten and taken away by thugs to the city outskirts. The next day they returned to the square in front of the National Palace in the centre of the city. The fired workers believed the problem required a political solution (Arteaga 1990b, 154).

The hunger strike was unsuccessful but the conflict intensified in December 1989 when the company paid a very low profit-share to the workers at Cuautitlán. The company argued that poor performance had weakened its financial situation. Management said the workers had already received a portion of their share of profits earlier in the year by Héctor Uriarte at the summer Union Congress. Because management arranged to have taxes taken from the traditional Christmas bonus workers were infuriated and initiated a wildcat strike.

By the end of 1989, a series of unresolved conflicts in the Cuautitlán plant made the labour relations situation unstable. The intensification of work led to a great deal of resentment, but workers were also upset because of the modifications to the collective agreement and because of the decline in their wages. The grievances were manifested in resistance on the line as well as actions in solidarity with the fired workers. The workers in the plant went on a one day collective fast. When the company refused to pay the workers the profits to which they felt entitled, workers immediately elected a Negotiating Committee comprised of 17 workers and five fired local executive members. The Committee demanded an increased payment of profit shares and threatened to change labour centrals if the CTM did not take a harder line with the company. As well, they demanded that Fidel Velázquez conduct a referendum on the legitimacy of the National Executive Committee (Arteaga 1990b, 161–2 n34).

In response, the company called a technical shutdown and closed the plant for longer than usual during the Christmas holidays. During the shutdown, the leadership of the Negotiating Committee met with Fidel Velázquez and signed an agreement to hold a January referendum on the legitimacy of the National Union leadership. If the result was to repudiate the leadership, new elections would be held. But, no sooner was the agreement signed than the dissidents had second thoughts. They realised that nothing had been clarified by this discussion. No one knew how the vote would be held, where it would be held, who would be able to vote, and what date had actually been set (Interview with Negotiating Committee 1992).

The conflict moved to a very violent confrontation. On 4 January, the company circulated a letter in which it indicated that 'outsiders had been attempting to destabilise production in the plant and distort information' (Talavera and Muñoz 1993, 51–3). The next day, the General Secretary of the National Union arrived at the plant with a group of 60 thugs, and for the second time, fired workers were severely beaten up at the Dignity Camp. These workers were taken away and brought to the police in the municipality of Cuautitlán Izcalli, where they were to be charged with damaging property and blocking the highways. Management argued that they had nothing to do with the conflict and that it was an intra-union matter in which they would not involve themselves. Later, the company was compelled to intervene since the Cuautitlán workers refused to work until those who had been taken away reappeared (*Movimiento Democrático de Ford* 1992, 1–16). Those detained were released and immediately brought their demands to the Human Rights Commission in Mexico City.

On Monday, 8 January, the General Secretary of the National Union was back with thugs in greater number as workers arrived at the plant:

> There were about 200 who came with sticks and tubes. I yelled at the *compañeros* on the lines to leave. They thought they had hit me, but thank God they didn't. Then [the *compañeros*] stopped the lines that had been running five minutes before and they gathered at the entrance to the plant near the Garage and Patio. There the fury to defend our jobs made us act without thinking of the consequences and we wanted lash out in our anger, falling into their game. But we controlled ourselves. They were completely drugged. A disaster was about to occur by the …door leading to the Garage, but it was locked and there was period of about a half hour until the goons left. We were able to catch two of them. We asked them, 'what do you want, *hijos de su pinche madre*' and they said, 'that you get back to work, *hijos de la chingada.*' They ran and we went after them…. The *compañeros* ahead went after these *cabrones* to confront them and when they reached Security they opened the door. That's when the shooting started with high-calibre bullets. With the fog all around, it was a nightmare. In a few seconds we disappeared …and we were about 2,300, but those who were in front were the ones who felt the consequences: more than 100 beaten, nine shot and one *compañero* fallen… I saw the one who killed Cleto running around. Cleto was hit in the backside and one shot in the abdomen. He fell on his way towards the cafeteria, but got up again and fell again, not to rise again. I tried to run to pick him up but the bullets were flying all around me. Other guys that were closer picked him up and took him to the infirmary. That's when the shooters left, when they saw that all the workers had hid to protect themselves. That was when the patrols

arrived outside without stopping anybody, acting in complicity with the government and the company. (*Movimiento Democrático de Ford* 1992, 5–6; Translated by the author)

One worker, Cleto Nigmo Urbina, was killed and many others wounded. Workers reported that the band of goons entered the plant, armed, in company uniforms and with credentials identifying them as Ford workers. Later, the workers used some of these credentials to show that they lacked a federal registration number which appears on all workers' badges. They argued that no one but the Ford Motor Company could have provided the aggressors with identification and old, used uniforms which they wore during the assault on the Cuautitlán workers (Talavera and Muñoz 1993, 55–6). Although the workers captured three men involved in the assault, no-one was ever brought to trial. The company announced that work would be stopped until it could guarantee secure working conditions. Workers occupied the plant, arguing that they would not leave the premises because after four days the Company could argue that they had abandoned their jobs and justify their dismissal. On 22 January, the workers were removed forcibly by over 3,000 police.

After the events of 8 January, the Negotiating Committee (CN) was seen by the Cuautitlán workers as their only legitimate representative, even though it existed outside of the formal union structure. The CN was recognised in Mexico as the leadership of the Ford workers movement. In the United States and Canada, they became known as the Ford Workers Democratic Movement (FWDM). The Committee fought a long legal battle contesting the lack of representation within the union and the state. It fought for the reincorporation of fired workers, a political solution to the conflict and a new definition of solidarity within the context of North American integration. Their battle culminated in a referendum within the plant over union affiliation.

At first, the Negotiating Committee demanded immediate union elections at the national and local level, as well as the full payment of lost wages and benefits as conditions for the return to work. Ford refused to talk with the Negotiating Committee until it was officially recognised by the CTM. The company also demanded that all individual contracts be rescinded since the workers had illegally occupied the plant. In defence, the Negotiating Committee argued that the Company had unilaterally abandoned the factory and decided to close it without the intervention of the labour authorities (Arteaga 1990b, 165–6).

Evidently, the Ford strategy was to wear the workers out; first of all, with a long shut down and then by de-legitimising the Negotiating Committee. Although Fidel Velázquez and the Ford Motor Company signed an agreement on 23 January, in which the company agreed to guarantee the security of the workers and to pay lost wages, the agreement was not made public until it became apparent that the Negotiating Committee was gathering support in its campaign against the CTM. During early negotiations the company refused to recognise the Committee as a legitimate interlocutor. It argued the union was not interested in talks and sent dismissal notices to the each worker's home. Almost immediately, the company hired back 300 workers each day to a total of only 1,500. The CTM required workers to reaffirm their loyalty to it as a condition of being hired back. The company eventually re-contracted 3,900 workers, leaving 750 workers with neither a contract nor a severance agreement (Arteaga 1990b, 167–8).

The workers who were not re-contracted tried to regain their jobs in a protracted battle under the leadership of the Negotiating Committee. The Committee decided to take the legal-institutional avenues open to them and found themselves in battle with the CTM, the National Executive Committee of their union, and the *Secretaría de Trabajo y Previsión Social* (STyPS) (Secretary of Labour). The Negotiating Committee mobilised the workers in mass demonstrations in support of their legal struggle. They marched the 36 km from Cuautitlán to the National Palace in order to gain a meeting with the President of the Republic. They were unsuccessful. On another occasion, while the leadership of the movement went into the offices of the Secretary of Labour, the workers maintained a large and noisy demonstration outside. While the leaders negotiated in the Federal District, the fired workers organised a blockade of the major highway outside the plant at Cuautitlán. As the weeks stretched into months, the resistance continued to take place largely within the labour law regime and through a public campaign which affirmed the need for a defence of individual rights. Acts of civil disobedience accompanied their legal battle. Fed up with the slow process, approximately one hundred fired workers appeared naked at the Federal Labour Board to protest the lack of results of their legal battle:

> So, we showed our nakedness in such a large group in order to express the unprotected state in which we, the Ford workers, found ourselves in. we wanted to let everyone see the monstrous transnational for what it was, a company which tramples over the labour laws of our country with impunity. (Talavera and Muñoz 1993, 73; Translated by the author)

Eventually, the Negotiating Committee and the corporation sat for direct talks. In July, the company offered a severance package on the condition that workers were required to desist from demanding changes in union centrals and that all remaining workers accept the severance package. They also demanded that the negotiating committee desist from making contact with workers in Canada and the United States (Interview with Negotiating Committee 1992).The Negotiating Committee considered these conditions to be anti-constitutional, seeing the first condition as a direct intervention by the company in union affairs, and the second condition as a repudiation of fired workers' rights to make up their own minds (Arteaga 1990b, 170–1).

For many workers, the issues had become fundamentally political ones. The Democratic Movement of Ford Workers demanded that those responsible for the attack on January 8th be brought to justice. They also refused to accept the legality of the company's refusal to hire them back and demanded that their petition to the Labour Board be heard (Interview with Negotiating Committee 1992). With this petition, the Negotiating Committee contested the entitlement of the CTM to the collective agreement. In effect, this demand was the means by which the movement would try to take the Ford Union out of the CTM.

The Labour Board finally heard the movement's petition. At the request of Ford, the Board rejected the workers arguments and closed the file. In response, the Ford Workers sought the intervention of the government's official National Commission on Human Rights (CNDH) in order to protest the lack of impartiality in the treatment of their case. At the same time, they appealed the decision of the Labour Board to the Supreme Court of Justice. In May of 1991, the Supreme Court ruled in their favour and the Secretary of Labour was required to set a date for a vote which would determine whether the CTM or the *Confederación Obrera Revolucionaria* (COR) had the right to represent the Ford workers. Once the date was set, the Democratic Movement of Ford Workers called for national and international observers at the referendum. The movement gathered support from many sectors (Talavera and Muñoz 1993, 81–3).

On 3 June 1991 the vote was held inside the heavily guarded factory. Representatives from the CTM, the company and the labour authorities watched each worker vote and asked each worker to call out which central they supported. Each decision was recorded on a list of employees and the proceedings were filmed by the authorities. The Negotiating Committee argued that non-union employees as well some individuals who were not Ford workers voted, while other workers were prevented from voting. The CTM won the referendum by a vote of 1,325 to 1,110. The Committee of Independent Observers, arguing that the vote was not a secret one, declared the vote null and void. The Observation Committee was comprised of national human rights activists, labour lawyers, union activists in Mexico, as well as UAW and CAW members, among others (Interview with Negotiating Committee 1993; see also Talavera and Muñoz 1993, 85–109).

Reprisals against those who voted for the COR were swift. The Secretary General of the national union demanded that all those who had voted in favour of the COR had 20 days to reincorporate into the CTM or they would be fired by means of the exclusion clause. Facing the threat of massive firings and having lost once again at the hearing into their appeal, the leadership of the Democratic movement faced the end of their struggle.

Still Worker-fathers, not *Cabrónes*

The members of the Committee engaged with every legal avenue available to them and they became experts in Mexican labour law. While waiting for their next court date, they continued to leaflet the workers in the plant, but despite the endless activism, and by the time the conflict had gone on for two years, the stress of living for so long without a job and without income caused problems for many families. As one Committee member described it:

> [A]fter we had been nearly two years without work, not having a salary, every day we would come home and the wife would ask: – When will it be over? Well, it's just that we have an audience. – But the audience was yesterday. No, now we have another. – Okay, so until when? Well, it's only the Labour Board decision now. And then when the decision was announced, – Good, now what? No, it's just that we have the appeal and the constitutional hearing after that. – Well that's just fine, but *me vale madres*; that matters nothing to me. You have to bring us something to eat. Then one day one of the brothers stood up and said, Look, brothers this already has gone too far. *Esto ya está de la chingada*. This can't get worse, because, look, I went to my house and my wife said

– Look *cabrón*, either you take care of your problems and you bring us something to eat, or you have to leave and let someone else in here who will bring something to swallow; So because of this, me, I'm leaving. I want to take the severance pay. (Talavera y Muñoz, 1993, 109; Translated by the author)

It wasn't the labour board or the company or the violent thugs that would dissuade this worker. It was the fact that his family could not survive and as a result, he was in danger of becoming a *cabrón*; a deceived man who knows he is being deceived and does nothing about it. By fighting so long against Ford and the CTM he was already refusing to be dishonoured and deceived at work but the battle had become yet another *chingada*, another imperial conquest, another violation.

As the conflict dragged on, Ford worker-fathers paid a heavy price:

The truth is that the democratic movement of Ford Workers was a very long conflict during which the *compañeros* spoke little about the repercussions we felt because of the movement. Because we never wanted to be seen like – Ah there go the Ford workers. *Hijole*, Here they come to complain like they were the Wailing Wall itself. We never spoke very much about what was happening in terms of morale and economic hardship, so things wouldn't be seen in that way. We have always believed that those are the costs of the struggle and the truth is that the costs were very high. Like, the *compañeros* sold their things. They sold their cars, those that had one. They sold their televisions. Many *compañeros* were abandoned by their families. One day a *compañero* came and said:

– They cleaned out the house.

Well, you have to go and lodge a complaint then.

– No man, my woman left a note and took off, taking my kids too. She left me a note in which she told me to go live with the movement, and if I couldn't, then bring them to live in the house.

All of us who lived in the movement had to pay very high costs. These are invisible costs because we didn't want to make public all that the Ford movement had cost us. At the end we had to find a way out because the people were abandoning the struggle, even without getting any money at all. (Talavera and Muñoz 1993, 110)

Regional, National and International Solidarity

Faced with delay after delay and dwindling resources, the Negotiating Committee organised a 'Kilo Campaign', during which it asked housewives from the Cuautitlán area to support their struggle by donating staple goods to the movement:

We organised a support campaign with housewives by producing various flyers calling on them to support us in our precarious situation. After 8 months of struggle already, we decided to keep on struggling. With our flyers, the people were asked to support in solidarity, the 'Kilo Campaign,' bringing rice, oil, beans, sugar and any dry goods we could bring to our homes. The campaign was a success I think, because it is at home that the economic policies of modernization are reflected and suffered. (Talavera y Muñoz 1993, 76; Translated by the author)

As the Negotiating Committee fought their battles, all other democratic labour organisations in the country watched with great interest and supported them strongly. The movement strengthened its solidarity with other democratic trade union movements at the national level by joining in the creation of the *Frente Sindical Unitario* (FSU) early in 1990. Together with workers from Tornel, Modelo Breweries, as well as the democratic section of the Teachers' Union, Ford Workers were able to increase their public presence while sharing information and supporting one another's struggles for democratic representation. Because they were part of the CTM, each member of the movement was also an official member of the PRI. Consequently, they were in a complicated position since they were supported by the broad centre-left coalition of the *Partido de la Revolución Democratica* (PRD), and by the *Partido de la Revolución de los Trabajadores* (PRT), among others. In the Chamber of Deputies, the opposition politicians tried to reform the Labour Law by establishing the right to a secret ballot in labour votes. The initiative was not passed.

There was wide support for the Ford workers at the international level as well, but this became a sensitive issue for unions affiliated with the International Confederation of Free Trade Unions (ICFTU) and its regional body in the Americas, the *Organisación Regional Interamericana de Trabajadores* (ORIT). At every opportunity, the CTM declared its opposition to any internationalism that would represent an incursion into the sovereign affairs of Mexico. The results of the final referendum, together with the information given by the international observers, were sent to the International Labour Organisation (ILO). In the petition, the leaders of the Democratic Movement asked the ILO to oblige the Mexican government to ensure the right to a secret ballot in labour matters.

With the beginning of North American Free Trade negotiations, the Ford Workers movement anticipated Mexican workers would face further attacks on their labour rights. In their meetings with national union and labour authorities the Negotiating Committee made their case:

> We could not tolerate what is now a reality – this free trade and the opening of borders. Even Salinas de Gortari was wandering around in foreign countries offering big capital everything so that they would come and invest in Mexico. [We pointed out] that we had already taken the transnational plants [and] it was not acceptable for everyone to see Mexico as a country where it was possible to trample all over the rights of workers in order to make the economy grow. We said that we were ready to produce with high levels of quality and productivity but only when there was social justice for us. And, as our top leader Fidel Velázquez said, we were not going to permit our national sovereignty to be violated. (Talavera and Muñoz 1993, 71; Translated by the author)

Regional and national issues developed an international character as the spectre of free trade began to take on more substance. Indeed, there was a general apprehension that the North American Free Trade Agreement would open the door to downward harmonisation and an even more restrictive notion of labour rights in Mexico, where US legal norms would be imported (Fuentes 1994). One of the Ford workers who travelled to the US on a solidarity tour comment on the restrictions facing US trade unionists:

So, people go to offer their services to the company even when there is a strike. Some continue working while the workers cannot even block the doors, nor put the red and black banners as we do in Mexico and in Latin America. They can't put their tents up in the factory permanently. They only thing they can do is put up a picket of people to try to keep the scabs out. Yes they do slow things down a bit, but nothing more.... So, I have the impression that with all these changes that they are thinking of making to the Federal Labour Law, they are trying to make us adjust to something similar to what they suffer there. (Talavera and Muñoz 1993, 123; Translated by the author)

The leadership of this movement encountered an unprecedented level of interest in Mexican labour issues among their counterparts in Canada and the United States. Links were formed between the three labour movements. The Cuautitlán Negotiating Committee, with the support of Transnational Information Exchange and Labor Notes in Detroit, developed an information network among North American auto workers. The Canadian Auto Workers supported the Ford Workers, as did the New Directions Movement of the United Auto Workers. Many of these trade unionists had long deplored the *maquiladoras* and the fact that much of the labour intensive work had been moved there, but this general uneasiness became more specific as the Big Three threatened workers with more plant closures and the movement of product lines. Because lean production demanded that plants compete with one another for contracts, Ford workers in Canada and the United States felt threatened by the company's restructuring plans for Mexico.

Representatives of the FWDM were invited to speak in at union gatherings in the United States and in Canada and they developed a network of contacts in Argentina, Brazil, Spain and England (Interview with Negotiating Committee 1992). The national and regional coalitions which organised in against the NAFTA, including the Mexican Action Network on Free Trade (RMALC), the Action Canada Network (ACN), the Coalition for Fair Trade (CFT), all took up the Cuautitlán story in their debates with the result that it became widely known in Canada and the United States. As the struggle continued, international solidarity became an important force that sustained the Committee, in financial terms and in terms of morale. Both CAW and UAW members went to Cuautitlán as an expression of solidarity and locals sent their support in the form of declarations as well as through financial donations to the Democratic Movement. For example, on the first anniversary of the attack, 8 January 1991, the Democratic Movement of Ford Workers brought together both national and international expressions of solidarity with the struggle and in memory of Cleto Nigmo. The 'International Day of the Ford Worker' was commemorated by trade unionists in Canada and the United States as Ford Workers wore black arm bands on the job.

In the context of the free trade debate, the Democratic Movement of Ford Workers offered trade unionists from Canada and the United States the opportunity to understand the dynamics of continental restructuring from the perspective of Mexican workers engaged in a serious conflict. The new internationalism of the Ford workers was based on a search for 'education, support, solidarity and exchange of experiences' (Talavera and Muñoz 1993, 120). With the Cuautitlán struggle, workers found the basis for solidarity around labour rights at the continental level. The struggle deepened the meaning of slogans such as '4 dollars a day, No Way' which the MEXUSCAN solidarity group first meant as a repudiation of the corporate search for cheap labour in the *maquiladora* industries. MEXUSCAN, a trinational organisation of Ford workers, developed a very thoughtful educational campaign in support of those workers from the industrial core of Mexico whose struggles had also been undermined by economic integration. As a Committee member reported:

> We explained that the transnational company in Canada, in Mexico, in the United States and in whatever part of the world violates the rights of workers. It is not us as workers from another country that take their jobs. We are not acting as scabs. On the contrary, this is a struggle of all workers in the auto industry and that struggle has to be for a guaranteed wage paid to all workers in the auto industry across the globe. (Talavera and Muñoz 1993, 108; Translated by the author)

Canadian and US trade unionists began to debate the question of whether and how labour rights had to be defended at the international level. From the perspective of one Canadian labour solidarity network: 'When they win, we win.'

Continuing the Crisis: Restructuring, Representation and Resistance in the Wake of Economic Crisis

After 1982, the Mexican state was remarkably vigorous in advancing economic restructuring along neo-liberal lines. In Mexico, state managers shifted their attention and public resources towards this new goal. President Migúel De la Madrid (1982–1988) submitted a series of Constitutional reforms to Congress asserting the state's right to intervene in economic development. The government introduced a National Development Plan which included austerity measures in the area of social programmes, together with policies aimed at developing the most highly internationalised economic sectors linked to the international economy (Bolívar Espinosa 1990, 27). The government announced its intention to expand the development of the northern border regions as sites for international investment, and to provide the opportunity for domestic capital to develop its export capabilities. Increasingly, government policy shifted away from the development of the internal market and moved towards external markets as the new focus for accumulation. It was not only the state, however, that oversaw the process. Given the new levers available to international financial institutions, economic restructuring closely followed the edicts proclaimed by the country's creditors.

The 1982 stabilisation agreement with the International Monetary Fund (IMF) meant that Mexico accepted certain conditions in exchange for the re-scheduling of its external debt, including deep cuts to public spending and reductions in subsidies for goods and services. The IMF insisted a broad program of structural adjustment including privatisation and decreased government intervention was needed to encourage a return to economic stability and private sector confidence. IMF imposed austerity was intended to ensure demand would be constrained, wages would not increase, imports would be limited and the currency would be devalued.

Between 1980 and 1989, a 50 per cent drop in real wages was reported and tens of thousands of jobs were lost in plant closures. In 1980 labour received 40 per cent of GNP. This percentage plummeted to less than 25 per cent in 1989 (Aguilar García and Arrieta 1990, 659). With the government declining to decree increases in the minimum wage and employers arguing wages had not fallen sufficiently from their high levels prior to the crisis, wages became the focus of contentious contract negotiations and strikes. As part of Miguel de la Madrid's response to the crisis and the International Monetary Fund, the population began to pay more for public services. Subsidies were reduced on basic foods, and the government also imposed wage controls. During the 1980s, indices marking poverty levels, nutrition, wage levels and employment, all deteriorated. The government turned increasingly to repression to contain the opposition generated by austerity. Social rights and individual political rights were diminished in the process.

In this context, the CTM's role as a mediating presence between the state and the working class declined, as did their claim to represent workers' interests. As wages were taken out of the realm of tripartite negotiations, the traditional role for the CTM in the *Comisión Nacional de Salarios Mínimos* (National Commission on Minimum Wages) was minimised. Meanwhile unemployment increased from 1.74 million in 1980, to almost 8 million at the end of 1988, while underemployment affected another 12 million workers, of a population of approximately 78 million (Aguilar García and Arrieta 1990, 668 and 671). The CTM neither objected to government policy, nor responded to workers' demands. Even in the public sector labour disputes where the official labour movement had considerable power as the representative of workers in national industries, the CTM stood by and watched as the government closed nuclear facilities, restricted the right to strike in airlines, closed publicly held steel mills, repressed the rights of striking electrical and telephone workers and destroyed the democratic character of their unions. At the national oil company, Pemex, workers were laid off and the government directly undermined the leadership of the union. At the national phone company, Telmex and in the airlines, the government imposed technological change and flexibilisation before privatising the services. In the publicly held mining sector, one of the main ways the government increased productivity and company finances was by reducing the union's right to dispute technological change (Bensusán 1990, 15–7).

Following from this attack on public sector unions, much of Mexico's extensive parastatal sector was privatised in the 1980s. Of the 1,155 state companies 773 were privatised between 1982 and 1989. Thousands of workers were dismissed (Aguilar García and Arrieta 1990, 670–73). In his first two years, Carlos Salinas de Gortari privatised 44 others through a process of liquidation, mergers, transfers and sales including the historic Cananea mine, the massive steel mill Sicartsa, and the national telephone company, Telmex (Bensusán 1990, 9). Privatisation, following from Mexico's entry into the General Agreement on Tariffs and Trade in 1985, was part of the 'modernisation' agenda which moved Mexico from protectionism and a nationally oriented economy, towards ongoing liberalisation which was, in many respects, state-led as well.

As the PRI turned toward liberalisation and worked to strengthen its alliance with national employers' groups and international capital, the CTM was increasingly marginalised from political decision-making. As the party moved away from 'revolutionary nationalism' to a discourse steeped in 'modernisation', labour's *caudillos* were evidently more uncomfortable with their own de-centring in political terms, than with the effect of the government's economic restructuring on the working class. For example, when the PRI announced that Carlos Salinas would be the PRI's candidate to succeed Miguel de la Madrid in 1988, the CTM had not yet consented to the idea. As a result, Fidel Velázquez walked out of Salinas' address the day of the announcement (Aguilar García and Arrieta 1990, 727). Cracks in the alliance began to appear as the PRI reduced its support for CTM candidates as deputies, senators and municipal presidents, The PRI manoevered to ensure the official labour bureaucracy, being unsure of its own future in changed circumstances, would prevent workers from resisting the neo-liberal direction of the government as well. In this sense then, the weakening of the CTM paradoxically maintained corporatist forms of control (Aguilar García and Arrieta 1990, 721–31).

During the 1980s, the line between international and national spheres of politics and economics became increasingly blurred. Each downturn in the international economy reverberated strongly through Mexico and thus became an aspect of domestic politics. The international financial disorder of October 1987 caused the value of the peso to be reduced in relation to the dollar and Mexicans felt its drastic effects on wages and living conditions. Once again, the country faced the problem of capital flight. Between two and three billion US dollars was taken out of the economy immediately. The annual rate of inflation ran up to 160 per cent and reached 14.8 per cent alone in the month of December. The peso lost approximately 35 per cent of its value in the last two months of the year and the population was faced with dramatic increases in domestic interest rates (Álvarez Béjar 1991, 6). In response to the ensuing national economic crisis, the government declared the *Pacto de Solidaridad Económica* (PASE) in December 1987, three days before a general strike called by the Labour Congress was to begin. This anti-inflation agreement was imposed by the government on the CTM. CTM Secretary-General Fidel Velázquez signed the pact, but trade union support was exceedingly low.

The Pact was announced on 15 December 1987. With this pact, the government agreed to increase prices for goods and services provided by the state, maintain its austerity program and divest itself of interests in the parastatal sector. The unions agreed to minimal increases in wages across the board and the employers' associations agreed to increase the supply of basic goods, increase productivity levels and moderate prices. The agreement on wage increases was a matter of moral suasion. Employers were not obliged but were exhorted to comply with fifteen per cent increase in wages under collective agreements. The minimum wage was also increased by fifteen per cent initially and twenty per cent again for January. The *Pacto de Solidaridad Economica* (PASE) was replaced by the *Pacto para la Estabilidad y el Crecimiento Economico* (PECE) in December 1988 (Bolívar Espinosa 1990, 55–6).

Representation, Resistance and New Social Forces

In 1985, a catastrophic natural disaster in the centre of Mexico together with deteriorating international economic conditions and an incompetent state response, provoked outrage in the urban population in the centre of the country. When the earthquake struck Mexico City on 19 September, the country was already reeling from the effects of continuing economic crisis. Garment workers felt the full blow. At least 600 women garment workers died in the earthquake and many bodies were not retrieved. Two hundred workshops were destroyed, 500 were damaged and 40,000 women were suddenly unemployed. There was very little help given. The Army came to cordon off the buildings, leaving the women still inside, both dead and alive. Novelist and journalist Elena Poniatowska spoke to the devastated garment workers:

> 'Our boss, he will come for us. Right now he's coming for us because he cares for us very much...' The boss, the masculine figure, the image of a father. He who gives a tap on the shoulder, permission to leave, he who doles out wages every 15 days in a brown paper envelope to those who have been working since they were 14 years old and who are single mothers; the boss is the point of reference.... For the garment workers, the whole world had given way: Their man who pretended to be helpless and then left them. The boss who took out the machinery first and asked them for help digging with their fingers to 'rescue their livelihood' until they realised. 'And the *companeras*?' 'First the machinery and then human life?' It was difficult to believe. Not only had the building collapsed, leaving a hull of concrete and rods entombing life, but another collapse hit them from within. – What are we then, garbage? 'My whole life is in there,' exclaimed [the boss]. And ours? And what about our lives? (Poniatowska 1988, 221–2; Translated by the author)

The urban popular movements were catalysed by the confluence of both issues – seeing the impacts of the earthquake as linked to the broader questions of citizenship and the need to strengthen civil society. The popular movement politicised the administration of municipal affairs in a new way, by demanding that the government respond to the urban crisis. We see an example of this in the successful campaign to expropriate abandoned damaged properties in the *Distrito Federal,* Mexico City. The *Regional de Mujeres de la Coordinadora Nacional del Movimiento Urbano Popular* (the Women's Regional section of the National Coordinating body of the Urban Popular Movement (CONAMUP)) proposed that these properties should be turned into public housing and cooperatives for the '*damnificados*', the victims of the earthquake. The *Regional* mobilised communities of women to fight for deeds for the new properties and it was successful in its organising and educational work (Villanueva 1992). As Poniatowska saw the transformation:

> The population at that moment took charge of itself. Those on the bottom are in any case accustomed to having no one throw even a lasso their way. The absolute dysfunction of the government was nothing new. They are so different from the apparatus of power, so much the defenceless spectators of government decisions, so thrown to one side that it is assumed they don't even speak the same language. Whatever happened 'out there' had nothing to do with what happened under the enormous umbrella, nothing. The language of power simply is 'other,' The people, although they speak a lot about them, are never considered for any other role than 'extras'; the leaders always have been there to get in the way, to paralyze, to close the door, to cultivate the sense of waiting. Otherwise, why aren't the protagonists of the tragedy here? Why, instead of hearing a garment worker, a victim, a rescuer speak, do we have to hear more politics as usual, from the bureaucrat, from the functionary with car and driver? (Poniatowska 1988, 101; Translated by the author)

From the rubble and destruction arose a powerful union of women garment workers. The *Sindicato Nacional de Trabajadoras de la Industria de la Costura, Confección y Vestido, Similares y Conexos,* (The September 19th Union of Women Garment Workers) demanded from employers and the government three months pay in wages, 20 days per year and lost wages from September until the negotiation was concluded and respect for their rights as set down in labour law (Poniatowska 1988, 222–3). The new union immediately began to play an important role in the independent trade union movement and were strongly supported by other independent unions and democratic labour sections.

The cross-sectoral alliances of the 1980s, having identified austerity and debt as the major problems facing the country, were strengthened by the inclusion of democracy as a central demand. The state could not suppress the urban popular movement which rose in the shadow of a disintegrating economic model. Nor was the government successful in making its claims for austerity appear to be in the general interest. IMF imposed structural adjustment obviously was not in the interests of the majority of the population. In the urban popular movements, the opposition took on the battle over ideas.

For example, one of the largest of the urban movements, the *Asemblea de Barrios* (Assembly of Neighbourhoods), added a symbolic level to its struggles with the government. It offered the public an image of a male All-Star Wrestler who would embody their demands and draw attention to their political project. *Superbarrio Gómez*, a wrestler in tights, red cape and red and yellow mask, was created to appear as a sort of gentle giant who was prepared to stand and fight on behalf of the people. This he often did as a passionate speaker at political rallies. He quickly became a thorn in the side of the government. *Superbarrio Gómez* ran for President in 1988 but became an effective supporter of Cuauhtémoc Cárdenas' actual campaign for the presidency. His public image complemented the reserved intellectual candidate of the opposition *Frente Democratico Nacional* (FDN) and afterwards, *Superbarrio*'s career continued to be linked to Cárdenas.

Meanwhile, modernisers within the PRI turned to 'technocratic' solutions to economic crisis which were thought to be more appropriate than `political' ones. The governing *Partido Revolucionario Institucional* (PRI) became alienated from its social base in the process. It was not so much the fact that the state responded with authoritarianism to economic crisis that caused a serious conflict within official *PRIista* circles. Rather, the Party's main constituent groups were completely passed over when President Miguel De la Madrid chose the official candidate for the 1988 Presidential elections, despite prior understanding that they would have a say in the process. Some of the Party's most recognised leaders who had comprised the Democratic Current within the PRI, among them Cuauhtémoc Cárdenas son of the ex-president General Lázaro Cárdenas, left the party in protest. With the split in the PRI, the prospect of a high profile oppositional candidate emerged. The question of whether to support a serious oppositional candidate was widely debated among all sectors critical of the PRI and a broad coalition formed behind the Cárdenas candidacy. A coalition of centre-left organisations created the *Frente Democratico Nacional* (FDN) in an unprecedented show of unity behind Cárdenas' campaign for the presidency in 1988.

Salinas de Gortari was declared President after the elections in July 1988, but not before the electoral computer system failed on the night of the elections and after only half the poll results were made public. It was widely held in the population that only massive fraud had defeated Cuauhtémoc Cárdenas and only deception brought Salinas to power. As described by Andrew Reding:

> When early returns on election night showed Cárdenas in the lead, the system went dead. Results were instead tabulated the old-fashioned way. After a week's delay in which Cárdenas ballots were found floating down rivers and smoldering in roadside bonfires, the Federal Electoral Commission released the official results: Salinas had won slightly more than 50 per cent of the vote. But the commission would not disclose details, and to this day the precinct tallies remain a state secret. (Reding 1991, 258)

The perception of fraud had so split the political elites that the outgoing President was unable to present his final *Informe de Gobierno* (State of the Union) address given the shouts from the opposition seats (Álvarez Béjar and Mendoza Pichardo 1991, 12).

This united opposition battled economic liberalisation as well as the abject deterioration in democratic practices that had accompanied the economic crisis. While De la Madrid left Salinas a legacy of dramatically lower rates of inflation, high international reserves, successful renegotiation of the external debt and lower interest rates, the population had paid the price in terms of an absolute decline in living standards (Bolívar Espinosa 1990, 63) and a crushing defeat of their democratic aspirations.

Maquiladorisation and Industrial Restructuring

In the 1980s, the *maquilas* began to lose their enclave status within the national economy and began to make inroads into the industrial centre of the country. As many observers have noted, women's unequal position in society and the labour market was one of the central prior conditions of this transformation (Carillo and Hernández 1982, 105–55; Fernández-Kelly, 1989, 125–82). As the *maquilas* themselves were restructured in the 1980s, it the woman as daughter-mother-wife remained the ideal polyvalent and flexible worker (Barajas Escamilla and Rodríguez Carrillo 1990, 335–367). The *maquila* model hastened the dismantling of labour rights in Mexico, not just because they began appearing alongside old industries in the interior of the country. Rather, the *maquilas* themselves became the new model of restructuring. The *maquilas* are critical to our analysis because theirs is the image in which labour relations were remade in Mexico. The feminised *maquila* worker laboured at the centre of the emerging model of development throughout the country in the 1980s. The old centre of auto production was reshaped such that the *maquila*, assembly and parts industries became more and more like one another. In fact, some observers had come to speak of the *maquilisation* of the auto Mexican industry:

> In general, we could say that as the auto industry was restructured, and was made more automated and flexible, it becomes ever more like a *maquiladora* in its social meaning.

That is, we are witnessing a process of '*maquilisation*' in the auto industry. Here we define a *maquiladora* as an industry in its social form and not as a tariff regime. Its central characteristics are as follows: feminine labour force, highly segmented skill levels, majority of workers in unskilled categories, relatively low wages and with an orientation towards de-unionisation. (Carrillo V. 1990b, 110; Ramírez 1988; Translated by the author)

In the assembly plants in the older, industrial centre of the country, the plants did not simply disappear as a result of the transformations in the industry, but were compelled to increase productivity and flexibility with minimal new technology (Arteaga 1989, 8). Men's work and women's work began to look more alike, if not through downward harmonisation, then through brutal repression. It was *maquilisation*, more than 'Japanese' forms of work organisation that restructured labour relations in Mexico during the 1980s. Even thought the main elements of 'continuous improvement', 'total quality management' and 'just-in-time' production were introduced into Mexican industry by transnational employers, it was a social struggle with an authoritarian state which ultimately defined the character of Mexico's increasing economic integration with the United States.

The *maquila* model was well suited to the auto industry, as far as employers were concerned. The *Secretaría de Comercio y Fomento Industrial* (SECOFI) figures reported that 10 per cent of those employed in industry in Mexico were located in the auto industry at the end of the decade. Of these 400,000 employees, approximately 60,000 were located in auto assembly; 140,000 in auto parts; 120,000 in the auto *maquilas* and 80,000 in auto distribution (SECOFI 1991, 9). Twenty per cent of those employed in the *maquilas* worked in auto production. 80.5 per cent of General Motors' 34,000 workers were found in the *maquilas*. For Ford, the percentage was 55.2 per cent of approximately 12,000 workers. Of Chrysler's 16,000 workers, 80.5 per cent were *maquila* workers (Carillo 1990b, 92). As a percentage of total employment in the auto industry, the *maquilas* became increasingly significant during this decade.

In the Mexican *maquiladora* industries, the labour force continued to be made up of workers who were both young and female. In the auto parts sector, traditionally a sector where women do not work, the percentage of women *maquila* workers continued to be significant. In the late 1980s Jorge Carrillo reported that 52.1 per cent of all workers in the auto *maquiladoras* were women. Arteaga, Carillo and Micheli found an average of 51.8 per cent female workforce in the GM *maquilas* they visited. Herrera Lima indicated that 37.5 per cent of all Ford *maquila* workers were women, while 58.5 per cent of General Motor *maquila* workers were women (Arteaga 1989, 34; V. Carrillo 1990, 94–5; Herrera Lima 1992, 30).

In Ford de México, as well as in other auto companies, managers sought to enhance their control over the production process by changing the gendered composition of the labour force in the auto plants (Carillo 1990, 94). At times this meant a feminisation and at other times a masculinisation of the labour force. In the old auto factories in the industrial core, the labour force was virtually all male. But in the new non-*maquila* factories, there were early indications of a feminisation of the labour force. The new engine plant at GM Ramos Arizpe, for example, employed a work force of 20 per cent women.

Nonetheless, at the Ford engine plant in Chihuaha, union officials indicated they expected gender relations to be maintained. For example, because employers had to pay three months wages as maternity benefits, the company was very hesitant to hire women. As well, as one official said, 'It is heavy work for women.' The local union at the Ford engine plant reported that their relations were good with the CTM:

> It's the same union structure, but with modern unionism. We are a young union and we are open to change… The difference between the north and the south is that in the south, the people are more political. In the north, the people like to work more. We like work more than politics. (Interview with union official, Chihuahua 1992; Translated by the author)

They argued that restructuring meant the end of paternalism: 'You have to fight for yourself.' The Ford – Chihuahua union saw the potential dangers in industrial restructuring, but they were nonetheless in agreement with the turn towards flexibility. They cautioned that it was important to keep in mind that over-work and flexible hours were difficult for the worker, and 'even if he earned more, it was the family that would lose out.' Moreover,

> We are not willing to run these risks for higher productivity. We are studying Kaizan and quality circles, but we don't think we will accept this in Mexico. It will tend to make the union disappear. We will get to a moment when the worker has his group, but he loses his commitment to his family, his society and the working class. (Ford-Chihuahua union official, interview with author, Chihuahua 1992; Translated by the author)

In the modern plant, the worker 'makes more decisions, has more responsibility and needs more training, therefore the union must ensure higher wages and benefits.' Before, as one official pointed out, there were strikes each time there was a wage revision: 'We had to change this awful custom. This isn't a vacation. You have to work' (Ford-Chihuahua union official, interview with author, Chihuahua 1992).

In 1979, the *maquiladora* industry as a whole employed 76.6 per cent women. But by 1984, the number of men had increased from 23.4 to over 30 per cent as a broader range of manufacturers entered the program. The International Labour Organisation suggested that, in part, this change might have been due to prolonged recession compelling men to accept 'women's work' (Pedrero Nieto and Norma Saavedra 1987, 42) By the late 1980s, the *maquiladora* industries grew at rates far exceeding national averages for industrial growth. Even so, this growth from 315,069 workers in 1988 to 452,000 workers in July 1990 was by no means an adequate solution to the employment problem in a country where one million young people became old enough to enter the labour market in every year (Álvarez Béjar 1993, 15). Furthermore, *maquila* employment levels remained susceptible to expansions and contractions in the US economy.

The expansion of the *maquila* sector depended upon the combination of low wages and rising productivity rates. The continued devaluation of the peso, which made the US dollar 100 times more valuable in Mexico between 1981 and 1988, resulted in lower wage rates in the *maquiladora* industries than those in export processing zones of South Korea, Taiwan and Singapore (Spelich 1988). But the low wages were not just in relation to international wage comparisons. In general, workers in the *maquila* auto parts industries made 60 per cent less in wages than autoworkers in the assembly plants in the centre of the country. In 1986, for example, an unskilled worker in Ford Cuautitlán earned the equivalent of 1.4 $US per hour. In Hermosillo, a Ford worker in the same category earned 0.56 $US, while a Ford worker in a *maquila* in Ciudad Júarez earned 0.36 $US per hour (Carillo 1990b,101). *Maquila* contracts provided benefits which were no better than those stipulated by federal law.

By the end of the 1980s, the restructuring of work along the lines of lean production were visible in many *maquiladora* industries. Together with a process of capital intensification, many *maquilas* were reorganised according to the demands of just-in-time processes, total quality, statistical process control and work teams. Neo-liberal arguments suggested that wage increases would accompany productivity increases achieved by these new developments. But wage rates in Mexico were not determined by the operation of the free market in this period. Apart from the dramatic decline in real wage rates following from structural adjustment, state coercion and the repression of labour rights also exerted downward pressure on wages. Wages did not directly reflect productivity rates. Ricardo Grinspun lists a large labour surplus and the co-optation of union leaders as two additional reasons for low wages that do not rise along with increased productivity levels (Grinspun and Cameron 1993, 114).

Maquiladora industries in the 1980s were notable for having no effective union representation. Even though many of the auto workers were organised into unions, those unions preferred to increase membership rather than fight for better working conditions and wages. In the *maquiladoras*, unionisation was not an obstacle for companies wishing to increase productivity levels. Official unions offered employers collective agreements protecting them against democratic labour movements (Carrillo and de la O 1992, 58–9). In the high-tech *maquiladoras*, 60 per cent of the companies had signed collective agreements, while in the low-tech *maquiladoras*, only 22.6 per cent did so (Carrillo and de la O 1992, 58). In sum, the low quality of labour representation in the *maquiladora* industries contributed to the maintenance of unilateral managerial control over the production process and provided for increased managerial prerogatives in this sector (Arteaga et al. 1989, 3; Quintero Ramírez 1990).

Beginning with the De la Madrid administration in 1982, the 'renovation' of the auto sector was deemed to be of central importance in the state's new export-oriented development strategy. Previous efforts to continue both import-substitution industrialisation as well as export-oriented production were at odds with the concern of transnational employers to rationalise production along continental lines. There was an undeniable crisis in the sector. Between 1981 and 1983, auto production dropped from 597,118 units to 285,485, or 48 per cent in two years (Arteaga García 1988, 166). Consequently, the 1983 Automotive Decree affirmed the state's objective to move the industry toward an export-oriented strategy and a positive commercial balance. The state lowered its demands for national content levels. Whereas the 1962 Decree set targets of 60 per cent national integration for the auto assemblers, the Decree of 1983 established new levels of national integration at only 50 per cent for autos (Arteaga García 1990a, 65 n1). New models did not have to comply with content requirements if 50 per cent were exported. The manufacture of eight cylinder engines was prohibited (Carillo 1990b, 75).

In 1989, the new administration of Carlos Salinas de Gortari introduced a Decree for the auto industry replacing the 50 per cent 'national integration' level with a minimum 'national aggregate value' of 36 per cent. Whereas the Decree of 1972 aimed to structure supply according to patterns of national demand, the objective of the 1989 Decree was to increase industry's participation in the international economy (Arteaga 1990a, 65n2). In accordance with the priority given to the auto industry as a source of foreign exchange, the state permitted the closure of some plants, the relocation of others, decreases in employment and radical changes to collective agreements (Carillo 1990b, 75). In this period we see the virtual disappearance of national auto producers (Herrera Lima 1992, 28).

Meanwhile, the government began to offer companies incentives to invest in production for export. Arteaga notes the *Decreto Para la Racionalización de la Industria Automotriz,* was declared on 15 September 1983, while the *Decreto Para el Fomento y Modernización de la Industria Automotriz* was announced on 11 December 1989 (Arteaga 1990b, 141). When Ford and Mazda indicated their interest in considering Hermosillo, Sonora as the site for a new auto assembly plant, the joint venture was granted a public credit of US$ 108 million, representing half of the companies' investment in machinery and equipment. The company had three years of grace and seven to pay it back. This sum of money was equal to that spent by the entire government of the state of Sonora that year. The state provided water, electricity, gas lines, and a four-lane highway for the company's use. These sorts of enticements for a company 100 per cent owned by foreign investors were previously unheard of, and contrary to the stated priorities of reductions in government spending (Carillo 1990b, 79).

Other producers opened facilities in Mexico. (Arteaga et al. 1989, 7). General Motors built an engine plant as well as an assembly plant in Ramos Arízpe. Ford constructed a new engine plant in Chihuahua and the assembly plant in Hermosillo. (Arteaga 1989, 77). Nissan built an engine plant in Aguascalientes and Renault established an engine plant in Gomez Palacios. From no exports at the beginning of the 1980s, Mexico became an exporter of 1,600,000 engines between 1985–1987 (Arteaga 1989, 76). Between 1982 and 1986, auto parts exports to the US increased from $550 million to $1.79 billion. In 1986, the trade balance in auto was $900 million in Mexico's favour (Shaiken 1990, 29). Mexico's export capacity increased to approximately 1.5 million engines in 1988. Between 1982 and 1987, automobiles became the second largest exports after oil (Arteaga et al. 1989, 8). This reorganisation of production relocated production from the centre to the northern periphery of the country.

The *maquila* option provided US auto manufacturers with low wage facilities for a share of Big Three parts production. The *maquilas* also pressured workers in the United States and Canada to consider the implications of widespread shifts in production. As the United Auto Workers (UAW) confronted Big Three employers in the early 1980s on issues surrounding technological change and work reorganisation, the threat of plant closures was a powerful incentive for the union to accept concessions in contract negotiations. The Canadian section of the UAW split from the union on precisely the issue of concessions. What is also true is that Mexican auto workers felt the same pressure. As Mexico became the site for Big Three investments in engine and auto assembly plants in the non-industrial northern states, established workers in auto plants of central Mexico were threatened by the relocation of production facilities to new 'greenfield' sites.

The Reorganisation of Work as another Challenge to State Corporatism

The restructuring of the North American auto industry was undertaken between countries and regions of widely divergent social and economic conditions. One of the most significant was the asymmetry in productivity levels that arose between national industries in the same sector. High growth rates accompanied by an increasingly unequal distribution of national income and low productivity rates characterised manufacturing under import-substitution industrialisation. In 1960, productivity in Mexican manufacturing was 70 per cent of the United States and by 1985 this figure had dropped to 53 per cent (Velásco Arregui 1993, 164). The disparity in productivity levels among the countries of North America was identified as one of the most serious problems facing Mexican producers as trade liberalisation was contemplated in North America. However, it became apparent that companies could diffuse advanced production practices. By the late 1980s, certain plants in the highly internationalised sectors of the Mexican economy, for example, had higher quality and productivity levels than comparable facilities in Canada and the United States (Shaiken 1990, 119–20). In both the new and old assembly plants, work was reorganised according to the central precepts of lean production practices. In the new northern plants, international levels of automation and robotisation were introduced along with rejection of corporatist labour practices. When Ford's Hermosillo plant was first built, for example, it was the most automated of any Ford plant in the world. The high level of capital investment, young labour force and reorganisation of work differentiated it quite significantly from the older Ford plant in Cuautitlán (Carillo 1990b, 72).

It is incorrect to assume that the new industrialisation in northern Mexico during the 1980s was restricted to low-wage, labour-intensive labour processes. In fact, much of the new investment was highly capital intensive (de la Garza 1990, 173–4). Competitiveness rested on a combination of transformations in work reorganisation and technological change and as a result there was not only one version of a competitive auto plant. As Jordy Micheli shows, auto assemblers reorganised the fit between technological and organisational factors in a variety of ways. Micheli suggests that the key factor in arriving at an international level of competitiveness was in the construction of a *nuevo modelo social de manufactura* (new social model of manufacturing) in which flexible labour relations became of utmost importance (Micheli 1994). By focussing on the national and plant level, both Micheli and de la Garza argue that productivity increases in the 1980s depended upon broad transformations including technical, social cultural and political factors (de la Garza, 1990, 163).

    As US employers found it increasingly difficult to wrest higher productivity levels out of the labour process, they argued that the once highly productive Fordist model of development had exhausted itself. It was said that the rigidities of its institutions, labour relations and ideas had reduced the vitality of the world's industrial heartland. The refrain was echoed in Mexico where the rigidities of corporatism were denounced. Auto manufacturers were among the first to demand that collective agreements be made more 'flexible' to achieve increased productivity increases. This solution to the productivity problem was dubbed 'Lean Production' by the organisers of the International Motor Vehicle Program (IMVP) at the Massachusetts Institute of Technology. Their five year, five million dollar international project was explicitly concerned with the ideological problem of convincing North Americans to accept 'lean production' as the solution to the lack of competitiveness of the North American auto industry As a result, it was not simply technological change that characterised the restructuring of production. Lean production, in ideology and practice, played a crucial role in the restructuring of North American industry during the 1980s (Womack, Jones and Roos 1990).

    Lean production was meant to do away with rigidities decried by theorists of work reorganisation. Enrique de la Garza Toledo argues that these included rigidities in the determination of product and product lines; in the ability of employers to increase or decrease the number of workers; in the division of labour; in seniority-based wage rages; in the protections guaranteed by the collective agreement; in labour culture; in the links between labour law, social security and the legal system and corporatism itself (de la Garza Toledo 1992, 12–14). De la Garza sums up the conflict as follows:

> In diagnosing the crisis as not only a crisis of productivity but also of rigidity, one would have to consider that the above mentioned elements (all or some in particular) would end up… impeding increased productivity, quality and competitiveness. (de la Garza Toledo 1992, 14; Translated by the author)

    As we have seen, restructuring did not happen automatically as Mexico became open to US economy. Flexibility was imposed with impunity. In Ford Cuautitlán, the result was that after the conflict, the new collective agreement institutionalised work reorganisation according to the precepts of lean production: Employers refused to pay severances 'when conditions beyond their control led them to suspend the collective agreement'; weekend overtime premium was reduced to 50 per cent; there would be no special arrangements made for absent workers; restrictions on management rights to move workers from position to position were eliminated; any worker refused a job by the employer would have to wait six months before applying again; the union's right to challenge the results of a worker's medical exam were eliminated; a new chapter in the collective agreement discussed the shared interests of workers and employer in quality and productivity increases; the union accepted the need for ongoing evaluations of workers and monitoring which would be done by both the union and the employer; the union agreed to work with the company to develop programs to encourage worker participation; the national union took on business which was previously conducted by the local union (Arteaga García 1990a, 71–4).

In sum, as productivity was identified as the crucial problem for the United States economy in the 1980s, this became the refrain in Mexico as well. The reclassification of jobs and skill, the intensification of work and the reduction of wages thus became the basis for international competitiveness. Restructuring entailed a new level of North American economic integration, defeats of struggles for democratic, autonomous and independent trade unionism, and the reorganisation of work in more intense and flexible directions. These three aspects of restructuring had a profound impact on working-class representation as Mexico became more outwardly oriented.

Caudillismo and Crisis

In this chapter, I have discussed the conflict which arose within the *Confederación de Trabajadores de México* (CTM) union at Ford-Cuautitlán in the late 1980s with the company's decision to close the plant and reopen it under a new flexible collective agreement in 1987. Workers immediately resisted the imposition of the reorganisation of work in the plant and the new working conditions which followed changes to their collective agreement. Since the national union leadership restrained the local union's attempts to contest the terms of these new conditions, the local found itself in direct conflict with the company and the national union leadership at the same time.

The conflict at Ford-Cuautitlán centred around the character of working-class representation within state corporatism as this productive mode, already in crisis, was brought into contact with neo-liberal restructuring. The state could no longer guarantee the minimal concessions from which the *caudillismo* of the worker-father had been constructed. Increasingly, the CTM turned towards authoritarianism to hold on to its membership, thus indicating that institutions of corporatist representation could no longer depend upon their traditional bases. For the most part, state officials supported the CTM against other reform movements within their ranks and heavily repressed oppositional labour and social movements. Lower salaries were one of the results, although labour's acquiescence to the reorganisation of work, including the team concept, just-in-time production, quality circles, Total Quality Management and zero error programmes was also sought. Employers prized the 'flexible' character of these new labour relations above all else.

The movement of Ford workers, as it resisted the restructuring of production relations, was also a movement of resistance against the authoritarian *caudillismo* of the official trade union leadership. Their direct challenge to the CTM was not an 'inter-union' dispute, but a contestation of internationalised production relations within the terrain of the state itself. Auto producers in the United States explained economic crisis in terms of the crisis of international competitiveness. Part of their solution was to impose a new form of labour relations. Yet, the restructuring of representation did not lead to cooperative labour relations, but more conflictual ones. Given the rigidity in wage levels and instability of employment, there was no stable resolution to the economic crisis (Carillo 1990b, 106). Cuautitlán was not the only place where older unions resisted the process of restructuring and acted in defence of their acquired rights. Meanwhile, unions in new assembly plants tried to improve their contracts, sometimes with devastating consequences. At General Motors in Ramos Arizpe and in Ford Chihuahua, for example, the company dismissed local executive committees. At Ford Hermosillo, management fired all departmental representatives and the members of the local executive committee (Covarrubias 1992; Sandoval Godoy 1990). This repression of labour rights became a defining characteristic of the process of seeking a new labour flexibility in Mexico. Under these circumstances, it seems more appropriate to think of *maquilisation* as a code word for increased control by management over workers. Workers were given more responsibility for the production process, but their power to negotiate the conditions within which they engage in production was weakened substantially (Carillo 1990b, 90).

The crisis deepened as the state turned increasingly towards policies advancing the integration of Mexico with the United States, as employers were able to dismantle many of the gains won by labour during mid-century, and as union leaders were unable to re-establish the legitimacy of their leadership or the politics of corporatism. Indeed, workers' opposition to the *maquilisation* of the industrial heartland would seem to indicate that *caudillismo* had lost its hegemonic character.

Chapter 5

Volkswagen, NAFTA and the Disintegration of Labour Rights in Mexico

In the Nissan workers' struggle we saw workers contest the *caudillismo* of an individual leader who advanced paternalistic economism over social unionism as the Mexican government faced a serious crisis of legitimacy. In the case of Ford, the official trade union *caudillos* conceded to the *maquilisation* of the auto industry and disrupted the position of the worker-father. The workers, in their resistance, put an end to the hegemonic character of official union leadership and endured the ensuing repression. This third moment in the crisis elaborates the gendered struggles of the men and women workers who defended their rights against the neo-liberal agenda and the President-as-*caudillo* who fought their Revolutionary claims. It was a Harvard-trained economist who carried the Washington Consensus from the centre of productive power as if there was no alternative to neo-liberalism; as if 'flexibility' was not forced on workers in the core by the threat of plant closures and ongoing deindustrialisation. It was an authoritarian state executive that imposed state-society 'concertation' to ensure corporate 'team-work' was established in Mexico. It was the President who, with impunity, privatised public companies and saw the nation's patrimony distributed regressively. With all the privileges of patriarchy and class, he oversaw the breaking of collective agreements, rather than democratically reforming the labour law. It was Salinas de Gortari who prepared the economic and political ground so that the North American Free Trade Agreement could be concluded.

The Anatomy of a Conflict: Summer 1992

The conflict at Volkswagen, which took place over the summer of 1992, may be divided into three stages. These will be discussed in detail below, but here I will give a short overview of the conflict. The first stage began with the negotiations for the 1992–1994 collective agreement. During negotiations, the union signed a side agreement with the company to restructure labour relations in the Puebla installations, within the parameters established by the National Agreement on Quality and Productivity Increases, but outside of the collective bargaining process. In the agreement, the union agreed to allow the introduction of 'work teams' throughout the plant and to modify any clauses in the collective agreement that would otherwise impede flexible work arrangements. This agreement was signed before the conclusion of collective agreement which it would then supersede. It also required that the collective agreement would be opened up subsequently, outside of the negotiation process and without ratification from the membership.

The second stage began when an oppositional movement arose within the membership after rumours of the agreement spread. Having no legal recourse to a ratification vote on the agreement, the Movement of July 20 organised within the parameters of the Federal Labour Law (LFT) to depose the union leadership. It held a vote of the membership and led a work stoppage, but the leadership resisted. The company responded by applying to the Labour Board to sever individual contracts and the collective agreement based on the argument that for 'reasons beyond our control', it was compelled to shut down production. As the Labour Board deliberated, the oppositional movement attempted to demonstrate the legality of its actions and receive the formal recognition which it was denied. The union, for its part, the union leadership sought out the support of the labour federation *Federación de Sindicatos de Empresas de Bienes y Servicios* (FESEBES).

The third stage of the conflict began with the mid-August labour board ruling in the company's favour. After negotiations with the company, the union immediately altered its own constitution, signed a new collective agreement with the company and thus retained its legal title to the contract. Subsequently, SITIAVW, the Volkswagen union, rescinded its status as an independent union and affiliated with FESEBES. In early September 1992, the Secretary of Labour granted FESEBES the legal registration it had been denied for two years. Most of the workers were hired back to the company after signing a document giving up their legal rights to contest the Board's decision. The leaders of the oppositional movement were not rehired under the new agreement.

Stage One: Contract Revision 1992

In preparation for negotiations in 1992, SITIAVW, the independent union of Volkswagen workers had already signalled acceptance of the discourse of modernisation. It spoke in favour of the re-organisation of work within the parameters of continuous improvement, cooperation and participation. This was further demonstrated in SITIAVW's own negotiating proposal for the 1992–1994 collective agreement. The union's definition of productivity, for example, reveals a wholly optimistic view of the dynamics involved in new work practices:

> The contracting parties conceive of productivity, in general terms, as the qualitative transformation of production systems and work methods, as well as collective and individual labour relations. This process tends towards a better and more rational utilisation of available resources to increase production with higher quality and with the same or less effort by the workers. It leads to a better implementation of technological innovations and advances; the more active and creative participation of the labour force in productive processes; and sharing economic and social benefits as determined by increases in productivity. Consequently the parties express their commitment to make their best efforts to increase productivity, quality and efficiency... adopting the best agreements to reach these ends, and will extend to workers their share of economic and social benefits. (SITIAVW, 1992a; Translated by the author)

The subsequent negotiations took place in the offices of the Federal Conciliation and Arbitration Board and eventually broke down. The company refused to accept the 35 per cent direct wage increase and the 20 per cent increase in benefits that the union demanded. It offered a 12 per cent direct wage increase instead. On 1 July, SITIAVW held a one-day strike during which it called together other regional union leaders who demonstrated their support for the Volkswagen workers. The strike was not expected to last more than a day and, in fact, lasted only a few hours before a settlement was reached (Rappo and Victoria 1992).

After the negotiations were completed, the Negotiating Commission characterised the contract negotiations as having been the most difficult that SITIAVW had ever faced. Noting the company's intransigence and the requirements of the changed economic situation, it announced that the union was successful in negotiating a 20 per cent wage increase and a 3 per cent increase in benefits. Punctuality and attendance bonuses were increased. Vacation days and bonuses were increased for those with more than three years seniority. The year end bonus was increased from the equivalent of 50 to 54 days wages and the expected amount of profit sharing was increased from 26 to 28 days. Food vouchers were increased by approximately 20 per cent (*La Jornada* 1992a; Rappo 1992).

The Negotiating Commission argued that they were able to fight back against the 'mutilation' of the collective agreement, but they reported that they had agreed to changes as a direct result of the federal government's *Acuerdo Nacional para la Elevación de la Calidad y la Productividad* (ANECP) which called for 'modernisation of organisational structures in the productive sphere' (National Agreement on Productivity and Quality Increases). SITIAVW's report to the membership noted that, among other things, the National Agreement called for:

> new work systems limiting repetitive and alienating work corresponding to the traditional methods... now can be transformed through work groups in order to continuously adjust the old labour relations of subordination and control [Supervisors or foremen – obedient and submissive workers] for new relations of coordination and agreement [coordinators – thinking and participatory workers]. (SITIAVW 1992b; Translated by the author)

In its report on negotiations, the Volkswagen union said it had agreed to conduct studies for the institution of work teams throughout the Puebla installations in the spirit of the ANECP. In its report to workers, SITIAVW argued it had been able to avoid the destructive tendency evident in other workplaces where companies ushered in the new labour relations through violence and coercion:

> [We concluded] a wide ranging and new kind of negotiation process that we think will transcend our labour relations. This constitutes proof that, with creativity and imagination, it is possible to carry out the change that modernisation requires. We can do this in a peaceful manner, with absolute respect for the acquired rights of workers and with full expectation for progress and improvements for the whole of the labour force. This process may assist changes in perspectives of the leaders of the company and all the workers. The future transformation of the contractual bases will take place in a negotiated manner, progressively and cautiously, with the democratic participation of the representatives of our organisation. (SITIAVW 1992b; Translated by the author)

With negotiations of the collective agreement concluded, it was immediately apparent that this negotiation had changed the character of labour relations in the plant. SITIAVW had, however, agreed to much more than it was willing to let on to the membership. In return for relatively substantial wage increases, the union leadership had fundamentally surrendered their own role in production relations as it had been understood historically. Subsequent events indicated that the negotiating committee had misjudged the membership which was unwilling to trade away their acquired rights for an increase in pay.

Stage Two: Deposing the Executive Committee

Workers were given very little information about the implications of the agreement that had been signed on work reorganisation, and with no process for contract ratification, were unable to hold the leadership accountable for the changes announced after the fact. The union refused to distribute the collective agreement, and dissent grew quickly as supervisors mocked workers, saying that the union had 'sold them out' (Fernández del Real 1993).

Workers were told that during the negotiations, SITIAVW had signed an agreement with Volkswagen permitting the limited trial of work reorganisation in the form of the Team Concept in Shop 6, on the monoblock line beginning 8 June and lasting six months (Junta Federal de Conciliación y Arbitraje 1992a). Even more galling was to find out the conflicting news that the trial had been superseded by the second agreement on the rapid introduction of lean production in the plant. Neither at the assembly notifying workers of the strike, nor in the presence of the other union leaders at the Solidarity rally during the strike, did the SITIAVW executive indicate that on 1 July, the same day that the union struck the plant, a document signed by the executive was deposited at the Labour Board in the Federal District. The preamble of the document reads as follows:

> Given the modernisation that the Company requires in its productive processes, as well as in its organisational structures; motivated by the trade liberalisation that the country is undergoing; as well as being motivated by the possible celebration of the Free Trade Agreement between Mexico, the United States and Canada; and based on the philosophy that people are the most important of any organisation; with the objective of looking for new forms of work organisation that permit the direct participation of workers in the search for higher quality and productivity, as well as continuous improvement in the process, and excellence of personnel, the parties agree to the following. (Junta Federal de Conciliación 1992a; Translated by the author)

This agreement established the bases for the institution of flexibilised production practices throughout the factory.

Based on the ideals of increased quality and continuous improvement, work would be re-organised according to the philosophy of a client-supplier relationship among workers in the production process. Work groups would be responsible for safety, order, cleanliness, minor adjustments to machinery and each group would be led by a non-union supervisor, now called a Coordinator. It was agreed that work groups were to be divided into cells in which one of the workers would be named a Facilitator and the rest, VW Technicians. The old auxiliaries were given the first option to become a Facilitator. These were not minor changes. Article 15 of the new agreement indicated that at least 14 of the 97 articles in the collective agreement, as well as the chapter dealing with the promotion list and seniority rights, and any other 'impeding' clauses, would be re-negotiated separately after the conclusion of contract negotiations:

> As the integration of groups is agreed upon in said work areas, both parties will establish the norms that will permit the establishment of the system and its development, independently of the text of the articles of the collective agreement governing the systems under which work have been developed to the present date. Once the groups have been instituted in all possible areas, the parties agree definitively to the modification of the articles of the Collective Agreement that do not conform to the work groups system. (Junta Federal de Conciliación 1992; Translated by the author)

The agreement stated that it was arrived at in the spirit of the National Agreement on Productivity and Quality Increases. It explicitly stated that no other ratification was necessary for the agreement to take effect than that concluded before the Labour Board.

With astonishing rapidity and very little discussion, SITIAVW accepted the arguments presented by both the government and the employer in two instances; within the framework of the National Accord and in the collective agreement itself. The union agreed to the complete restructuring of shop-floor relations even before a pilot project on teams had even begun, and with little information on the possible ramifications that the project might have for workers and the union (*La Jornada* 1992a; Rappo 1992).

The union executive's response did nothing to diminish the growing discontent within the rank and file. On the afternoon of 20 July, 170 of the 204 sectional delegates of the union attended an assembly at which they agreed to begin proceedings which would dismiss the Executive Committee, according to the provisions in their union statutes. Since the company refused to allow an assembly to be held in the factory, the sectional delegates then went through the factory lines and called the workers to a meeting outside of the factory to take the formal resolution to dismiss the committee. The sectional delegates collected signatures during the second and third shifts, and during the first shift of the following day. By 11am on 21 July, they had collected almost 9,000 signatures.

The leaders of the oppositional movement, which took the name of the 'July 20th Movement', travelled immediately to Mexico City to submit documentation to the *Junta Federal de Conciliación y Arbitraje* (Federal Conciliation and Arbitration Board). In their deposition, the movement leaders argued that the document approving the institution of work teams signed by the SITIAVW and the employer was deposited without their knowledge at the Labour Board in the Federal District on 1 July, the same day that SITIAVW led the strike against the company. The workers argued that they had no information about the clauses in the collective agreement that were to be changed to prepare for the reorganisation of production. They raised questions about the lack of training for the new work arrangements, and they complained that there was a discrepancy between the company's practice and the union's statements regarding the actual wage increase. While the company indicated that the wage increase was 15 per cent plus a 5 per cent increase based on productivity, the SITIAVW claimed that it was a 20 per cent direct increase. The opposition leaders argued the new conditions meant the disappearance of the inspectors and auxiliary workers, the sub-contracting of the wire harness department, and a new work day of two shifts of 11 hours each, with straight compensation for the two extra hours worked.[1]

When they returned from Mexico City, the leadership of the oppositional movement discovered that the company had locked them out and stopped the buses from transporting workers to the factory. The leaders called a meeting of workers outside the plant. Having reached quorum, and after the vote to dismiss the SITIAVW's executive and the legal advisor was taken, the workers declared a Permanent Assembly outside of the factory. There 7,000 workers proposed a full referendum be held and demanded that the Secretary of Labour 'take note' of the change in union leadership that had taken place at the factory. The leadership of the July 20th Movement denounced threats that had been made against it. For its part, the SITIAVW executive, under the direction of Secretary-General Gaspar Bueno, declared that it would not resign, having been elected in fair elections in December 1991 (Rappo 1992).

Volkswagen stated that it was in a legal position to sever relations with SITIAVW and rescind individual workers' contracts four days after the shutdown of production (Calderón 1992). The Executive Administrative Committee of Volkswagen argued that the company had lost 30 thousand million pesos in the first 40 hours of the work stoppage and demanded that the federal and state authorities provide 'guarantees of security to renew activities immediately' (*La Jornada de Oriente* 1992a). The company claimed that this was an inter-union conflict and they would not intervene.[2] They did intervene, however, by calling police who arrived armed with M-16s. In response, nine thousand workers marched to the centre of the city to hold a demonstration at the Government's Palace (Guillén and Mendez 1992).

A group of sectional delegates went to talk to a commission of PRI deputies of the state of Puebla. They were advised to return to work, call sectional assemblies and make the SITIAVW executive convene an assembly headed by the Commission of Honour and Justice, before the Labour Authorities. The PRI deputies suggested that they protest like the Japanese, and wear an armband while they work, to show their displeasure. In response, a sectional delegate stated: 'It is not because of ignorance that we proceed in this way. We know our statutes and the Federal Labour Law very well, but when the authorities have no will then we reach an impasse' (Guillén and Mendez 1992).

---

1   Previously, the first shift ran from 6am-3pm, the second from 3pm-11:30pm and the third from 11:30pm-6am. The new hours fixed the day at 6am-5pm and from 3pm-1:30am (Lucero and Guillén 1992).

2   This indicated a shift in the company's position since the time four years previously, when a three day work stoppage resulted in the dismissal of General Secretary Rodolfo Contreras. On that occasion, the company was flexible (Calderón 1992a).

Wives of the dissident workers held a demonstration in the streets of Puebla and met with officials from the Department of the Interior, asking the authorities to find a solution to the conflict and ensure the safety of the unionists. The workers held a demonstration on the highway linking Puebla and Mexico City and were publicly supported by workers in the textile, steel and petroleum industries (*La Jornada* 1992b).

The Secretary of Labour, Arsenio Farell, called together the parties to discuss the conflict. He met with Gaspar Bueno (General Secretary SITIAVW), Héctor Barba (SITIAVW counsel), Martin Josephi (President of the Administrative council of VW), Jesús Valencia (July 20th Movement leader) and Carlos Fernández del Real (July 20th Movement counsel). The opposition presented their two demands. The leaders agreed the workers would to go back to work if a referendum were held to permit workers to declare their positions with respect to the conflict. Second, they demanded that an interim commission be formed to call new Executive Committee elections. After six hours of discussions, SITIAVW General Secretary Bueno agreed to hold an assembly to discuss the sanctions against the dissident leaders; discuss the ratification or dismissal of his leadership by the membership and call new elections if the membership decided to dismiss him. He then changed his mind, abruptly walked out of the meeting with his contingent and thus broke the agreement (Fernández del Real 1993).

At the same time, the company presented the Federal Conciliation and Arbitration Board with a request to terminate the collective agreement with the union representing 14,500 workers, for 'reasons beyond their control' (*La Jornada de Oriente* 1992b). On announcing this decision at a press conference on 27 July, the President of the Administration Council of the company, Martin Josephi, asserted:

> We are deeply sorry that certain workers... have not understood that the modernization of the country and the challenges of opening of our economy imply profound changes in worker-employer relations, but before all else, the adherence to and respect for the law. (*La Jornada* 1992b; Translated by the author)

Under the labour law, the Board had 11 days to consider the request. If the argument based on 'reasons beyond our control' were accepted, the company would be able to dismiss the workers according to the terms of Federal Labour Law which would grant workers three months wages and 12 days of pay for each year of seniority.[3] Immediately following this announcement, the 14 leaders of the movement were fired by the company and expelled by the union under the exclusion clause (Calderón 1992).

On 2 August, at a rally in Puebla's central square, the July 20th Movement held a rally to call for a formal General Assembly that would have the power to form an interim commission which would then call for new elections. Following the union constitution on the procedure for the dismissal of an executive committee, the dissidents collected signatures from the workers for a second time. To call a General Assembly, they had to demonstrate the support of 33 per cent of the unionised workers and this they did by collecting the signatures of 158 sectional delegates and

---

3   *Causa de fuerza mayor* also translates as an 'act of God'.

309 sheets of paper recording the signatures and identification numbers of 6,760 unionised workers. They then had to give ample notice of the General Assembly which was called for 15 August 1992. The signatures, along with examples of three newspapers where notice for the Assembly was published were deposited with the labour authorities. As well, they requested that officials from the Secretary of Labour present observers.[4] They decided to begin a permanent encampment outside the office of the Secretary of Labour in Mexico City, until the conflict was resolved. As a result, 5,000 workers stayed outside at the encampment during the first days of August (Vázquez 1992).

The hearing at the Federal Labour Board was held on 7 August. The company presented its reasons for wanting to break off labour relations with SITIAVW. The company indicated that it was held up in its plans and was losing six million dollars each day as a result of the conflict.[5] The hearing lasted for almost 15 hours, with the legal advisor for SITIAVW speaking for nearly ten hours, arguing against the company's position. He argued that the hearing itself was illegal and ought to be cancelled, since the parties were not given the required notice of ten working days. The oppositional leadership, as well as labour lawyers external to the conflict, concurred, arguing that this violated Article 763 of the Labour Law (de Buen 1992). But they also argued that the federal labour law was contravened since the company had already, in fact, terminated labour relations long before any judgement had been made by the Board. The SITIAVW legal advisor, Héctor Barba, stated that it was not *fuerza mayor* (reasons beyond their control), but the fact that the company had cancelled the buses to the factory that prevented workers from returning to work and resulted in the cancellation of production. Barba demanded that the employers pay all of the lost wages and open the plant immediately. He declared that if they lost, and if all relations with the union were ended, they would go to the Supreme Court of Appeal (Arrona 1992a).

The fired leadership of the oppositional movement was not given legal status at the hearing, but they continued to demand legal recognition and the 'taking of note' by the Secretary of Labour (Arrona 1992b). Their lawyer, Carlos Fernández del Real, argued that Article 433 of the Federal Labour Law permits the termination of the collective agreement only if the plant is completely shut down. Yet throughout the conflict, non-unionised workers, including office staff, were working at the plant. Obviously, 'an act of God' had not closed the plant (Piedrahita 1992).

After the audience, Volkswagen indicated that it would await the decision of the Labour Board before trying to come to any resolution with the union. But the company also hinted that it would consider a new kind of 'concerted' agreement, as a satisfactory outcome for the conflict (*Síntesis* 1992). The following day, at a rally of about 2,000 workers, the General Secretary of the union, Gaspar Bueno, reported on this meeting and was accompanied to the podium by the Francisco Hernández

---

4   The documentation was presented to the Dirección General de Registro y Associaciones of the Secretaría Federal de Trabajo y Prevision Social (see Vásquez 1992).

5   Volkswagen had been producing 400 Golfs, 400 Sedans and 65 vans, as well as 2,000 engines each day, with stated plans to invest one thousand million dollars in Mexico over the next five years (Vásquez 1992).

Juárez, the General Secretary of the *Federación de Sindicatos de Empreses de Bienes y Servicios* (FESEBES) (Federation of Unions in Goods and Services Companies); and the other leaders of FESEBES, as well as Antonio Durán, Secretary of External Relations of the *Sindicato Mexicano de Electricistas*. Hernández Juárez noted that FESEBES had sent 18 tons of food to the embattled union as an expression of solidarity. They had invited the independent Volkswagen union to work with FESEBES, he stated, not in order to control it, but so that they could work together (Becerril 1992a; Victoria 1992).

The July 20th Movement held its assembly on 15 August as planned, and for the third time, workers demonstrated their intentions to depose the union executive. According to the documentation submitted to the Secretary of Labour, 9,494 of the total 14,233 unionised workers attended the assembly. At the meeting, 9,301 workers, including 152 sectional leaders, voted to dismiss the Executive Committee of Gaspar Bueno and all the Union Commissions (Lovera 1992). Voters deposited their ballots, on which were written 'yes' or 'no', in urns that were sealed; ballots were then counted by press photographers. The assembly elected a provisional Executive Committee headed by Jesús Valencia that would be responsible for holding new union elections. The ballots and attendance cards which indicated that the voters were union members were brought to the Secretary of Labour (Becerril 1992b; Arrona 1992c; Chavarría Díaz 1992; Vázquez 1992). Secretary General Gaspar Bueno responded by arguing that the assembly was illegal, that there was a lack of security at the meeting and that many of the people who voted were not union members (SITIAVW 1992c).

Stage Three: Termination: The Labour Board brings down its Ruling

The Board ruling was delayed long past its expected date and brought down its ruling on 17 August. It accepted Volkswagen's arguments for the suspension of labour relations and gave the company 72 hours to sever its relations with its 14,233 workers (Junta Federal de Conciliación and Arbitraje 1992). The Board ruled that the inter-union conflict had produced an 'irreparable condition' that resulted in the shut down of production.

With the news that the oppositional movement had lost, the SITIAVW executive called a meeting of approximately 7,000 workers for that same day where a package of proposed modifications to the union statutes was presented to the workers for their approval. SITIAVW announced that the company required it to reform its internal union statutes if it wanted to avoid firings. The union formed a commission to take the reformed statutes to the labour authorities and the company offices (Escobar 1992). The new union statutes were intended to reflect the new flexible working conditions, according to reports by SITIAVW's legal advisor, Hector Barba. In the new constitution, 40 of the 100 clauses of the union constitution had been altered. Among other things, the practice of forming opposing slates in union elections was ended. The new statutes terminated the practice of calling General Assemblies and eliminated sectional delegates. The 214 sectional delegates were replaced by 14 secretaries who control approximately 1,000 workers each. The practice of granting severances to outgoing union members was also ended (Calderón Gómez 1992b; Guillén 1992b).

Six hours after the Labour Board brought down its ruling, the Secretary of Labour, Arsenio Farell Cubillas, called a meeting of the Volkswagen officials and Gaspar Bueno to conduct negotiations on the re-hiring of the workers under the new contract (Calderón Gómez 1992b). Secretary General of FESEBES Francisco Hernández Juárez attended the meeting on SITIAVW's behalf. A completely new collective agreement was signed just before 4am the next day, 18 August. The new collective agreement prepared for the immediate imposition of work teams. The union's legal advisor, Barba, argued that the collective agreement was the same as the old one with respect to wages and benefits. It included a 20 per cent direct increase in wages, 4 per cent increase in benefits and the equivalent of 28 days wages pay for profit sharing, paid in December and May (Guillén 1992c; Juárez 1992). When asked for corroboration of Barba's announcement, the Secretary of Press and Information of SITIAVW Fausto Lara Paisano, indicated that the new contract had not been distributed, saying, 'It's not even printed yet, anyway why would we give it out if they are not even interested in it and wouldn't even read it anyway?' (Becerril 1992d).

The rehiring process caused immediate concern among the workers returning to the plant. Not everyone was rehired, and those who were had to give up one of their rights under labour law: workers had to sign a statement agreeing not to appeal the decision made by the Labour Board. Workers were required to hand in their old identification card that indicated seniority levels. This caused immediate alarm, since the new cards did not record seniority and were similar to those given out to temporary workers in the past. Workers in the maintenance and wire harness departments were not listed among those to whom the new hiring process applied (Becerril 1992d).

On 19 August, the day workers returned to the factory, 300 dissidents tried to organise a meeting in the early morning but were attacked by guard dogs and beaten by soldiers. Eleven were arrested. After a meeting between their lawyer and the state governor, the detained were released. The government agreed to pay their medical costs (Becerril 1992e). The next day, Volkswagen took out advertisements in national newspapers with the following message:

> *Home sweet Home*: Unity will strengthen our family. Now we will be able to see, once again, the fruits of our talents, creativity and imagination. We will hear again, the movement of the line that transports parts, engines and automobiles from one work group to the next. We will continue to offer the results of our abilities and our efforts. It fills us with enthusiasm to return. But we are most proud to know that we will continue being a family: The great Volkswagen family. (Volkswagen de México 1992a; Translated by the author)

By early September, the 400 remaining members of the July 20th Movement were able to negotiate their severances with the labour authorities according to the conditions of the old collective agreement. The 600 workers who were not re-hired signed over all their rights to appeal and agreed to be represented only by the SITIAVW's legal advisor in the negotiations with the company over severances (*La Jornada de Oriente* 1992c, 16).

When the workers were being hired back, the company stated that dissident leaders would not be re-hired since they had received economic support from the same international organisations that had participated in the Ford conflict. Thus, they were not to be given access to the plant again (Calderón Gómez 1992c). The presence of ex-Ford workers at earlier rallies, as well as the support from the United Auto Workers (UAW) and the Canadian Auto Workers (CAW-TCA) was criticised in the official press as an interventionist attempt by Canadian and US workers to destabilise Volkswagen and turn the conflict over to foreign hands (Bustillos 1992, 1; see also Luis Sierra 1992).

Public Reflections on the Conflict

The conflict at Volkswagen was watched widely within Mexico and ignited much discussion in public discourse. Labour lawyers, academics, labour leaders, politicians and industry leaders commented on it. In the shadow of the NAFTA negotiations, the Volkswagen story appeared as a harbinger of things to come and fuelled much debate. Whether the 'lesson' was that labour law was not respected, or labour law ought to be reformed, or the dynamic was located in the imperatives of free trade, or that state authoritarianism was increasing, or that participation in management's restructuring plans was the only alternative, the conflict touched a national nerve. Labour lawyers deplored the attack on the right to association, arbitrary detention and violation of the Constitution. In a public denunciation, the *Asociación Nacional de Abogados Democráticos* (National Association of Democratic Lawyers) stated:

> We call on all workers and the people of Mexico to consider the seriousness of this Resolution in terms of the annulment of Constitutional rights established in their favour. We call on the Mexican government to rectify the violations committed, thus restoring the constitutional order. (Asociación Nacional de Abogados Democráticos 1992; Translated by the author)

The *Asociación* launched a public campaign arguing that it was 'absolutely false' to suggest that the movement of workers had impeded the access to the plant and shut down production. No 'Act of God' could be proved. Rather, argued the lawyers, the company had achieved its objective which was to terminate labour relations in the plant, with the complicity of the *Junta Federal de Conciliación y Arbitraje*, and the *Secretaría del Trabajo y Previsión Social*. Further, without any basis in jurisprudence, the labour authorities interfered with internal union affairs by refusing to 'take note' of the change in union leadership that had been concluded according to the union's own constitution. At the same time, the labour authorities recognised the changes to the union constitution submitted by the deposed union leadership without any ratification by the membership on 18 August (Krieger 1992).

The *Asociación* indicated its concern for the rule of law given the decisions sanctioned by the President of the Republic during the NAFTA negotiations. In part, their concern reflected a broader debate about the reform of labour law in Mexico.

Although labour law reform had been contemplated in Salinas's Reform of the State, it was not carried out. Labour lawyers argued that, in fact, the labour law had already been altered through concertation at the national level and coerced changes to collective agreements. Unwilling to risk an overt conflict, Salinas reformed the law in this indirect manner. As labour lawyer Néstor De Buen commented:

> There are some who worry themselves- even me as a case in point, -about reforms to the Federal Labour Law; idiots that we are. Because our political system has invented a much better formula: throw the law into the garbage and make a new one every day according to the whims of the client...And this is why Volkswagen merits special attention. After the beating that it received as a result of NAFTA and content requirements of 62.5 per cent, all this was worth the consolation prize – that's it for labour relations, the union and the collective agreement. So, everyone lives happily ever after. Amen. (de Buen 1992; Translated by the author)

Although SITIAVW was already an independent union and not a member of the CTM, the labour authorities dealt a serious blow to the old corporatist trade union structures and official trade unionism by promoting the new labour federation. FESEBES, formed in 1990, was closely aligned with Salinas's policies. The President of the Labour Congress (CT), Mario Suárez, recognised the threat, condemned the union's advisors and urged the workers to appeal the Board's decision. The CTM took its traditional position by playing both sides of the field. Fidel Velázquez, leader of the *Confederación de Trabajadores de México*, announced that the decision of the Labour Board was an 'ominous and ill-fated precedent for the labour movement that might be repeated in other conflicts' (Becerril 1992c). Juan Moises Calleja, deputy and legal advisor to the CTM, took the opposite position by defending the legality of the decision and the role played by Secretary of Labour Arsenio Farell Cubillas. Calleja argued that the conflict was an inter-union one promoted by people external to the company; the same ones who interfered in the Ford movement (Camacho Guzman 1992; Sánchez Rebolledo 1992). Juan Ortega Arenas, who played a decidedly inactive role during the conflict, denounced the decision as fascist (Becerril 1992c).

After a series of events in which the Secretary General of FESEBES, Francisco Hernández Juárez, publicly demonstrated his support for Gaspar Bueno and his Executive Committee, it became clear that SITIAVW would enter into a new relationship with the Federation. Crediting the company with a conciliatory attitude during the conflict, Hernández Juárez stated that FESEBES promoted unity and 'identified with those unions wanting change' along the lines offered by the modernisation agenda (Guillén 1992b). Among labour leaders, Hernández Juárez, stood alone:

> The truth is, I have to say, that the attitude of the company was very positive ...in order to resolve this. The truth is that this has been a very important experience for us. It is an excellent precedent that perhaps will serve as a demonstration that it is possible, even under the most difficult conditions, to find solutions acceptable to everyone. (Becerril 1992c; Translated by the author)

Hernández Juarez's declaration was in concert with that of the president of the Administrative Council of Volkswagen of Mexico, Martin Josephi, who hoped that other companies would follow VW's example:

> [T]he changes that were made to the collective agreement are reflected in other labour relations, since there is liberty to exercise the productivity and quality programs, these are very important aspects to be able to compete in international markets. (Becerril 1992e; Translated by the author)

Indicating his support for FESEBES, Josephi stated that SITIAVW ought to belong to a federation or union central. This senior company official applauded the reform of the union constitution that extended the executive's term of office from three to six years (Becerril 1992e). FESEBES was granted its official registration by the labour authorities in early September.

Representation and Presidential *Caudillismo*

It was unlikely that Carlos Salinas de Gortari took office by means of a democratic election, and it was not popular support which kept him in power from 1988–1994. Rather, he reproduced a highly illiberal form of politics to promote the neo-liberal restructuring of the Mexican economy. This was *caudillo* politics at its best. His leadership depended upon his ability to command the loyalty of other groups of men. He was able to see his National Development Plan through because he concluded 'concerted' agreements with the men who were leaders of the most important social forces. Throughout his six year tenure, Salinas de Gortari was aware he would need to generate wealth and ensure it was distributed such that the loyalty of his 'group' would be solidified. For example, he privatised most of the state-owned corporations, including Telmex, and permitted Carlos Slim Helú to profit dramatically (Slim Helú has since become the wealthiest man in the world). Salinas built cross-class alliances with other men, as demonstrated by his relationship with the General Secretary of the Telephone Workers union, who then became General Secretary of the newly consecrated labour federation, FESEBES. In this way, Salinas manoeuvred so as to displace and then exclude the CTM *caudillos* from the centres of power. He was willing to use police as well as judicial violence to both co-opt and control working-class movements. He accepted the fact that coalition building did not necessarily mean a consensus was in the offing. As President, it did not seem to matter whether this system of patriarchal power was hegemonic or not. *Caudillismo* was expressed in the Salinas's years as conflict between men resulting from intense competition and a deep restructuring within the state itself.

Carlos Salinas de Gortari announced in his first annual report of his government a National Development Plan in which the themes of sovereignty, democratisation, non-inflationary growth and improvements in the general standard of living would take priority (Salinas de Gortari 1989, 1–62). In particular, the reform of the state took a central place in this Plan. Salinas declared himself a defender of the rule of law, and committed to the democratic exercise of authority as reflected in the 1989 Electoral Law reform (Trejo Delarbre 1991, 59). Salinas's objectives were made clear to Mexicans as well as to interested observers in Canada and the United States (Presidencia de la República 1991a). The President argued that a modern state required increased levels of efficiency. In other words, he equated privatisation with modernisation: 'Not only because of the complexity of demand and the poorly regulated growth of the State apparatus, but the concept of the State as an exclusive provider in itself inhibits the organised forces of society' (Salinas de Gortari 1990, 6). Salinas called for a change in the national objectives contained in the Constitution. In true neo-liberal fashion he wanted to dispense with national programmes, nationalisation and public enterprises. *Salinisimo* would reduce federal authority and protectionism in the areas of 'industry and trade, urban and social services, labour and ownership relations, both in the countryside and in the field of industry.' Instead, he argued in favour of programmes that would strengthen the modern state by enhancing:

> coordination, democratic exercise of authority, rationalization and encouragement of autonomy, stimulation of popular participation and organization in social programs, privatisation of non-strategic public enterprises with workers having a share in their ownership and the product of their sales being channelled into social programs, and transparency in the State's relations with all those active in the social sectors and with all its citizens. (Salinas de Gortari 1990, 13–14; Translated by the author)

One of the most significant changes coming from Salinas's reforms concerned the National Solidarity Programme (PRONASOL). Using funds derived from the privatisation of parastatal enterprises, PRONASOL was organised as a poverty alleviation programme in which targeted communities and programmes directed towards work projects and social services provision (Salinas de Gortari 1990, 16–18).[6]

Salinas followed International Monetary Fund (IMF) and World Bank (WB) directives on reductions in public spending, deregulated key sectors of the economy, reformed central Constitutional articles and unilaterally decreased tariffs on trade before the negotiations for the North American Free Trade Agreement (NAFTA) were completed.[7] In order to facilitate liberalisation, the Salinas government undertook to alter the regulatory framework governing economic relations. It deregulated almost every sector of the Mexican economy including agriculture, where it rescinded the central tenets of the much beloved Constitutional Article 27 on common agricultural lands. The changes promoted under the PRI were preceded by a decade of moves toward economic liberalisation, but in no other six-year presidential term since General Lázaro Cárdenas established corporatist institutions in the 1930s has the relationship between state institutions and the economy been so dramatically restructured.

---

6   For a critical discussion of this programme see Valdés Ugalde (1994, 232); see also Dresser (1991).

7   See Trejo Delarbre (1991) for a sympathetic analysis of the outcomes from the first half of Salinas' government; for a more critical view, see Álvarez Béjar and Mendoza Pichardo (1991).

One of the most significant contradictions of this moment was that neo-liberal reforms were constructed within the ambit of 'concertation', the sealing of alliances with major social forces through national agreements. In this sense, they gave new life to corporatism, but this was not the corporatism of old. For example, the administration extended its neo-liberal agenda by removing wage bargaining from collective negotiations and imposing an incomes policy within the national pacts, or *Pactos*. As a result, the national leadership of labour organisations signed agreements with the government that were tremendously unpopular with the membership (Bolívar Espinoza 1990, 36, 42). Whereas labour once played a role, albeit a constrained one, in adjustments and negotiations over the setting of priorities within the government, in the 1990s official labour became not only a rubber stamp for agreements formulated at other levels in the state but the mechanism through which economic restructuring was imposed on the working class. Salinas deepened the strategy established by De la Madrid, and institutionalised neo-liberalism much more profoundly at the national and North American level.

Corporatist institutional relationships were not laid to rest in the process of globalisation. They were put to different purposes. National sectoral associations were brought to participate in national agreements on the implementation of modernising strategies in the country. Although the top leadership in the official labour body of the governing party, the *Confederación de Trabajadores de México* (CTM) opposed the process by which their preferential location in the labour movement and within the state was eroded, the CTM acquiesced to most of the significant governmental policies. In the Volkswagen conflict we have an example of how the Salinas government was able to obtain relative compliance within the labour sector, even with a union that had maintained its independence from the official labour movement for over 20 years.

From the beginning of its term, the Salinas administration promoted a series of national agreements in which key organisations from the business, union and peasant sectors agreed to work with the state and each other to promote economic growth and modernisation in preparation for a new phase of continental integration. In the economic sphere, the umbrella agreement was known as the *Pacto para la Estabilidad y el Crecimiento Económico* (PECE). This 'Pact for Economic Stability and Growth' was signed immediately after Salinas took office in 1988 and was renewed during the years of his presidency (1988–1994). The goals of the PECE were to reduce inflation while increasing productivity, savings and competitiveness. The signatories agreed to a program which limited public spending, reduced the value-added tax from 15 per cent to 10 per cent and brought fuel prices closer to market levels. The government agreed to an ongoing but slight devaluation of the peso (.20 daily) and to end exchange controls. The minimum wage was increased by twelve per cent for all workers except those with a collective agreement. All parties to the agreement made a general commitment to economic deregulation with the aim of promoting increases in quality and productivity levels. The parties agreed to conduct studies on price increases if deemed necessary during the duration of the Pact while the Department of Industry and Trade (SECOFI) agreed to conduct industry studies in specific areas. The version of this national agreement in effect during the summer of 1992 was signed on 10 November 1991 and lasted until January 1993 (*Pacto Para La Estabilidad y El Crecimiento Economico* 1991).

Under the terms of these arrangements, another agreement dealt specifically with labour relations. The *Acuerdo Nacional para la Elevación de la Calidad y Productividad* (ANECP). This 'National Agreement on the Increase in Quality and Productivity' was an agreement for wages and price controls but it was much more than that.[8] The ANECP articulated the dominant ideas of lean production centred in the goals of increased productivity and quality levels. It stated categorically that 'Productivity cannot be imposed; its essence stems from the will of all parties contributing to the productive process and depends upon a highly participatory process' (Acuerdo Nacional para la Elevación de la Productividad).

The Agreement referred to the importance of technological modernisation, research, training and human resource development. It included a declaration that each of the parties to the agreement would promote a new 'culture of work' in the country. Labour organisations agreed to promote educational programs in order to educate members about the imperatives of new economic conditions. These educational programs were meant to diffuse information about new forms of production and the changing role of labour organisations in the new context. The government agreed to link macroeconomic policy to the promotion of productivity and quality while the national business organisations agreed to establish support programs for companies and to work with unions and peasant organisations to develop human resources programmes.[9] The ANECP framed the solution to the productivity problem in the language of lean production and international competitiveness.

Apart from the ideological importance of this agreement, there were two other aspects that became significant. First of all, the state, together with the national associations of labour and business, agreed to modernise the organisational structures within the labour relations regime. This was what opened the door to the national debate on labour law reform and its foundations in Constitutional Article 123 and the 1931 Federal Labour Law. This part of the agreement also brought into question the internal representational structure of trade unions as they had developed over time. This was certainly a contentious issue since the terms of the debate were dominated by concerns with productivity not democracy.

No less important was the fact that national labour and business organisations agreed that unions and employers would sign productivity and quality agreements in each unionised workplace:

> The labour and business sectors promise to conclude agreements and productivity clauses in collective agreements in which the measure of productivity and economic stimuli derived from these increases will be precisely determined. These will become normalised through an ongoing process of concertation and evaluation by the parties. The government assumes the commitment to contribute to the creation of the necessary conditions for

---

8　This national agreement was introduced on 27 January 1992, amended and then signed by the largest union, peasant and business organisations as well as the Secretary of Labour, on 25 May 1992 after months of contentious discussion.

9　A Follow-up and Evaluation Commission was formed to ensure that the parties complied with their obligations (de la Luz Arriaga Lemus 1992, 7–12).

the concertation of such agreements and clauses. (Alzaga 1992, i-viii; Translated by the author)

This mandate framed the context within which the Volkswagen conflict originated. Work reorganisation was undertaken by authoritarian means even in the midst of a severe crisis of representation. The oppositional movement at Volkswagen was defeated, not because lean production had won the hearts of the workers, but because the government was willing to risk deepening the crisis of representation by being seen to undermine the Constitution itself. The conflict at Volkswagen had an impact at the national level and reinforced the demands of the opposition for a reform of the state.

Under Salinas's reforms, the powerful official trade union leaders were obliged to yield to a new cadre of technocratic foreign educated leadership within state-party institutions. The struggle between 'dinosaurs' and 'technocrats' within the PRI was demonstrated by the emergence of the new labour federation during Salinas's term. The *Federación de Sindicatos de Empresas de Bienes y Servicios* (FESEBES) replaced the CTM as the embodiment of the favoured model of labour relations as soon as it was formed in April 1990. FESEBES was a labour federation composed of six organisations with more than 100,000 members in the early 1990s. Membership derived from many of recently privatised state companies and para-statal corporations. Among its founding members were the *Sindicato de Telefonistas* (Telephone Workers), the *Sindicato Mexicano de Electricistas* (Electrical Workers), *Sindicato Técnicos y Manuales de la Producción Cinematográfica* (Film Technicians), *Alianza de Tranviarios de México* (Transportation Workers), and the *Asociación de Sobrecargos y Pilotos de Aviación* (Airline Workers). Fully supportive of the globalising policies of the Salinista government, FESEBES emerged in direct opposition to the CTM on the national political scene and was prohibited from joining the *Congreso del Trabajo* (CT) (Trejo Delarbre 1991, 319–22).

Salinas's view of a modern labour sector was elaborated in his 1 May 1990 speech. Here Salinas indicated that he was prepared to support the restructuring of the labour movement in support of economic modernisation. He rejected 'confrontational' trade unionism and called for labour's affirmation of the need for increased productivity, realised in alliance with a reformed and strengthened state. Along with recommendations in favour of reformed trade unionism, Salinas also referred to the need for a reform of the administration of labour relations. Finally, he emphasised the importance of developing a new labour culture in which participation and dialogue would characterise labour relations. For instance, as part of the effort to broaden support for state reform, certain distinguished people were invited by the President to contribute to the production of a series of books reflecting on the modernisation project. Francisco Hernández Juárez was the only labour leader invited to participate in the project (Hernández Juárez and Xelhuantzi López 1992, 7). The invitation was extended one month after the end of the conflict at Volkswagen. Hernández Juárez stated his position on the crisis of labour relations in Mexico at that time:

> In essence, the labour conflict within the crisis is an eminently political conflict. It puts into question those exhausted labour systems that generate less production, less human

well-being, concentrating it in the hands of fewer and fewer groups and individuals. It also limits the social capacity for the transformation of unions and workers, limiting their participation within social and labour structures that are hierarchical, centralised and inflexible. (Hernández Juárez and Xelhuantzi López 1992, 17; Translated by the author)

Hernández Juárez's appreciation of the virtues of Salinas's initiatives in the areas of free trade in particular and globalisation more generally was apparent throughout, but it was his discussion of the new unionism that was most illuminating. For him, labour must participate in the reform of the state, but its participation must be based upon a redefinition of its own institutions in order to permit increased 'participation', 'consensus' and 'commitment' with respect to the modernisation project (Hernández Juárez and Xelhuantzi López 1992, 150–51). Hernández Juárez suggested: 'Even if the Labour Congress (CT) continues to forbid itself from becoming the foundation and the catalyst for this restructuring, this does not mean unionism cannot, or should not, change by other means' (Hernández Juárez and Xelhuantzi López 1992, 151). Newly anointed by the power of the federal executive, Hernández Juárez was speaking the new 'official' line to the labour sector. If the official labour movement would not reform itself according to the demands of lean production, state reform and free trade, through Hernández Juárez, the President would impose reform.

Deepening the Crisis: NAFTA

In June 1990, the United States and Mexico announced they would begin discussions leading towards a free trade agreement. They were joined by Canada in October 1990. After the US Congress approved 'Fast Track' negotiations, formal negotiations began in June 1991.[10] An agreement was reached on 12 August 1992 and signed on 17 December 1992 (Grinspun and Cameron 1993, 3).

Recalling the legitimating power of Constitutional discourse, Mexican President Carlos Salinas de Gortari announced that Mexico's objectives in participating in North American Free Trade Agreement (TLC or TLCAN) negotiations were compatible with the goals of Revolutionary Nationalism. In a promotional booklet published during the negotiations, *Secretaría de Comercio y Fomento Industrial* (SECOFI) stated:

> For Mexico, the objective is to reach an Agreement that corresponds to the interests of its society. The Treaty will respect inherently the text of our Constitution and our laws, permitting us to fulfil the great objectives that Mexicans have entrusted us with: consolidate sovereignty, promote development and attain justice. (Secretaría de Comercio y Fomento Industrial 1992, 4; Translated by the author)

---

10 In the United States, 'Fast Track' refers to the 'authority that Congress may give the Administration to negotiate a trade agreement and present the legislation. Once negotiations are completed, Congress has 60 days to vote yes or no on the whole agreement and the implementing legislation.' The fast-track authorisation won by a vote of 23 in the House of Representatives in the spring of 1991 (Citizens Trade Campaign 1993; Translated by the author).

For its part, Canada argued that the government's objectives were simply to increase exports and jobs. In the words of Finance Minister Michael Wilson, 'Nations and peoples have resoundingly said no to the policies of the past, so discredited in eastern Europe and elsewhere: closed economies, central planning, policies which are anti-business and policies which undermine the incentive to work are recipes for economic and environmental hardship'(Wilson 1992, 8). Government discourse consistently obscured the link between trade and investment that had become a defining characteristic of North American negotiations since the onset of the Canada-US Free Trade Agreement.[11]

Throughout the 1980s, Canadian business leaders kept pressing for a free trade agreement with the United States. The federal government called a Royal Commission on the subject and by 1988, the country was embroiled in an intense national debate that extended through a hotly contested federal election. Ronald Reagan was in the White House, and his administration wanted:

> to make sure that the outcome provides for comparable treatments for American and Canadian investment and intellectual property rights (copyright and patent questions) in both countries. We will also want to eliminate or reduce tariffs imposed on our exports and to gain increased access to government procurement opportunities in the Canadian market...reduction of government subsidies and support to industry, non-discriminatory treatment of suppliers of services, and effective protection against transhipment problems.... We continue to retain full access to multilaterally sanctioned United States trade remedies. (Reagan 1986, 43–5)

The Progressive Conservative party won the election and the Canada-U.S. Free Trade Agreement came into effect on January 1, 1989.

The NAFTA built on the model of trade negotiations established in the Canada-US deal. It went well beyond lowering tariff barriers and set down the parameters of state action in setting national economic policies. The CUFTA, limited the scope of government procurement, introduced for the first time disciplines covering the treatment of services and provided for special access for business persons. It undermined the system of managed trade in automotive products and it pushed back against 'non-tariff barriers' to trade. Most importantly, the CUFTA established a 'proportional sharing' agreement in energy resources which compelled Canada to ensure that:

> export restrictions not be designed to disrupt normal channels of supply or alter the product mix as between various types of specific energy good exported to the other country. For example, if Canada in future decides to implement measures to limit the consumption of oil, it can reduce exports to the United States proportional to the total supply of oil available in Canada. Any such restriction must not be designed to disrupt normal trade patterns. (External Affairs Canada 1987, 142)

---

11 Ken Traynor cites R.K. Morris, head of the National Association of Manufacturers in the United States on this point (see Traynor 1992, 11).

The Mexican government agreed to no such clause in the North American Free Trade Agreement and access to the Mexican oil fields remained a goal of the United States thereafter.

The Mexican government did, however, agree to a chapter on investment which went well beyond the CUFTA framework. In CUFTA, the Investment Chapter mandated national treatment for foreign investors. It prohibited performance requirements like those Mexico had used to establish its Auto Policies. It prohibited nationalisation or expropriation, or actions considered 'tantamount to an expropriation'. It prohibited governments from limiting the flow of capital across their borders. The NAFTA went beyond these provisions to establish the 'investor-state' clause which for the first time permitted an investor to sue a state. In other words, since 1994 corporations have been permitted to take governments to court for having 'breached their obligations' under the agreement and causing damages to the investor as a result (North American Free Trade Agreement 1992, Art. 1116 and 1117).

In the auto industry, the NAFTA liberalised trade but also entrenched the terms of North American production patterns (Márquez 1993). After a transition period of ten years, goods produced in Canada, the US or Mexico would be traded duty-free within the region. The definition of authorised goods depended upon the 'rules of origin'. According to SECOFI:

> The rules of origin designate goods 'originating' in the region when they are produced completely in North America. Goods containing materials from outside this zone are also considered originating, if foreign materials are transformed in one of the countries party to the agreement. Said transformation must be enough to modify the tariff classification according to the provisions of the Agreement. (Secretaría de Comercio y Fomento Industrial 1993, 1; Translated by the author)

In some cases, including the auto sector, goods incorporating a designated level of 'regional content' could be considered originating, even when the final product maintained the same tariff classification as its component parts. Based on the method of 'net costs', auto producers gained preferential market treatment if they incorporated 62.5 per cent regional content for passenger cars and light trucks, engines, and transmissions for these same vehicles. Sixty per cent regional content was required for duty-free access for all other vehicles and auto parts.[12] Tariffs were lifted on goods produced in the auto industry over a period of ten years. After ten years, restrictions on new auto imports were lifted. After 16 years, used cars would be imported on a gradual basis (Secretaría de Comercio y Fomento Industrial 1993, 1).

The *Decreto para el fomento y modernización de la industria automotriz* was to be modified and phased out over the transition period. The obligations to maintain a 'trade balance' were lifted for auto producers located in Mexico. So too the NAFTA lifted restrictions preventing auto producers not located in Mexico from selling

---

12 The method of net costs subtracts the total cost of the good, royalties, advertising, packing and shipping. With this method, financial charges are reduced (Secretaría de Comercio y Fomento Industrial 1993, 1).

vehicles in the Mexican market. The level of 'aggregate national value' (VAN) requiring auto assemblers to incorporate auto parts produced by Mexican companies into their end product was to be reduced in the course of the transition period. Changes permitted certain *maquila* products to be incorporated into the VAN for the transition period (Secretaría de Comercio y Fomento Industrial 1993, 4–6).

Furthermore, Mexico agreed to permit foreign investors 100 per cent ownership in companies deemed to be 'national suppliers' of autoparts. As per other trade-related investment measures, the auto sector came under the purview of the Investment Chapter of NAFTA (Canada, 1992, 11.1–11.10). After the phase-in period, US regulations on fuel efficiency (Corporate Average Fuel Efficiency CAFE) began to consider Mexican exports on the same terms as Canadian and US products Secretaría de Comercio y Fomento Industrial 1993, 4–6). These provisions reflected not a weakened Mexican state so much as a state in which the executive power retains for itself a vital role in privatising the character of economic decision-making.[13] No longer were governments permitted to negotiate commitments from corporations to provide jobs and fixed investment in exchange for access to a national market, without violating the terms of the agreement (Canadian Centre for Policy Alternatives 1992, 48). While globalisation under NAFTA terms reduced government's role in managing foreign investment and trade, the state became more active in managing the relations of production. The clearest example of this was exhibited in Salinas's own priorities for state reform.

Resistance to NAFTA's Corporate Constitution for the Americas

With NAFTA, a particular form of restructuring was institutionalised having implications for political as well as economic structures. Opponents and supporters of the NAFTA argued that globalisation was 'constitutionalised' within this tri-national agreement.[14] While pro-free trade forces argued that NAFTA 'locked-in' economic reforms, opponents countered with the charge that the institutionalisation of one dominant or 'corporate' agenda, precluded the possibilities for democratic participation in future social reforms (Red Mexcana de Acción Frente al Libre Comercio 1992a, 83). The *Red Mexcana de Acción Frente al Libre Comercio* (RMALC) argued, for example, that matters previously considered to be within the public domain were being taken over by the executive power of governments

---

13 For further discussion of this point, see Panitch (1996).

14 The term has been attributed to Ronald Reagan who called the Canada–US Free Trade Agreement 'an economic constitution for North America' (Laxer 1992, 209; see also McBride and Shields 1993, 157). Stephen Gill refers to 'the new constitutionalism' found in the NAFTA, as well as the Maastricht Treaty and the Gatt Uruguay round, which makes it increasingly difficult for governments to direct trade, monetary or investment policy in the direction of 'social protection' in the Polanyian sense (Gill 1996, 216; for an earlier reference, see Gill 1992, 157–96). As Maude Barlow and Tony Clarke report, the director-general of the World Trade Organization opened the first ministerial meeting with a declaration that drafting a global investment treaty was like 'writing the constitution of a single global economy' (Ruggerio, as cited by Barlow and Clarke 1997, 30).

and corporations. Citizens in general, as well as workers, peasants and indigenous peoples in particular, were excluded from shaping the priorities under negotiation by the three governments. In a letter to Jaime Serra Puche, Minister for SECOFI, RMALC argued:

> We are concerned, as you know, with the lack of recognition of the asymmetries in the negotiation and, consequently, with the absence of the compensatory mechanisms and social safety nets that would lessen the effects of the NAFTA. Above all, we are concerned with the inability to establish different premises concerned with the social agenda and the autonomous and plural participation of organisations representing society. Such participation would be directed to achieving an agreement able to respond to a sustainable model of development and not merely to economic growth at any cost. (Red Mexicana de Acción Frente al Libre Comercio 1992b; Translated by the author)

Canadian and US social movements and coalitions made similar statements. In a widely publicised letter to Prime Minister Brian Mulroney, Robert White, President of the Canadian Labour Congress urged the Canadian Government to withdraw from the negotiations. He argued:

> Expanded trade has a significant role to play in development. But governments in all countries must retain the ability to manage trade and to regulate investment if they are to build stable and productive economies. The FTA/NAFTA is wrong because it sacrifices the sovereignty of governments to so called market freedoms, which in reality amount to the freedom of transnational corporations to operate just as they please.... The NAFTA would have profound impacts upon our economy and our society, adding to the major changes of the recent past. Yet the process of negotiation has been shrouded in secrecy. There has been no meaningful opportunity for public participation in the drafting of what has been called 'a new economic constitution for North America,' and no meaningful public debate. (White 1992, 14–15)

In fact, opponents quite accurately pointed out that some of the items under negotiation were intended to impose strict limitations on future political developments in each of the three countries. For example, NAFTA's promotion of 'national treatment clauses' limited the ability of the state to support national economic development in the face of asymmetrical foreign investment flows.

Under NAFTA, governments faced restrictions on their already weakened ability to control foreign investment. Intellectual property rights were strengthened, which had the effect of making it more difficult to counter-act the tendency towards monopolisation with efforts to socialise the transfer of technology. As coalitions of social movements organised trilateral meetings to consider the implications of NAFTA during the negotiations, they were very concerned with effects of 're-privatisation' on national state structures (Brodie 1996, 389). An emphasis on gender on the part of feminist activists revealed the link between economic restructuring at the level of world order, and the restructuring of the state.

During the negotiations, the strongest expressions of resistance to globalisation on the part of oppositional social forces emerged from, and referred back to, a critique at the level of the nation state. Far from being seen as irrelevant in the context of globalisation, social movements called on the state to be democratically accountable in virtually every *fora* where national social movements issued joint demands and alternative propositions at the international level. The anti-free trade movements in Canada, the US and Mexico did not, as some have suggested, direct their local organising efforts to the 'global' sphere (Brecher and Costello 1994, 97–102). During the NAFTA debate, 'internationalism' emerged from ongoing sharing of information about specific national and local and workplace experiences.

In October 1990, 30 Canadians representing 26 organisations met with 104 Mexican participants representing 60 organisations in the first of a series of trinational cross-sectoral meetings including labour and popular movement representatives which took place over the next few years (Seymour and Wolfarth 1990). In this sharing of common experiences of the effects of globalisation on their communities, working lives, national political economies, the tri-national work, when it was most effective, was able to integrate these different sites or spheres into their analysis and action proposals.

The first tri-national *Encuentro* between NAFTA's opponents was followed by another which took place in Zacatecas, Mexico in the fall of 1991, while the trade ministers of the Canada the United States and Mexico met in an official NAFTA negotiation session. The alternative Zacatecas Declaration stated that the NAFTA negotiations lacked a commitment to 'development with democracy favouring the participation of society in national decisions, in which the right of peoples to freely elect their representatives and governors is respected.' The Declaration demanded that the governments of the three countries respond to their fifteen proposals for a 'Continental Development Agreement'. The proposals ranged from the protection of existing and acquired social rights within the context of national sovereignty to new mechanisms for the management of economic integration at the regional and continental level. Under the general assumption that 'interdependence has to be determined according to national necessities and strategies', the proposals called for activist states which would not only preserve acquired rights but also to extend their areas of responsibility so as to manage economic integration according to the needs of the majority of their populations (Red Mexicana de Acción Frente al Libre Comercio 1992a, 84–5).

Specifically, the coalitions proposed that level of wages in Mexico be raised and that social security programs not be considered 'unfair competition'. They sought a prohibition on any undermining of Constitutional guarantees through the NAFTA, and supported calls for the recognition of collective labour rights, protective legislation for women, self-determination over natural resources, and agricultural policies which attended to the satisfaction of basic needs of each nation's population. They demanded that NAFTA expressly exclude any requirements for liberalisation in the area of culture, education or communications (Red Mexicana de Acción Frente al Libre Comercio 1992a, 85–6). Despite an excellent analysis of the gendered dimensions of economic restructuring presented by *Mujeres en Acción Sindical* and *Mujer a Mujer* and found in the text of Conference proceedings, the final Declaration did not reflect a feminist analysis.

All these proposals were raised in response to the effects of continental integration, and thus embodied a 'continental' dimension to them. Yet each required active state intervention to manage this integration and so were directed towards national levels of contestation in particular. Clearly, these provisions could not emerge without the efforts of representative states responding to the needs of the majority of their populations. This insight was most clearly articulated in the 'Trinational Working Women's Conference on Economic Integration and Free Trade' held in Valle de Bravo in February 1992. Over 100 women representatives of unions and other labour organisations from Canada, the US and Mexico participated. The conference was divided between a sharing of information and experiences of globalisation on the lives of working women, as well as a concern to advance mutually supportive strategies of contestation.

The consensus of participants in this conference was that economic integration would be challenged by making demands on each national government as regards their domestic responsibilities to guarantee social rights as well through its role as negotiator of international trade agreements:

> Because economic integration is based explicitly on women's exploitation in the paid labour force, we – women of Mexico, Canada and the United States – demand that our respective governments guarantee basic rights to adequate education, health care, food, nutrition, housing, stability of employment, living salaries and training, voluntary maternity, and peace (that is the ability to live free from violence) within any trilateral agreement. (Women's Plan of Action 1992)

Insofar as social inequality between nations promoted the increased exploitation of women workers, participants argued for the upward harmonisation of wages and working conditions as well as the maintenance of social services provided by the state:

> If we propose that salaries be harmonized upwards, we will question the very foundation of the NAFTA. Its very reason for being are the low wages in Mexico. To demand the upward harmonization of salaries is the same thing as opposing the Treaty, which is totally unrealistic.
> [A] very obvious demand that we need to be insisting upon now in the context of the negotiations is that basic services in each country not be dismantled – services like child care, health and educational systems, without which we cannot work. One demand that we can make is that the permissible levels for workplace toxics be standardized. Our bodies are the same – it doesn't make sense that the permissible levels in Mexico be so high. (Women's Plan of Action 1992)

Throughout this discussion, conference participants raised the issue of democracy, at the national and international level and within unions as well.

> In the unions in California, we have problems with the lack of democracy. The unions lost their power 20 years ago. Those of us who are new, in middle-level positions, decide to organize. We made our own analysis: We had forgotten the rank-and-file, direct representation. We are now re-organizing. We began by training membership, preparing them, making sure they can read and speak in Spanish and English. We teach them the history of unions, their achievements. And we prepare them to demand accountability from their leaders, from our superiors, from us. (Samano, Women's Plan of Action 1992)

This project of labour rights and modernization cannot be separated from the dispute regarding our very nationhood. Only a democratic government elected by Mexican women and men, with respect for suffrage, is capable of respecting and building on workers' rights. (Ortíz, Women's Plan of Action 1992)

We have to demand full democratic participation. We must have information regarding the NAFTA negotiations and any treaty or agreement should guarantee the rights of the most marginalized in all three countries. (Canadian Delegation, Women's Plan of Action 1992)

The internationalist movement is more and more necessary for the democratic movement, and especially for women. (Mexico, Women's Plan of Action 1992)

Despite the differences in union histories in each of the three countries, each delegation reflected on women's working lives by analysing the gendered division of labour in the household, as well as the similarities and differences of experiences in the marginal workplaces where women tend to be located. In general, participants shared the view that unions must move beyond the workplace to represent working women's issues effectively:

Our goal is to renew the alliance between mothers and teachers. Teachers can call the community together – to speak of what is happening locally and seek solutions to local problems. Our strategy is not to fight with the union, but to work outside of it. (Member of Teachers' Union, Women's Plan of Action 1992)

In the sewing workshops in Los Angeles, every time the workers try to organize, the owners close up shop and open up again around the corner. Moreover, workers have an aversion to unions. So we decided to organize our Garment Worker's Justice Centre. We hold workshops on immigrants' rights, and that's how we attract new members. We are unionizing people without unionizing their workplaces. They can begin to organize themselves without endangering their jobs. (Representative from the Justice Center, Women's Plan of Action 1992)

We're seeing creative organizing, innovation among workers based on their own needs- with or without the support of unions... working in coalitions with women's organizations, churches, community-based organizations. We are taking up the challenge of organizing with a view of the whole community. (Villasin, Women's Plan of Action 1992)

We hold workshops in which women reflect on the double day, how many hours they sleep, how many they work, what they like and don't like... We begin each session with group exercises which warm women up before beginning our analyses, games to help women talk. If we don't do that, they don't open up, few of them even speak Spanish. (Cervantes Rojas, Women's Plan of Action 1992)

Participants called on popular sector organisations to advance 'new and creative collective organising initiatives and solidarity' so that women would not bear the brunt of economic restructuring. The principles set down in the 'Women's Plan of Action' included calls to organise the unorganised, strengthen existing unions, promote women's research and create trinational links among women and women's organisations. These calls came out of successful prior experiences of new working relationships across national borders. On the issue of international alliances and information exchange between unions, participants reflected on the success of past experiences of sectoral meetings.

> We saw how 100,000 jobs had been lost AT&T in New York in the last ten years. In Boston and New York, the operators have a campaign- 'Say No to the Robot, Yes to the Human Voice.' They received support to keep their jobs, but the general public still was in favour of implementing the latest technologies. It's a real dilemma. The same changes that were implemented there over a ten year period are being carried out here in three. We have to stay in touch so that we can develop strategies to confront the transformation of our work…. Next week, the leadership of our respective unions will meet in Miami to sign an agreement defending wages, jobs, and the work process. (Ortíz)

> But these relations should not be taking place only at the top because that would serve only to strengthen elites and not involve the rank-and-file. One way or another, we need to be promoting grassroots-level connections, promoting contact among our locals. (Telephone worker, Women's Plan of Action 1992)

It was suggested that ongoing communication might be facilitated through electronic communication. Educational campaigns and worker exchanges were also encouraged. The conference was evaluated as having been a very useful opportunity for discussions among women workers. As the evaluation, *Memoria Testimonial*, expressed it, 'It has been important to begin putting together the puzzle of our three countries, so geographically close, but so culturally, economically and politically different.' (Women's Plan of Action 1992)

Labour and NAFTA's Side-Agreements

Immediately after NAFTA was signed in 1992, a new President took power in the United States. In the context of widespread and highly organised oppositional campaigns, President Bill Clinton was held to a campaign promise that he would not bring any deal to the US Congress to be ratified if it threatened labour or environmental standards (Stanford, Elwell and Sinclair 1993, 56). During the first half of 1993, negotiators in Canada, the US and Mexico worked to conclude side-deals on labour and the environment. These were announced on 13 August 1993, and the Agreement was ratified in the legislatures of each country. The Agreement came into effect on 1 January 1994 (Canada 1993).

The free trade debate and negotiations continued for a year after the Volkswagen conflict was concluded. The debate over labour's ability to defend workers' rights in the face of the NAFTA was highly contentious. In the United States, the AFL-CIO, along with other citizens groups and coalitions of social movements, expressed fears that NAFTA would mean the loss of jobs to low wage zones in Mexico where corporations would not have to contend with effective environmental and labour standards. However, the AFL-CIO expressed its support for the addition of side-agreements which would limit the possibility of companies moving to take advantage of these conditions (*La Jornada* 1993).

The Canadian labour movement refused to become involved in the negotiations of parallel accords to the NAFTA. In general, the position of the CLC and its member unions was one of outright rejection of the FTA, the NAFTA and the proposed environmental and labour side agreements. The Canadian labour movement, along with the Action Canada Network (ACN), expressed its lack of confidence in the negotiations on the side agreements, arguing that they could not alter the fundamental character of NAFTA the labour and environmental problems inherent in it. The ACN denounced the anti-democratic character of the negotiations (López Espinosa 1993). In Mexico, the official labour movement rejected any attempts to infringe on the sovereignty of Mexico with the use of labour and environmental side-agreements. A more progressive labour perspective was advanced within the *Red Mexicana de Acción Frente al Libre Comercio* (RMALC). RMALC is a coalition of groups that developed a strong criticism of the NAFTA's asymmetries and inherent degradation of democracy (Monroy 1993). They recognised the changing context given the extent of economic integration and advocated a critical politics of *propuesta y protesta*; in other words they decided to engage in the debate by promoting alternative proposals over protest alone.

According to Berta Luján, the RMALC insisted throughout the NAFTA negotiations that the social aspects of NAFTA have to be examined: protection of workers, social agenda, labour and environmental issues, free movement of peoples, discussion of the foreign debt, compensatory funds, and consideration of low wages as an unfair trading subsidy. During the debate on the side agreements, RMALC proposed three objectives: to improve working conditions, to provide for the upwards harmonisation of standards, to allow national legislation to regulate the side agreements (Luján 1993). They argued that the governmental lack of interest in these matters confirmed argument that NAFTA advanced the interests of transnational corporations at the expense of labour and popular groups in all three countries.

Although consultations were held as early as the middle of February 1993, the formal process of meetings and negotiations with respect to parallel accords on environment and labour began on 17 March 1993 in Washington. Canada and México began from the premise that the accord would not be reopened, nor a 'comma changed'. Both countries announced their intention that the parallel accords would respect national sovereignty and would not imply changes to labour or environmental laws (Aponte 1993). In an effort to appease national opposition while not alienating Republican members, the Clinton administration proposed that the Trilateral Commissions on labour and the environment be endowed with enforcement powers (Behr 1993). In the end, an agreement was reached. The central premise of the side agreements was to consider, in a non-adversarial way, whether or not a country's domestic laws have been complied with. The Labour Side Agreement imposed no transnational labour standards, but dealt with alleged failures to enforce national laws regarding child labour, minimum wage standards, forced labour, discrimination and other issues touching on basic liberal freedoms such as the right to organise, bargain and strike.

The many contentious issues raised in the debate on the side agreements raised broader questions concerning social movements' focus on the state in their opposition to globalisation. During the debate, issues of democracy and sovereignty were at times constructed as opposing precepts. Arturo Alcalde, of the *Asociación Nacional de Abogados Democráticos*, described the conflict; 'When governments talk about free trade, sovereignty is outdated. When they talk about labour rights, sovereignty becomes important again' (Alcalde 1993). Despite strengthening the visibility of international labour solidarity in the context of NAFTA, with the conclusion of these agreements on labour and the environment, the national juridical-institutional framework was affirmed as the primary site of struggle for labour movements' struggles against globalisation.

In the United States, the North American free trade negotiations were linked with a broader hemispheric agenda originally set out in George Bush's 'Enterprise for the Americas Initiative'. A free trade area from Alaska to Tierra del Fuego was the goal (Grinspun and Cameron 1993, 16). The Clinton Administration eventually took on this agenda itself. The Democrats proposed that neo-liberal reforms be 'locked in' through a series of Free Trade Agreements throughout the hemisphere. Clinton's trade representative declared that any country wishing to be considered for NAFTA membership must demonstrate that they had already undertaken substantive economic restructuring:

> While political considerations would play a role in the selection process – eg., a democratic government would probably be a necessity – they should not override economic 'readiness.' (United States Trade Representative 1994, 18–19)

As a template for agreements throughout the Americas, it was agreed that NAFTA would be expanded if other countries accepted the basic formula already negotiated between Canada, the United States and Mexico.

¡Ya Basta! Enough is Enough!

On 1 January 1994, the day NAFTA came into effect, Mexico woke up to news of a rebellion in the southeastern state of Chiapas. From the Lacondonan jungle, the *Ejercito Zapatista de Liberación Nacional* (EZLN) issued a call to arms and invited all Mexicans to rise in rebellion against an illegitimate state (Ejercito Zapatista de Liberación Nacional 1994). After preparing for ten years, it was not simply the Salinas government that they rebelled against, but a much longer history of disenfranchisement that had crystallised in the state itself. The EZLN did not speak for itself only. It spoke from the margins of Mexican society to a national problem and addressed its demands to the broadest sectors of civil society. From the centre of a direct confrontation with the state, the Zapatistas called for struggle for democracy within civil society (Reygadas, Gómezcesar and Kravzov 1994).

Within dominant groups, there was intense conflict as well. Nothing demonstrates this like the assassination of the PRI's presidential candidate, Luis Donaldo Colosio just months before the federal election. In the midst of a profound crisis of legitimacy, the political order degenerated rapidly. Another prominent leader of the PRI was killed a few months later; in August 1994, José Francisco Ruíz Massieu, the Secretary General of the PRI and the ex-brother-in-law of the president was assassinated in Mexico City. Raúl Salinas de Gortari, brother of Carlos was sentenced to 50 years in prison for masterminding the murder. In 2005, after ten years, he was released on appeal. The investigations into these assassinations, implicating the highest levels of political power in Mexico, are still not resolved.

The organisations of civil society looked for opportunity within these degenerating circumstances. There was massive support for the EZLN in every state across the country. After years of organising in defence of the vote in gubernatorial elections, non-governmental organisations stepped up the pressure for free and fair elections. They argued that if the liberals were really serious about destroying the corporatist system and supporting individual rights, then the government would be compelled to permit the opening of new spaces on this political terrain. In this demand they were partially successful. Organisations defending the vote sprang up to extend this new political space.

Multi-sectoral coalitions were organised in preparation for the decisive election of 1994. The coalitions in defence of the vote created the *Alianza Cívica*, and drew over 12,000 national observers to its 1994 election-day task. The *Alianza Cívica* was formed as a diverse coalition representing more than 400 non-governmental and civic organisations from all 31 states and the Federal District of Mexico. Members worked to defend the vote by conducting their own educational and media campaigns. With the oppositional parties, they obliged the PRI to accept electoral reforms, including the presence of national observers and international visitors (Alianza Cívica 1994c).

In turn, Salinas conceded to the multi-party accord when it was agreed that the observers would have limited responsibilities. The amendment to the electoral code permitted international visitors who were invited by the government or Mexican NGOs to 'come to learn about the development of the electoral process', under the condition that they would not interfere in national politics in any way.[15] As far as officials in the Federal Electoral Institute were concerned, observers were restricted to accredited Mexican citizens and non-governmental organisations (NGOs) and registered political parties. Neither observers nor visitors had any officially recognised role in affirming the final outcome. The electoral authorities were responsible for certifying the elections while the Chamber of Deputies would validate the election of the President (Instituto Federal Electoral 1994).

At the same time, the Zapatistas engaged civil society in an initiative in support of the election. They called for the creation of the *Convención Nacional Democrática* (CND) a National Democratic Convention which hearkened back to the Revolutionary Convention in Aguascalientes. Participants in the 1994 *Convención* continued to organise themselves as social, rather than individual subjects (i.e., constituted around a defence of social rights). After having responded to the Zapatista invitation by electing representatives from social movements to state-level congresses during the early summer of 1994, these representatives of civil society met in the capital of Chiapas, San Cristóbal de las Casas. For two days,

---

15 The amendment to Article 82 Paragraph 2 of the Federal Code for Electoral Institutions and Proceedings (COFIPE) was approved on May 18 1994 by Congress. The prohibition on foreign interference in national politics is set out in Article 22 of the Political Constitution of the United States of Mexico (Alianza Cívica 1994c).

6,000 delegates met in workshops to contemplate resolutions for the reform of the state. Following that, the *Conventionistas* travelled by buses to the Convention site in the Lacandonan jungle inside Zapatista territory. The site, cleared from the side of a mountain, was christened 'Aguascalientes' by the Zapatistas in memory of the first *Convención* that formed its popular Revolutionary platform at the beginning of the century (Tacho 1994).

Having been trampled in the Salinas years, these activists from a wide range of social organisations asserted their argument that effective democratisation would require a new form of state. In the context of the Zapatista uprising, it was inconceivable that the federal election could be held without the social movements mobilising to make their demands heard. They did so in relation to the centre-left oppositional party, the PRD and with the support of other democratic organisations. The CND, however, also organised massive and continuous expressions of support for the social demands outside of any political party. Not unrelated to the struggle for electoral democracy, the CND attempted to build a movement in support of the struggle for a new form of state.

The Two Elections of 21 August

The 1994 election was lost by the popular forces in Mexico, and the PRI emerged triumphant. In its election report, Alianza Cívica gave the following assessment:

> The political rights of Mexican citizens are not yet guaranteed, and unfortunately, in Mexico a culture of respect for the personal, free and secret vote does not yet exist. Those who today try, ingenuously or in self-interest, to celebrate the quality of this election, contribute to widening the abyss that separates us from effective suffrage and credible and transparent electoral processes. That is not how democracy is constructed. (*Alianza Cívica* 1994a, 17; Translated by the author)

The *Alianza Cívica* findings indicate that there tended to be two different electoral experiences in Mexico. The *Alianza* found that the rate of irregularities was consistently higher in most rural and southern regions of the country, than that of northern and urban areas. While the incidence of violations in the secret vote of urban and northern regions was itself high (22.34 per cent), the fact that observers in 59.89 per cent of the polls in most southern and rural region reported such violations is staggering. Similarly, with respect to the evidence of coercion of voters, the discrepancy is enormous. Observers reported irregularities in 12.53 per cent of polls in the most urban-northern region, while 46.03 per cent of polls in the most southern-rural regions reported coercion of voters.[16]

---

16 The Civic Alliance Election Day report was based on the results of 62 questions answered in 1,810 observer reports. The reports were chosen in advance of the election to permit a sample national profile. The questions asked whether there was evidence of irregularities in the polls being observed and do not refer to percentages of votes cast. The results were tabulated according to national totals and according to municipal populations. This division by population gives an indication of variations between urban and rural areas (Alianza Cívica 1994a).

However striking these results, the 'two elections' theory does not go far enough in explaining the results of the election. The pre-electoral conditions were such that voters went to the polls fearful of future reprisals were the PRI to be defeated or even weakened in the election. *Alianza Cívica* opinion polls indicated that 47 per cent of the population believed that there would be electoral fraud and 70 per cent of these believed that the PRI would be responsible (Alianza Cívica 1994b, 4). The Mexican Institute on Public Opinion (IMOP), for example, released its report in which it estimated that the PRI outspent the PRD by 354 times during the campaign. It cited the case of one campaign for Senator in the Federal District where the PRI spent more money than in all of the PRD campaigns combined (see Equipo Pueblo 1994a). The PRI government was able to manipulate the timing of expenditures for the PRONASOL and PROCAMPO programs. Its disproportionate access to, and control of, the media limited the public's access to other parties. The PRI created fear in the electorate by suggesting that voters would choose political instability if the PRI lost.

Despite the concentrated efforts of opposition political parties and citizen's organisations, the credibility and impartiality of electoral bodies remained in question. In the months following the election more information became available. For example, the National Chamber of Radio and Television formally instructed all its affiliates on 22 August 'not to discuss post-election protests, and not to use the word fraud' (Equipo Pueblo 1994a).

The media paid a lot of attention to those international visitors who declared a free and fair election. Most of these visitors, who had not strayed far from the hotels of Mexico City and the offices of the Federal Electoral Institute (IFE), made their declarations long before the ballots were counted. Even after groups of national observers had issued preliminary reports questioning the legitimacy of the election, despite the fact that the two main oppositional political parties continued to raise serious allegations of election day fraud and even though it was abundantly clear that the 'international visitors' did not speak with one voice, criticisms were given only cursory treatment in the international press.

In their Election Day Report, the Civic Alliance argued while millions of citizens voted freely, electoral irregularities were more than isolated incidents, had clearly distinguishable patterns that systematically violated citizens' electoral rights. As a result, they asserted, millions of Mexicans were subject to intimidation, denied their right to vote or denied a secret ballot (Alianza Cívica 1994a, 16). With the Federal Electoral Court (TRIFE) receiving 1,229 complaints and the PRD's evidence challenging the results in 190 of 300 districts, the elections raised more questions than they answered (Equipo Pueblo 1994a, b).

The Mexican economy collapsed in December 1994. Within a few months, the stock market fell 35 per cent. Inflation reached 50 per cent, interest rates increased to 80 per cent and the peso lost almost half of its value in relation to the US dollar (Heredia and Purcell 1995, 3). This collapse, appearing as a currency crisis, had its roots in the unsustainable deficit in the current account. Despite the restructuring of industry, Mexico was still importing more than it exported (Chávez 1995, 1). The significance of the crash was that, after more than 30 years of restructuring meant to overcome the balance of payments problems of import-substitution industrialisation, export-oriented development was not able to solve the country's current account difficulties.[17] As an outcome of restructuring, manufactured products had increased to 83 per cent of Mexico's exports, thus diminishing the significance of primary products exports, including oil. Nevertheless, over half of the country's manufactured goods were from the *maquiladora* sector which uses less than 1.5 per cent of national inputs in its production (Arroyo 1995, 3). Without counting *maquiladoras*, between 1988 and 1994 manufacturing imports increased at an average annual rate of 41.3 per cent, while exports average annual growth of 22.2 per cent. The oil industry was unable to cover the difference (Chávez 1995, 5). As a result, the current account deficit grew 11.4 times between 1988 and 1994 and rose by 37 per cent in 1994 alone. In the auto industry we see an example of the severity of the problem. In 1994, the auto industry exported goods worth 4,607 million US dollars, while it imported materials worth 5,487 million US dollars (Álvarez Béjar 1995, 8).

The deficit was financed by an influx of foreign direct and portfolio investment capital supported by high interest rates. This strategy produced a surplus on the capital account that financed the disequilibrium. The surplus was produced, not through investments that represented long term commitments to Mexico, but through a strategy that left Mexico vulnerable to the discipline of foreign investors. In the 1990s, portfolio investment became increasingly important as a percentage of foreign investment. In 1990, 44 per cent of foreign investment was direct (stocks). In 1993, this level fell to 15 per cent, as the importance of the more volatile investment in government bonds increased (Arroyo 1995, 3). By the end of the second quarter 1994, portfolio investment had dropped by 82 per cent, while foreign direct investment dropped by 25 per cent (Chávez 1995, 6).

Many economists critical of the government argue convincingly that the deterioration in the current account during the 1990s was to be expected, given the opening of domestic markets under conditions of structural adjustment in the 1980–1990s.[18] Instead of responding to the problems that were visible and anticipated, the government paid for the deficit with its foreign reserves and waited months after the federal elections until the new President was installed before overseeing a chaotic devaluation set within a deflationary economic program.[19] The US administration, for its part, had long accepted the over valued peso while it sold the benefits of NAFTA to the US Congress (Laxer 1995).

It was after the crisis, however, that the impact of internationalisation under the North American Free Trade Agreement (NAFTA) became more apparent. In 1995, the Mexican government sold 29 billion dollars worth of *Tesobonos* (bonds) indexed to the price of US dollars (Álvarez Béjar 1995, 4). As a result, foreign investors

---

17 From 1991 to 1994, only petroleum, primary products, livestock, apiculture, construction and fishing generated a trade surplus. All manufacturing sectors produced trade deficits (see Arroyo 1995, 3).

18 Álvarez Béjar points out that the deficit in the current account reached 30 billion US dollars in 1993 and 27 billion US dollars in the third quarter of 1994 (Álvarez Béjar 1995, 6).

19 The government decreased public spending and imposed wage ceilings of 7 per cent, making growth projections impossible to meet (Álvarez Béjar 1995; Chávez 1995, 2).

were guaranteed that public money would be used to underwrite their security. This act alone increased the indebtedness of the Mexican government in a way that raised the ire of many non-investing Mexicans. Securing the interests of private investors in Mexico was also a priority of the US government. Not only did the 40 billion US dollars in loans received from the US government bail-out support the interests of foreign investors in Mexico, the loans were guaranteed by four years of oil exports (Álvarez Béjar, 1995, 45). Mexico signed away sovereignty in the process. Furthermore according to an economist with the *Red Mexicana de Acción Frente al Libre Comercio*, given the restrictions on governments entrenched within the investment provisions of NAFTA, foreign investors have 'absolute liberty':

> They are not required to fulfil any obligations. They cannot be regulated or oriented according to a national project. All limitations on the free transference of resources and foreign exchange, etc are prohibited. Which is to say that foreign investment may be attracted, but it is forbidden to direct, or regulate it. Neither are there any instruments to distribute its location and duration. (Arroyo 1995, 1; Translated by the author)

The problems with currency speculation and financial panic at the end of 1994 were manifestations of the problems of globalisation which, as Fernando Chavez argues quite convincingly:

> originated in 1983 and was reinforced financially towards the end of 1987 until the beginning of 1994.... The ingredients that were lacking and finally made neoliberalism unviable as an historic project were evident from the beginning of its launching: political democracy and income redistribution. These could not be the results or the awards at the end of a long period of modernising transformation in the country. They were the hinges of a structural change in Mexican society. Without them, the cataclysm was inevitable. (Chávez 1995, 2; Translated by the author)

Once again, questions of representation were seen to be wrapped up with the problems of restructuring.

The Mexican state played a definitive role in shaping these transformed relations. Insofar as it mandated the transformation of production through concerted national agreements, concealed the administration of justice, sanctioned the use of violence against workers, mounted a thorough restructuring of state-labour relations and forestalled an open debate on the merits of the existing labour law, the 'reformed' Mexican state institutionalised the new order. As demonstrated by the Volkswagen conflict, the 'reformation' did not resolve anything. It contributed to the erosion of confidence in the very institutions the government placed at the centre of the modernisation project. Although presidential *caudillismo* institutionalised globalisation in Mexico, the legitimacy of the Mexican state was undermined in the process and Salinas left office disgraced and retreated to a self-imposed exile in Ireland soon afterwards.

Chapter 6

Globalisation and the Gendering of Working-Class Politics

In the first moment of crisis, the radical movement in the Nissan union was defeated, in part, by a highly gendered, paternalistic ideology that shored up a narrow economistic form of trade unionism against a more broadly constructed social unionism. In the second moment of crisis, the Ford Workers' democratic movement was defeated as *maquilised* forms of production were imposed in the heart of the auto industry. In the third moment of crisis, the radical movement in the Volkswagen union was defeated by the institutionalisation of work reorganisation in law, the collective agreement and trade union constitution. This was accomplished under the masculinised, authoritarianism of the executive level of government and justified by 'cooperative, family-values'. Just as gendered social relations played an important role in stabilising the Revolutionary Nationalist social compromise, gendered social relations were bound up in the long crisis that destroyed it. Running through all of these stories were conflicts between different groups of men over the terms of production. The *caudillo* and the worker-father were the two most important masculinities in play.

In this discussion of Mexican labour struggles I have elaborated upon some of the complexities of globalisation by showing how relations of power other than social class are involved in the constitution and transformation of historical structures. Working-class men are enmeshed in gendered social relations, although theirs is a position of privilege relative to working-class women, and subordination relative to their employers and the state. I have argued that we may recognise the hegemonic character of masculinity during times when men's privilege is considered so 'natural' as to be quite invisible, but that does not mean that all men partake in all the privileges of hegemony. Nor does it mean that hegemony is fixed. These gendered struggles of working-class men suggest that masculine hegemony, like other kinds of hegemony, exists along a continuum of experience. Perhaps, instead of identifying oppositional categories such as 'hegemonic' and 'non-hegemonic' it would be more useful to look to the 'condition of hegemony' which would suggest more variation in experiences, more space for contestation, more subtlety and ambivalence especially in periods of great global transformation like the one we are experiencing at the moment (Healy 2006).

At the level of world order, gender is a fundamental but overlooked dynamic (Enloe 1993; Peterson 1992, 1997; Peterson and Runyan 1993; Tickner 1992). At the level of the state, gendered identities became part of Mexican state structure and the organisation of the economy in all of its twentieth-century transitions. At the level of production, the worker-father existed in relation to his family and the auto assembly plant, which also existed in relation to export-processing zones. These structures have not only been marked by gender and class. Colonialism continues to leave its imprint even under conditions of 'post'-colonialism, and the international gender division of labour is built upon such structures (Bannerji 1987, 11).

When capitalists build new plants in the middle of a desert they are not filling up empty space. Yet even while NAFTA was being negotiated, it was not uncommon to encounter the perception in Canada and the United States that the new factories on Mexico's northern border were springing up in a context of absence: absence of community, absence of union struggle and absence of history. The reality is that these plants arrived into a whole nexus of social relations within which production was already occurring. Otherwise, the fact that a young, educated, Spanish-speaking woman of colour was chosen the preferred worker would have no meaning at all. The location of new investments in the 'greenfield' was an overt repudiation by globalising capitalists, of the social structures that had once been central to their own interests during the period of social compromise. Subsequently, *maquilisation* shaped the restructuring of the older, industrial centre. There, degraded labour relations became normalised; first because feminisation had already made flexibilised labour relations viable and second, because the internationalisation of dominant patriarchal ideas had made flexibility desirable.

In Mexico, gendered representations have been intertwined with post-colonial symbols challenging the power of the priest, the conqueror, the *guero* (white man), the boss, the landlord and the father. These symbols of contested masculine power are accompanied by symbols of layered femininity as well. This is seen in the national symbol of the *Virgen de Guadalupe* superimposed on the Aztec goddess Tonantzin; *La Llorona* who is both abandoned lover and murderous mother; as well as Cortés' indigenous lover and translator, *La Malinche*. In these icons of Mexican femininity, mythical images of female suffering, resistance and treachery are intertwined. For Octavio Paz, there is also the ever present symbol of *La Chingada*, the violated mother (Paz 1993, 81–97). In Paz's view, the *chingada* resides in 'the violent, sarcastic humiliation of the Mother and the no less violent affirmation of the Father' (Paz 1993, 88; Translated by the author). The *chingada*, he says, is wrought by the *macho* foreigner who, through violation and conquest, destroyed indigenous community. In English, *macho* may be translated simply as 'male', but Paz argued that *machismo* attains meaning in relation to the legacy of colonialism in which the '*Macho*' is seen as the foreigner who opens all that is familiar to external assault. *La Chingada*, if she tolerates the intervention, is never forgiven. The violated one is blamed, responsible, made culpable.

Paz's analysis of Mexico's colonial legacy became highly influential after its appearance in the 1950s, but he is not without his critics. Paz reinforced the view of women and all workers as submissive. He ignored the agency of those who have been dominated by authoritarianism and paternalism. He was, as Alfredo Tecla Jiménez argues, more likely to see the worker as one who 'cannot realise any change, cannot be a protagonist in history, but can only be used, manipulated' (Tecla Jiménez 1992, 117; Translated by the author). What is important for us here, is that Paz contested the commonly held idea that Mexican *machismo* may be understood in national terms, or in terms of some caricature of *latino* gender relations. In locating *machismo* in the identity of the coloniser, Paz suggests a re-reading of more recent conditions.

The terrifying affirmation of a direct relationship between globalisation-as-*machismo* and violence against women lies in the underside of the *maquila* city of Ciudad Juarez. Between 1993 and 2003, the National Commission on Human Rights reported 263 unprosecuted cases of murdered women and 4,500 disappearances of women and girls from the city. Amnesty International reported the number of murdered women at 370 in the same period and the murders continue with impunity. A United Nations Commission reported in 2003 on the state's incapacity of to investigate and prosecute the guilty. Marcela Lagarde y de los Ríos discusses the issue:

> Femicide spreads in an ideological and social climate of 'machismo' and misogyny, of normalized violence against women, and in the absence of legal and governmental policies; conditions that generate an insecure environment for women, putting their lives in danger and favoring the conjuncture of crimes which we demand be clarified and eliminated. (Lagarde y de los Ríos 2005, 73)

The only thing that could be worse would be to blame women workers for being modern day Malinches and that is the very thing impunity does.

Globalisation and the Ideology of the Family

It was through the discourse of the family that the idealism of progressive capitalism took hold in Mexico in the early twentieth century. The family was the prism through which the international was refracted as national; the constructed became natural; the new became enduring; and authoritarianism was presented as paternalism. Later, the cooperative ideology of the factory and the family re-emerged with the imposition of new forms of work organisation and new representative structures within the work place at the end of the century.[1] This ideological commitment to 'cooperation' is important to the globalisation of 'flexibilised' labour relations. The ideology is, on the surface, highly paternalistic but, as we have seen, workers within the mode are subject to new forms of colonialism and gendered inequalities. Its material base is rooted in globalised production oriented to export and depends upon the defeat of independent trade unionism through the authoritarianism of the state and employers. The authority of the worker-father is de-centred not because gendered relations have become more equal, but because he has been beaten by more powerful groups of men. We have to think very carefully about the meaning and implications of this.

When the level of violence against women in actual families is astonishingly high, we must ask what kind of unity is the corporate family calling upon? A 2003 study found that 44 per cent of Mexican women living with their partner had experienced some kind of domestic violence in the previous twelve months. More than half

---

1   Although sometimes referred to as a 'Japanese' method, global corporatism has strong roots in the ideology of enterprise corporatism which played an important role in North American industrial development (Cox 1987, 70–74).

of these (23 per cent), had experienced more than one type of violence including emotional, economic, sexual or physical (Instituto Nacional de las Mujeres 2004). Every time a corporation appeals to the unity of the family, it attempts to justify much more than its internal hierarchy. As Doreen Massey points out, 'representation is not merely reflection; it is in itself an active form in moulding social relations and social understanding' (Massey, 1994, 213). The corporation which buys unity with repression ends up sanctioning violence in the home.

Martha Guadalupe Figuroa Mier analyses the problem of violence against women in Mexican society and more broadly:

> Those of us working with women who are victims of violence observe how men practice unequal, abusive and violent power relationships against women in order to preserve their gender privilege in the street, at home and at work; we see how governments use their armies, marines, police forces and repressive bodies (in Chiapas, even paramilitary) and militarize the region to ensure their hegemonic place in the world or in the country and how multinational corporations abuse their economic power, which becomes a social and political power, to maintain and accumulate their profits and other powers. Gender violence against women is the expression of the masculine culture of fear. It is linked to the existing hierarchies between countries, between men, between men and women, between human beings and other living being, or the violence of men against other men or against themselves. Thus violence among men is a tool used since childhood to impose a hierarchic order, with elements assigned to masculinity, such as competitiveness, repression of emotional feelings, domination and power. This is precisely why wars are linked to a collective image of hegemonic masculinity. (Figuroa Mier 2005, 81–2)

Mexican free-trade critics also argue that 'globalization has a masculine and patriarchal character, since under its logic values of competition, individualism, commercial trade and inequality are generated' (Villamar and Atilano 2005, 4). For decades, feminists have criticised liberal economics for its tendency to neutralise the specific impacts of economic restructuring on men and women workers (Sanchís 2001). Certainly one of the most gender-specific antecedents to globalisation was the effort of the corporations formerly-known-as-the Big Three US auto producers to shift their competitiveness problem to Mexico. They took advantage of the *maquiladora* program to open export-processing zones along the northern border region.

Leslie Salzinger says that it took, and continues to take, effort to feminise the *maquiladoras*. Working women femininities are not simply transferred from household to factory. Indeed, it is in the factory and as a result of managers' fantasy and intention, argues Salzinger, that 'productive femininities' are sought after and fought over: 'On *maquila* shop floors, it is the insistent invocation of femininity, rather than its consistent enactment, which is most striking. Assuming gender's essential rigidity makes this process impossible to perceive.' She goes on to observe that:

> ... gender is indeed a fundamental element of global production... Femininity is a trope – a structure of meaning through which workers, potential and actual, are addressed and understood, and around which production itself is designed. The notion of 'productive femininity' thus crystallizes through a process of repetitive citation by transnational

managers, and the imperative to hire such workers operates as a creative force, shaping both workers and the technical structure within which they work. (Salzinger 2003, 15)

By building upon and imposing unequal gender relations, *maquila* managers prepared the way for 'creative force' to be used to model the re-gendering of plants in the industrial south. The *maquila* model was a productive one which could be used to restructure the Mexican industry well beyond the boundaries of the northern free-trade zones.

Already by the late 1980s, changes in the international gender division of labour were clearly affecting both men and women workers. Mexican men were losing their industrial jobs in massive numbers and men began to look for work in the *maquila* autoparts plants. In the process, women's participation fell from 66.5 per cent in 1980 to 52 per cent in 1986 (Rocío et al. 1989; see also Mercado 1992, 79). There was nothing straightforward about the changing gendered segmentation of work, except for the fact that both men and women faced declining quality of work. According to the analysis of *Mujeres en Acción Sindical* (MAS) (Women in Union Action), 'paradoxically, at the same time that men's workplaces are closing down, new occupations for women are being created' (Mujeres en Acción Sindical 1989). It was not modernisation, they argued, but economic restructuring that was generating increasing numbers of poor jobs for women. This included the transference of jobs from workplaces to household production, and the redefinition of 'gender assignments' in other occupations.

In the restructured economy, the feminised workplace could not simply be defined by how many women worked there, but by the absence of the worker-father. There was a cynical circularity to this process: The worker-father model had legitimised sub-standard wages and working conditions of maquiladorised women which were then used to undermine the masculinised model. Thus, the *maquila* model becomes the model more generally. Salzinger's trope of productive femininity is visited upon the men who 'make trouble' not only in the *maquila* where disruptive men workers are put on the soldering line with the women, but in whole factories where men are 'feminised' as work is restructured, acquired rights undermined, seniority rejected, democratic models of representation prevented from being. It was not the hegemonic, but one of the subordinated masculinities, that of the worker-father, which was feminised. The hegemonic masculinity quite clearly became less hegemonic and more coercive. As Mexico itself moved further and further away from becoming a hegemonic society, so too did the prevailing masculinity.

As processes, feminisation and masculinisation are not 'sexed' characteristics inherently carried in the bodies of workers, but socially constructed in the workplace and through the practices of labour law, trade unionism, and political activity at all levels. In V. Spike Peterson's view:

Women and feminised others constitute the vast majority of the world's population, as well as the vast majority of poor, less skilled, insecure, informalised and flexibilised workers: and the global economy absolutely depends upon the work that they do…. The key point here is that feminisation devalorises not only women but also racially, culturally and economically marginalised man *and* work that is deemed unskilled, menial and 'merely' reproductive. (Peterson 2006, 88–9)

Additionally, part of the 'devalorisation', is the process of rendering feminisation among women and among men, in women's work and in men's work.

To move beyond the category of 'man' to the situated man; to the located, historicised man is to ask questions about the power relations in which he is enmeshed (Hooper 2001). How does the 'worker-father' confront the *caudillo* despite the threat of losing everything, of being expelled from the union and fired? What gendered values are implied in the threat of his being turned into the *muchacha* in the *maquila*; the young woman *maquila* worker? What should he do when neoliberalism fails to deliver democratic citizenship to him or members of his family, or when state authoritarianism destroys his reason to consent?

This brings us to the question of the state. In the 1980s and 1990s, the welfare-state in North America, whether Keynesian or corporatist, came under attack by neo-liberalism and ended up profoundly restructured. It would be a mistake to blame external forces for having imposed this eventuality. Despite its subordinate position in relation to the United States, globalisation did not 'happen' to the Mexican state. As Maxine Molyneaux argues, states are not neutral in this process.

> Whether through intention, through the effects of policies, or through an indifference and inaction that maintain the power relations enshrined by the status quo, states are implicated in the ordering of gender relations in the societies over which they preside. (Molyneux 2000, 39)

Critics of globalisation in Mexico discuss the state's contribution to the gendering of globalisation in the privatisation of public services, sanctioning of violence and discrimination, opening of the agricultural sector to liberalisation, strengthening intellectual property rights to the detriment of indigenous women, permitting increasing levels of poverty among women, and resisting the democratisation of trade union representation in the *maquilas* in particular. (National Network on Gender and Economy 2005). Social movements identified the problems for women with what Janine Brodie discussed as the expansion and re-regulation of the private sphere that accompanied the contraction of the public sphere (Brodie 1996, 383–4). In Brodie's view:

> Critical governing instruments of the KWS [Keynesian welfare state] such as public corporations and social welfare programmes are said to be 're'-privatized to the market or the home, thereby creating the illusion that they are being returned to some place they naturally belong. This reprivatization has been enforced through two other 'res' – the 're-commodification' of claims and the 're-constitution' of domestic enclaves. (Brodie 1996, 389)

As an aspect of globalisation, the restructured state brought women's work out of the public sphere and into the private sector or private home in very particular, specific and historically contingent ways. The inequalities between men and women were sharpened in this respect. As we have seen, there was nothing passive about the Mexican state as regards these issues.

In the ongoing construction of historical structures in Mexico, race and gender are intertwined with class, yet the image of the Revolutionary Worker who is not-woman, not-peasant and not-indigenous remained within trade unions for too long. Comfortable in their role as representatives of a highly masculinised 'universal' worker, most official trade unions, as well as oppositional movements of working-class men did not sufficiently address the question of women's representation and leadership within working-class organisations. Despite their conflicts, the worker-father and the *caudillo* could share a commitment to many of the central elements of Revolutionary Nationalism. Globalisation, as North American integration, fractured their shared understanding and the re-gendering of the economy has made new alliances and forms of representation absolutely imperative (González Nicolás 2006).

Inequalities between men and women, continued to be used against workers to weaken and divide, restructure and re-gender. This was something the practices surrounding the 'worker-father' shielded from men, and something which might now be shielded from the 'modern' individual woman as she increasingly becomes the political subject favoured by the neo-liberal state. Many alternatives are possible, however. As working-class organisations strengthen their internal structures of representation so as to confront the gendered dimensions of their work, it is more likely they will achieve their long sought after goals of union independence, autonomy and democracy. When they build stronger alliances with other democratic forces, they come that much closer.

In retrospect we can see the path that was taken in these years of crisis and how it ended up in the North American Free Trade Agreement, but there was no necessary reason why. What is very clear, is that Mexican workers fought hard in these years for the things liberalism promised: the defence of individual rights, a share in a growing economy, transparent government, clean elections, decent work, freedom from violence at home and beyond, and respect for contracts. In fighting for the fulfilment of Revolutionary promises as well, they made demands upon the state that went well beyond the neoliberal paradigm. In response, they faced a frontal attack by the state and global capital. In these years, the politics of economic liberalisation established no necessary link between democracy and the market-place. Working-class struggles however, did establish the connection between internal democracy and the realisation of collective power. In the urgency of their demands to have a voice, both within and without their organisations, in the home and in the community, facing their employers and making demands of their governments, these movements revealed some of the most fundamental contradictions of globalisation itself.

Bibliography[1]

Abogado, G. (1992), Interview by author, México DF, 12 May.

Acedo Angulo, B. et al. (1979), 'Unidad Obrera Independiente (UOI)', in *2o Coloquio Regional de Historia Obrero* (vol 1; Mérida Yuc: CEHSMO), 1369–75.

Aguilar Camín, H. and Meyer, L. (1993), *In the Shadow of the Mexican Revolution: Contemporary Mexican History 1910–1989* (Austin TX: University of Texas Press).

Aguilar García, J. (1982), *La Política Sindical en México: Industria del Automóvil* (México DF: Ediciones Era).

—— (ed.) (1990), *Historia de la CTM: 1936–1990* (vols 1–2; México DF: Instituto de Investigaciones Sociales, Facultad de Economía, Facultad de Ciencias Políticas y Sociales UNAM).

—— and Arrieta, L. (1990), 'En la fase más aguda de la crisis y en el inicio de la reestructuración o modernización', in Aguilar García, J.(ed), *Historia de la CTM: 1936–1990* (vols 1–2; México DF: Instituto de Investigaciones Sociales, Facultad de Economía, Facultad de Ciencias Políticas y Sociales UNAM), 657–731.

Alcalde, A. (1993), 'Los Acuerdos Paralelos del TLC: Laboral y Ambiental', Presentation for Ciclo de Mesas Redondas, Red Mexicana de Accion Frente al Libre Comercio, México DF, miércoles 16 de junio.

Alianza Cívica (1994a), 'La Calidad de la Jornada Electoral del 21 de agosto de 1994: Informe', Observación 94, 19 de septiembre.

—— (1994b), 'Las elecciones presidenciales de agosto de 1994' (Mexico DF: Alianza Cívica).

—— (1994c), 'Guidelines for International Visitors: Respect for Mexican Law and the Guidelines of the Civic Alliance', in *Mexican Elections 1994: International Visitors Infopak: Alianza Cívica Observación 94* (México DF: Alianza Cívica).

Alonso, A.M. (1995), 'Rationalizing Patriarchy: Gender, Domestic Violence, and Law in Mexico', *Identidades* 2:1–2, 29–47.

Altshuler, A. et al. (1984), *The Future of the Automobile* (Cambridge: MIT Press).

---

1 The research drew on various issues of the following Mexican journals and newspapers: *Corre la Voz* (1992–1994); *Cotidiano* (1992–1994); *Economía Informa* (1992–1994); *El Nacional* (1992–1994); *El Financiero* (1992–1994); *El Sol de Puebla* (1992–1994); *Investigación Económica* (1992–1994); *La Jornada* (1992–1994); *La Jornada de Oriente* (1992–1994); *Punto Crítico* (1972–1976); *Síntesis* (Puebla) summer 1992; *Trabajo* (1992–1994); *Uno Más Uno* (1992–1994). I also gratefully acknowledge the material obtained from the archives of Javier Aguilar García, Alejandro Álvarez, Béjar, Carlos Fernández del Real, Frente Auténtico del Trabajo, and Karen Hadley.

—— (1995), 'Cinco enseñanzas del fracaso ecónomico neoliberal en México', unpublished paper, Facultad de economía, UNAM.

Alvarez Béjar, A. (1987), *La Crisis Global del Capitalismo en Mexico: 1968– 1985* (México DF: Ediciones Era).

—— (1993), 'Economic Integration, Social Dislocation and Political Challenges in North America', Paper presented at the 34th Annual Convention of the International Studies Association, Acapulco, Guerrero, México, March 23–27.

—— and Mendoza Pichardo, G. (1991), *México 1988–1991: ¿Un ajuste económico exitoso?* (México DF: Facultad de Economía, Universidad Nacional Autónoma de México).

—— and Mendoza Pichardo, G. (1992), 'Mexico: Neo-liberal Disaster Zone', in Sinclair, J. (ed.), *Crossing the Line* (Vancouver BC: New Star Books), 26–37.

Álvarez Garín, R. (1970), 'Alegato de Defensa: 18 de septiembre 1970 antes Eduardo Ferrer MacGregor, Juez 1o Distrito Federal en Materia Penal', in *Tiempo de Hablar...: los procesos de México 68* (México DF: Editorial Estudiantes) 43–76.

—— (1993), 'Las Ondas Expansivas', in Bellinghausen, H. and Hiriart, H. (eds), *Pensar el 68*, 4th Edition (México DF: Cal y Arena).

Alzaga, O. (1992), 'El Acuerdo para Elevar la Productividad reforma la legislación laboral', *Trabajo y Democracia Hoy* 7:2, i–viii.

Amnesty International (1998), 'Human Rights in Jeopardy: Oral Statement made to Non-Governmental Organisations in Geneva, Switzerland', 1 April; available online at http://www.amnesty.it.

Aponte, D. (1993), 'Las plácticas paralelas al TLC comenzarán el 15 de marzo en EU', *La Jornada* Jueves 18 de Febrero.

Arriaga Lemus, M. (1992), 'El Acuerdo Nacional de Productividad y la Política Laboral Salinista', in *Economía Informa* (México DF: UNAM), 7–12.

Arrona, M.E. (1992a), 'Anulación de la Audiencia ante la Junta Federal de Conciliación Demando el Sindicato de la VW', *El Sol de Puebla*, domingo 9 de agosto.

—— (1992b), 'Reconocimiento Legal Buscara el Movimiento "20 de Julio,"' *El Sol de Puebla*, domingo 9 de agosto.

—— (1992c), 'Aprobaron la Destitución de Bueno, Miembros del Movimiento "20 de Julio,"' *El Sol de Puebla*, 16 de agosto.

Arroyo, A. (1995), 'Hacía un Diagnóstico de la Crisis y Propuesta de Condiciones Mínimas para Enfrentarla', unpublished paper.

Arteaga García, A. (1985), 'Innovación Tecnológica y Clase Obrera en la Industria Automotriz', in Gutiérrez Garza, E. (ed.), *Testimonios de la Crisis: Reestructuración Productiva y Clase Obrera* (vol 1; México DF: Siglo Veintiuno), 166–87.

—— (1988), 'Reconversión Industrial y Flexibilidad del Trabajo en la Industria Automotriz en México, 1981–1986', in Gutiérrez Garza, E. (ed.), *Testimonios de la Crisis: 3. Austeridad y Reconversión* (México DF: Siglo Veintiuno Editores), 166–87.

—— (1989), 'Reestructuración y Periodización en la Industria Automotriz', in Gutiérrez Garza, E. (ed.), *Reconversión Industrial y Lucha Sindical* (México DF: Fundación Friedrich Ebert), 75–78.

—— (1990a), 'Nacido Ford, Crecido Flexible', *Trabajo* 2, 64–74.

—— (1990b), 'Ford: un largo y sinuoso conflicto', in Bensusán, G. and León, S. (eds), *Negociación y Conflicto Laboral en México* (México DF: Friedrich Ebert Siftung), 141–74.

—— (ed.) (1992), Proceso de Trabajo y Relaciones Laborales en la Industria Automotriz en México (México: Universidad Autónoma Metropolitana-Iztapalapa.

—— et al. (1989), 'Transformaciones Tecnológicas y Relaciones Laborales en la Industria Automotriz', in *Documentos de Trabajo 19* (México, DF: Fundación Friedrich Ebert).

Asociación Mexicana de la Industria Automotriz (1982), *Industria Automotriz en Cifras* (México DF: AMIA).

—— (1988), Industria Automotriz Mexicana en Cifras (México DF: AMIA).

Asociación Nacional de Abogados Democráticos (1992), 'Ruptura del Orden Constitucional en VW a La Opinion Publica', *La Jornada*, 19 de agosto.

Banco de México (1989), 'Dirección de Operaciones Internacionales, Oficina de Cambios Nacionales', in *La Industria Maquiladora de Exportación* (Mexico DF: Gobierno de México).

Bannerji, H. (1987), 'Introducing Racism: Notes Towards an Anti- Racist Feminism', *Resources for Feminist Research* 16:1, 10–13.

Barajas Escamilla, R. and Rodríguez Carrillo, C. (1990), 'La mujer ante la reconversión productiva: el caso de la maquiladora electrónica' in González-Aréchiga, B. and Carlos Ramírez, J. (eds), *Subcontractión y Empresas Transnacionales: Apertura y Restructuración en la Maquiladora* (México DF: El Colegio de la Frontera Norte), 335–67.

Barbosa Cano, F. (1980), *La C.R.O.M, de Luis N. Morones a Antonio J. Hernandez* (Puebla: Editorial Universidad Autonoma de Puebla).

Barlow, M. and Clarke, T. (1997), *The Multilateral Agreement on Investment and the Threat to Canadian Sovereignty* (Toronto: Stoddart).

Bazán, L. (1980), 'El Sindicato Independiente de Nissan Mexicana' in *Memorias Del Encuentro sobre Historia del Movimiento Obrero* (vol. 3; Puebla: Universidad Autónoma de Puebla).

Becerril, A. (1992a) 'Podría VW recontratar buen número de obreros, pero en forma personal, advierte su presidente', *La Jornada* miercoles 12 de agosto.

—— (1992b), 'Ratifican por unanimidad destituir a Gaspar Bueno en la Volkswagen', *La Jornada*, domingo 16 de agosto.

—— (1992c), 'Precedente nefasto, el fallo contra obreros de VW', *La Jornada* miercoles 19 de agosto.

—— (1992d), 'Hoy reanuda labores la VW; 12 mil 265 obreros fueron recontratados ayer', *La Jornada*, jueves 20 de agosto.

—— (1992e), 'Lanzan perros de ataque contra disidentes de Volkswagen', *La Jornada*, viernes 21 de agosto.

Behr, P. (1993), 'New Powers Sought for Trade Pact: White House Moves to Bolster Support', *Washington Post*, 14 May.

Bellinghausen, H. and Hiriart, H. (eds) (1993), *Pensar el 68* (México DF: Cal y Arena).

Benería, L. and Roldán, M. (1987), *Crossroads of Class and Gender: Industrial Homework, Subcontracting and Household Dynamics in Mexico City* (Chicago: University of Chicago Press).

Bennett, D. and Sharpe, K. (1984), 'Agenda Setting and Bargaining Power: the Mexican State versus the Transnational Automobile Corporations', in Kronish, R. and Mericle, K. (eds), *The Political Economy of the Latin American Motor Vehicle Industry* (Cambridge: MIT Press).

—— (1985), Transnational Corporations versus the State: The Political Economy of the Mexican Auto Industry (Princeton NJ: Princeton University Press).

Bensusán A.G. (1989), 'La Ley Federal del Trabajo: Una Visión Retrospectiva', in *Documentos de Trabajo 24* (México DF: Fundación Ebert).

—— (1990), 'Políticas de Modernización y Relaciones Laborales en el Sector-Parasestatal', in Graciela Bensusán, A.G. and Carlos García, C. (eds), *Relaciones Laborales en las Empresas Paraestatales* (Mexico DF: Fundación Ebert, 1990), 9–22.

Bizberg, I. (1990), *Estado y Sindicalismo en México* (México DF: El Colegio de México).

Block, F. (1977), *The Origins of International Economic Disorder: A Study of United States International Monetary Policy from World War II to the Present* (Berkeley CA: University of California Press).

Bluestone, B. and Harrison, B. (1982), *The Deindustrialization of America: Plant Closings, Community Abandonment and the Dismantling of Basic Industry* (New York: Basic Books).

Bolívar Espinoza, A. (1990), 'Primera Parte: El periódo de la transición a la modernidad', in Garavito Elías, E.A. and Bolívar Espinoza, A. (eds), *México en la Década de los Ochenta: La modernización en Cifras* (México DF: El Cotidiano, Universidad Autónoma Metropolitana/ Azcapotzalco).

Brandenburg, F.R. (1969), 'Causes of the Revolution', in Wilkie J. and Michaels, A. (eds), *Revolution in Mexico* (New York: Alfred A. Knopf).

Brecher, J. and Costello, T. (1994), *Global Village or Global Pillage* (Boston: South End).

Brenner, R. and Glick, M. (1991), 'The Regulation School and the West's Economic Impasse', *New Left Review* 188.

Brodie, J. (1996), 'New State Forms, New Political Spaces', in Boyer, R. and Drache, D. (eds), *States Against Markets: The Limits of Globalization* (London: Routledge).

Bustamante Fernández, J. (1983), '*Maquiladoras*: A New Face of International Capitalism on Mexico's Northern Frontier', in Nash, J. and Fernandez-Kelly, M.P. (eds), *Women, Men and the International Division of Labour* (Albany: State University of New York Press), 232–33.

—— (1989), 'El programa fronterizo de maquiladoras: Observaciones para una evaluación', in Carillo, J. (ed.), *Reestructuración industrial: Maquiladoras en la Frontera México-Estados Unidos* (México DF: Consejo Nacional para la Cultura y las Artes and Colegio de la Frontera Norte), 97–122.

Bustillos, J. (1992). 'Pasarela Política', *El Universal*, Domingo 9 de agosto as cited in Jorge Luis Sierra, *Síntesis,* Lunes 10 de Agosto de 1992.

Calderón Gómez, J. (1992a) 'Volkswagen despide a 14 de los disidentes; el sindicato los expulsa', *La Jornada*, miercoles 29 de julio.

—— (1992b), 'Empresa y Gaspar Bueno negocian ya nuevo contrato', *La Jornada*, martes 18 de agosto.

—— (1992c), 'Se recontrataría a 90 de trabajadores: beneplácito de Farel', *La Jornada*, martes 18 de agosto.

Campero, G. et al. (1976), *La incorporación obrera en un medio de industrialización reciente: estudio de casos en la Ciudad Industrial del Valle de Cuernavaca (CIVAC)* (Mexico DF: Secretaria del Trabajo y Prevision Social/INET.

Canada, Department of External Affairs (1987), 'Chapter Nine: Energy', *The Canada – U.S. Free Trade Agreement* Ottawa.

Canada (1992), 'The Government of the United Mexican States and the Government of the United States of America', *North American Free Trade Agreement* (Ottawa: Minister of Supply and Services).

—— (1993), 'Canada's Objectives met in the North American Agreement on Environmental Co-operation and the North American Agreement on Labour Co-operation', News Release, 13 August.

Canadian Auto Workers (1992), 'Synchronous Manufacturing', CAW-Research Department Presentation.

Canadian Centre for Policy Alternatives (1992), *Which Way for the Americas: Analysis of NAFTA Proposals and the Impact on Canada* (Ottawa: CCPA).

Carne, F. (1987), 'Estereotipos Femininos en el Siglo XiX', in Ramos Escandón, C. et.al. *Presensia y Transperencia: La Mujer en la Historia de México* (México D.F.: El Colegio de México) (Mexico: El Colegio de México), 95–109.

Carr, B. (1976), *El Movimiento Obrero y la Política en México: 1910–1929* (México DF: Ediciones Era).

—— (1981), *El Movimiento Obrero y la Política en México: 1910–1929* (México DF: Ediciones Era).

—— (1986), 'The Mexican Left, the Popular Movements and the Politics of Austerity1982–1985', in Carr, B. and Montoya, R. A. (eds), *The Mexican Left, the Popular Movements, and the Politics of Austerity* (San Diego CA: Center for US–Mexican Studies, University of California), 1–18.

—— (1991), 'Labour and the Political Left in Mexico', in Middlebrook, K. (ed.), *Unions, Workers, and the State in Mexico* (San Diego CA: Center for US–Mexican Studies, University of California), 121–52.

Carrillo V. J. (ed.) (1990a), *La Nueva Era de la Industria Automotriz en México* (Tijuana: El Colegio de la Frontera Norte).

—— (1990b), 'Maquilización de la industria automotriz en Mexico: De la industria terminal a la industria de ensamble', in Carillo, V. J. (ed.), *La Nueva Era de la Industria Automotriz en México: Cambio Tecnológico, Organizacional y en las Estructuras de Control* (Tijuana: El Colegio de la Frontera Norte), 67–114.

—— and de la O, M.E. (1992), 'La reestructuración en la industria maquiladora', *El Cotidiano* 46, 54–9.

—— and Hernández, A. (1982), 'Sindicatos y Control Obrero en las Plantas Maquiladoras Fronterizas', *Economía* 161, 105–55.

Castro, G. (1998), 'Boletin', *Chiapas* 133.

Centro Nacional de Comunicación Social (1972a), 'Laborales: Panorama Nacional, Trabajadores de Nissan Mexican Desmienten a Fidel Velázquez', México DF, febrero.

—— (1972b), 'El Comité Ejecutivo: Trabajadores de Nissan Mexicana SA sufren violaciones al contrato colectivo de trabajo y atropellos por parte de la empresa', in *Fuerza de Trabajo: Panorama Nacional* (CENCOS: Cuernavaca).

Chavarría Díaz, R. (1992), 'Desconocen en la VW a Gaspar Bueno: eligirán un líder interino', *El Nacional*, domingo 16 de agosto.

Chávez, F. (1995), 'Colapso cambiario y ajustes macroeconómicos', *El Cotidiano* 68, 1

Chávez Samano, F. (1993), Interview by author, Cuernavaca, Morelos, 8 June.

Citizens Trade Campaign (1993), 'Nuestros Trabajos, Nuestro Medio Ambiente, Nuestro Futuro: Una Introducción a la Campaña Cívica Sobre el Comercio', Washington DC.

Cockcroft, J. (1968), *Intellectual precursors of the Mexican Revolution: 1900–1913* (Austin TX: Institute of Latin American Studies, University of Texas Press).

Connell, R.W. (1987), *Gender and Power: Society, the Person and Sexual Politics* (Stanford: Stanford University Press).

—— and Messerschmidt, J.W. (2005), 'Hegemonic Masculinity: Rethinking the Concept', *Gender and Society* 19, 829–59.

Córdova, A. (1990), 'La política de masas y el futuro de la izquierda', in González Casanova, P. and Florescano, E. (eds), *México Hoy*, 13th Edition (México DF: Siglo Veintiuno Editores), 385–404).

Covarrubias, A. (1992), *La Flexibilidad Laboral en Sonora* (México DF: El Colegio de Sonora y Fundación Friedrich Ebert).

Cox, R.W. (1986), 'Social Forces, States and World Orders: Beyond International Relations Theory', in Keohane, R.O. (ed.), *Neorealism and its Critics* (New York: Columbia University Press), 204–254.

—— (1987), *Production, Power and World Order: Social Forces in the Making of History* (New York: Columbia University Press).

—— (1993), 'Gramsci, Hegemony and International Relations: An Essay in Method', in Gill, S. (ed.), *Gramsci, Historical Materialism and International Relations* (Cambridge: Cambridge University Press), 49–66.

—— (1996), 'The Global Political Economy and Social Choice', in *Approaches to World Order* (Cambridge: Cambridge University Press), 191–208.

Cypher, J. (1990), *State and Capital in Mexico: Development Policy since 1940* (Boulder CO: Westview).

de Buen, N. (1992), 'Laudo habemus', *La Jornada*, martes 18 de agosto.

de la Garza Toledo, E. (1990), 'Siete Tesis Equivocadas de la Reconversión Industrial en un País Subdesarrollado: El caso de México', in Carillo, J.V. (ed.), *La Nueva Era de la Industria Automotriz en México* (Tijuana: El Colegio de la Frontera Norte), 151–86.

—— (1992), 'Prólogo', in Covarrubias, A. (ed.), *La Flexibilidad Laboral en Sonora* (México DF: Fundación Ebert and Colegio de Sonora), 9–28.

—— and Bouzas, A. (1999), 'El Cambio en la Contración Colectiva de Jurisdicciones Federal y Local', in de la Garza Toledo, E. and Alfonso Bouzas, J. (eds), *Cambios en las Relaciones Laborales* (México DF: UNAM), 29–80.

Díaz, F. and Álvarez, J. (1972), *Caudillos y Caciques: Antonio López de Santa Anna* (Mexico DF: El Colegio de México).

Domínguez, A. (1972), 'El FAT con Punto Crítico: entrevista con Alfredo Domínguez', *Punto Crítico* 1:6, 33–9.

—— (1992), Interview by author, Mexico DF, 22 April.

—— (1993), Interview by author, Mexico DF, 14 April.

Dresser, D. (1991), *Neopopulist Solutions to Neoliberal Problems: Mexico's National Solidarity Program* (La Jolla CA: Center for US–Mexican Studies, University of California).

Echeverría Álvarez, L. (1971–1976), *Informes Presidenciales* (México DF: El Gobierno de Mexico, Presidencia de la Republica).

Ejercito Zapatista de Liberación Nacional (1994), 'Declaración de La Selva Lacondona: ¡Hoy decimos Basta!' 1o de enero.

Escobar F. R. (1992), 'Acuerda el Sindicato Independiente de la Volkswagen modificaciones a los estatutos', *Unomásuno*, martes 18 de agosto.

Enloe, C. (1993), *The Morning After: Sexual Politics at the End of the Cold War* (Berkeley CA: University of California Press).

Equipo Pueblo (1994a), *Mexico Update* 2:3; available online at web:carnet. mexnews.

—— (1994b), *Mexico Update* 2:4; available online at web:carnet.mexnews.

Fernández del Real, C. (1993), Interview by author, Puebla, Puebla, 30 August.

Fernández-Kelly, M.P. (1980), 'The Maquila Women', *Nacla Report on the Americas* 14:5.

—— (1983), 'Mexican Border Industrialization, Female Labor Force Participation and Migration', in Nash, J. and Fernandez-Kelly, M.P. (eds), *Women, Men and the International Division of Labor* (Albany NY: State University of New York Press).

—— (1989), 'Asia y Frontera México-Estados Unidos', in Carillo, J. (ed.), *Reestructuración industrial: Maquiladoras en la Frontera México-Estados Unidos* (México DF: Consejo Nacional para la Cultura y las Artes and Colegio de la Frontera Norte), 125–82.

Freyre Rubio, J. (1983), *Las Organizaciones Sindicales, Obreras y Burocráticas Contemporáneas en México* (México DF: Universidad Autonoma Metropolitana-Azcapotzalco).

Frobel, F. (1978), 'The World Market for Labor and the World Market for Industrial Sites', *Journal of Economic Issues* 12:4, 843–58.

—— et al. (1980), *The New International Division of Labour: Structural Unemployment in Industrial Countries and Industrialisation in Developing Countries* (Cambridge: Cambridge University Press).

Fuentes, M. (1994), *La Imposición Laboral que nos viene del Norte* (México DF: Comisión Mexicana de Defensa y Promoción de los Derechos Humanos).

Furtado, C. (1976), *Economic Development of Latin America: Historical Background and Contemporary Problems*, 2nd Edition (Cambridge: Cambridge University Press).

Garner, P. (1985), 'Federalism and *Caudillismo* in the Mexican Revolution: The Genesis of the Oaxaca Sovereignty Movement (1915–20)', *Journal of Latin American Studies* 17:1, 111–33.

Gelderman, C. (1981), *Henry Ford: The Wayward Capitalist* (New York: Dial Press).

General Motors Mechanical Components Division (1992), 'Synchronous Manufacturing Definition and Scope', Synchronous Manufacturing Training Course notes, as reproduced in 'Synchronous Manufacturing', CAW-Research Department Presentation.

Gill, S. (1992), 'The Emerging World Order and European Change', in Miliband, R. and Panitch, L. (eds), *New World Order? The Socialist Register 1992* (London: Merlin), 157–96.

—— (1996), 'Globalization, Democratization and the Politics of Indifference', in Mittelman, J. (ed.), *Globalization: Critical Reflections* (Boulder CO: Lynne Rienner), 205–228.

Gilly, A. (2005), *The Mexican Revolution* (New York; London: The New Press).

Gindin, S. (1989), 'Breaking Away: The Formation of the Canadian Auto Workers', *Studies in Political Economy* 29, 63–89.

—— (1994), 'Cars and Continentalism', Presentation for Harold Innis Centenary Celebration Conference, University College, University of Toronto, Toronto, May.

—— (1995), *The Canadian Auto Workers: The Birth and Transformation of a Union* (Toronto: James Lorimer).

González Nicolás, I. (2006), 'Presentación', in *Deconstruyendo Paradigmas del Poder Sindical* (México DF: Fundación Friedrich Ebert, 2006), 9–13.

Grinspun, R. (1993), 'The Economics of Free Trade in Canada', in Grinspun, R. and Cameron, M. (eds), *The Political Economy of North American Free Trade* (Montreal: Canadian Centre for Policy Alternatives, McGill-Queen's University Press), 105–124.

—— and Cameron, M. (1993), 'The Political Economy of North American Integration: Diverse Perspectives, Converging Criticisms', in Grinspun, R. and Cameron, M. (eds), *The Political Economy of North American Free Trade* (Montreal: Canadian Centre for Policy Alternatives, McGill-Queen's University Press), 3–25.

Guerra, F-X. (1988), *México: del Antiguo Régimen a la Revolución* (vol. 2; México: Fondo de Cultura Económica).

Guevera Niebla, G. (1993), 'El Movimiento a la ofensiva', in Bellinghausen, H. and Hiriart, H. (eds) *Pensar el 68*, 4th Edition (México DF: Cal y Arena).

Guillén, B. (1992a), 'No regresaron al trabajo pese al ulitmatum de Volkswagen', *Síntesis*, 27 de julio.

—— (1992b), 'Arreglo ajustado a derecho y con respeto al trabajo: Héctor Barba', *Síntesis*, 18 de agosto.

—— (1992c), 'Desde ayer: opera ya en VW la nueva organización del trabajo', *Síntesis*, 25 agosto.

—— and Alberto Mendez, A. (1992), 'VW: al trabajo por la fuerza', *Sintesis*, 24 de julio.

Gutmann, M. (1996), *The Meaning of Macho: Being a Man in Mexico City* (Berkeley CA: University of California Press).

Hadley, K. (1994), 'Working Lean and Mean: A Gendered Experience of Restructuring in an Electronics Manufacturing Plant', PhD dissertation, University of Toronto.

Hansen, R. (1971), *The Politics of Mexican Development* (Baltimore: The Johns Hopkins University Press).

Healy, T. (2006), 'The Condition of Hegemony and Labour Militancy: The Restructuring of Gender and Production Patterns in Mexico', in Davies M. and Ryner, M. (eds), *Poverty and the Production of World Politics: Unprotected Workers in the Global Political Economy* (Houndmills, Basingstoke, UK; New York: Palgrave Macmilllan), 178–203.

Helleiner, E. (1994), *States and the Re-emergence of Global Finance* (Ithaca, NY: Cornell University Press).

Hellman, J. (1983), *Mexico in Crisis*, 2nd Edition (New York: Holmes and Meier).

Heredia, C. and Purcell, M. (1995), 'Structural Adjustment in Mexico: The Root of the Crisis', in *Structural Adjustment and the Spreading Crisis in Latin America* (Washington DC: The Development GAP).

Hernández Juárez, F. and Xelhuantzi López, M. (1992), *El Sindicalismo en la Reforma del Estado: Una visión de la Modernización de México* (México DF: Fondo de Cultura Económica).

Herrera Lima, F. (1992), 'Reestructuración de la Industria Automotriz en México y Respuesta Sindical', *El Cotidiano* 46.

Herzenberg, S. (1996), 'Calling Maggie's Bluff: The NAFTA Labor Agreement and the Development of an Alternative to Neoliberalism', *Canadian–American Public Policy 28*, Occasional Paper Series, Canadian–American Centre University of Maine.

Hiriart, H. (1993), 'La Revuelta Antiautoritaria', in Bellinghausen, H. and Hiriart, H. (eds), *Pensar el 68*, 4th Edition (México DF: Cal y Arena).

Hooper, C. (1998), 'Masculinist Practices and Gender Politics: The Operation of Multiple Masculinities in International Relations', in Zalewski, M. and J. Parpart (eds), *The 'Man' Question in International Relations* (Boulder CO: Westview), 22–58.

—— (2001), *Manly States: Masculinities, International Relations and Gender Politics* (New York: Columbia University Press).

Instituto Federal Electoral (1994), *The Mexican Electoral System* (México DF: Instituto Federal Electoral).

Instituto Mexicano del Seguro Social (1993), 'Exposition de motivos de la Ley del Seguro Social de 1973', in *Diario Oficial de la Federación*, 12 de marzo de 1973 (México DF: Editorial Alco), 11.

Instituto Nacional de Estadística, Geografía e Informática (1991), *Estadística de la Industria Maquiladora de Exportación: 1979–1989* (México DF: Instituto Nacional de Estadística, Geografía e Informática).

Instituto Nacional de las Mujeres (2004), 'Violencia de género en las parejas mexicanas: Resultados de la Encuesta Nacional sobre la Dinámica de las Relaciones en los Hogares' 2003* (México DF: Instituto Nacional de las Mujeres).

Jaimes, R. (1993), Interview by author, Cuernavaca, Morelos, 10 June.

Jary, D. and Jary, J. (1991), *Dictionary of Sociology* (New York: Harper Collins).

Jenson, J. (1992), 'Gender and Reproduction, or Babies and the State', in Connelly, M.P. and Armstrong, P. (eds), *Feminism in Action: Studies in Political Economy* (Toronto: Canadian Scholars' Press).

Juárez, H. (1993), Interview by author, Puebla, Puebla, August.

Juárez M. V. (1992), 'Sigo Siendo el Líder de VW: Bueno A', *Momento*, miercoles 19 de agosto.

Junta Federal de Conciliación y Arbitraje, Secretaría Auxiliar de Conflictos Colectivos (1992a), 'Convenio entre VW and SITIAVW', Exp. III-244/92, Mexico DF, 1 de julio.

—— (1992b), Junta Especial Número 15. Expediente Numero 579/92, Volkswagen de México, SA de CV vs Sindicato Independiente de Trabajadores de la Industria Automotriz, Similares y Conexos Volkswagen de México y otros, México DF, 17 de agosto.

Kaufman, M. (1993), *Cracking the Armour: Power, Pain and the Lives of Men* (Toronto: Penguin).

Knox, P. (1988), 'Mexican workers show the strain', *Globe and Mail*, 27 February.

Krieger, E. (1992). 'Violación del estado de derecho en Volkswagen,: Laudo de la JFCA', *La Jornada* lunes 31 de agosto.

La Botz, D. (1988), *The Crisis of Mexican Labour* (New York: Praeger).

—— (1992), *Mask of Democracy: Labor Suppression in Mexico Today* (Boston: South End).

La Jornada (1992a), 'Levantaron ayer su huelga los trabajadores de la Volkswagen', *La Jornada*, viernes 3 de julio.

La Jornada (1992b), 'Dio entrada la JFCA a la demanda de la VW', *La Jornada*, miercoles 29 de julio.

La Jornada (1993), 'La AFL-CIO pidió a Clinton renegociar el TLC' jueves 18 de Febrero.

La Jornada de Oriente (1992a), 'Asegura Volkswagen que el paro ya causo pérdidas por 30 mil millones', *La Jornada*, jueves 23 de julio.

La Jornada de Oriente (1992b) 'Volkswagen da por terminada su relación laboral con el sindicato', *La Jornada*, martes 28 de julio.

La Jornada de Oriente (1992c), 'Líquida la VW a los 400 obreros del Movimiento 20 de Julio', *La Jornada*, martes 8 de septiembre, 16.

Lagarde y de los Ríos, M. (2005), 'An end to the Feminicide: V-Day, Unitil Violence Ends', Ciudad Juarex, Chihuahua, February 14, 2004', in Aída, L. and Labelle, G. (eds), *Women's Resistance and Alternatives to the Globalizing Model* (Mexico DF: National Network on Gender and Economy), 67–79.

Laxer, J. (1995), 'Straight Talk on Mexico, not another amigo', *Toronto Star*, 2 April.

Lerner, B. and Ralsky, S. (1976), *El Poder de los Presidentes: Alcances y Perspectivas (1910–1973)* (México: Instituto Mexicano de Estudios Políticos).

Ley de Seguro Social (1993), 'Exposition de motivos de la Ley del Seguro Social de 1973', in *Diario Oficial de la Federación, 12 de marzo de 1973* (México DF: Editorial Alco).

Lipietz, A. (1986), 'New Tendencies in the International Division of Labour: Regimes of Accumulation and Modes of Regulation', in Scott, A.J. and Storper, M. (eds), *Production, Work, Territory: The Geographical Anatomy of Industrial Capitalism* (Boston: Allen and Unwin), 16–40.

Loaeza, S. (1993), 'La Memoria Protectora', in Bellinghausen, H. and Hiriart, H. (eds), *Pensar el 68*, 4th Edition (México DF: Cal y Arena).

López Espinosa, S. (1993), 'Que los Complementarios Sean un "Parche", Temor de los Opositores Canadiense al TLC', *El Financiero* (México, DF), miercoles 31 de marzo.

López, G. (1993), Interview by author, Mexico DF, 26 August.

Lovera, S. (1992), 'Fuerza mayor: razón del fallo; plazo de 72 horas para indemnizar', *La Jornada*, martes 18 de agosto.

Lucero, A. and Guillén, B. (1992), 'Resistiremos, Dicen los Trabajadores Disidentes', *Sintesis*, 23 de julio.

Luján, B. (1993), 'Los Acuerdos Paralelos del TLC: Laboral y Ambiental', Presentation for Ciclo de Mesas Redondas, Red Mexicana de Accion Frente al Libre Comercio, México DF, miércoles 16 de junio.

Macías, A. (1982), *Against All Odds: The Feminist Movement in Mexico to 1940* (Westport; London: Greenwood).

Mahon, R. (1987), 'From Fordism to ?: New Technology, Labour Markets and Unions', *Economic and Industrial Democracy* 8:1, 5–60.

—— Jenson, J. and Bienefeld, M. (eds) (1992), *Production, Space and Identity: Political Economy Faces the 21ˢᵗ Century* (Toronto: Canadian Scholars' Press).

Marquis, S.S. (1923), *Henry Ford: An Interpretation* (Boston).

Márquez, H. (1993), Interview by author, México DF, 6 April.

Martínez, F. and Urrutia, A. (1997), 'Combatir corporativismo y pactos, fines de la UNT', *La Jornada*, 26 de noviembre.

Martínez-Assad, C. (1978), 'Alternativas de poder regional en México', *Revista Mexicana de Sociología* 40:4, 1411–28.

Martínez Cruz, J. (1983), 'Quince Años de Lucha Proletaria en Morelos (1969–1983)', *La Batalla* 5.

Massey, D. (1994), *Space, Place and Gender* (Minneapolis: University of Minnesota Press).

México (1992), Nueva Ley Federal del Trabajo, Ley del Infonavit: Vista Panorámica y Leyes Complementarias. 16o Edición (México DF: Editorial Olguin).

—— (1993), 'Objetivos y procedimientos de huelga, Capítulo II Artículo 450:I', in *Nueva Ley Federal del Trabajo* (México: Berbera Editores).

Meza Ponce, A. (1984), *Fábrica y Poder, Mecanismos de Control Empresarial: El Caso de la Ensambladora deAautomóviles Ford* (México DF: Centro de Investigaciones y Estudios Superiores en Antropología Social).

Mercado, P. (1992), 'Contratos Colectivos y Trabajo Femenino',in *Documentos de Trabajo 39* (México DF: Fundación Friedrich Ebert).

Micheli, J. (1994), *Nueva Manufactura, Globalización y Producción de Automóviles en México* (México DF: Universidad Autónoma de México, Facultad de Economía).

Middlebrook, K. (1991), 'The Politics of Industrial Restructuring: Transnational Firms Search for Flexible Production in the Mexican Automobile Industry', *Comparative Politics* 23:3, 275–97.

—— (1995), *The Paradox of Revolution: Labor, the State and Authoritarianism in Mexico* (Baltimore: Johns Hopkins University Press).

Mies, M. (1986), *Patriarchy and Accumulation on a World Scale: Women in the International Division of Labour* (London: Zed Books).

Mitter, S. (1996), *Common Fate, Common Bond: Women in the Global Economy* (London: Pluto).

Molot, M. (ed.) (1993), *Driving Continentally: National Policies and the North American Auto Industry* (Ottawa: Carleton University Press).

Molyneux, M. (2000), 'Twentieth-century State Formations in Latin America', in Dore, E. and Molyneux, M. (eds), *Hidden Histories of Gender and the State in Latin America* (Durham & London: Duke University Press), 33–81.

Monden, Y. (1983), *Toyota Production System: Practical Approach to Production Management* (Norcross GA: Industrial Engineering and Management Press and Institute of Industrial Engineers).

Monroy, M. (1993), *¿Socios? ¿Asociados? ¿en Sociedad?: Asimetrías entre Canadá, EEUU, México* (México DF: Red Mexicana de Acción Frente al Libre Comercio).

Monsiváis, C. (1993), '¿También las multitudes son históricas?' in Bellinghausen, H. and Hiriart, H. (eds), *Pensar el 68*, 4th Edition (México DF: Cal y Arena).

Montiel, Y. (1991), *Proceso de Trabajo, Acción Sindical y Nuevas Tecnologías en Volkswagen de México* (México DF: Centro de Investigaciones y Estudios Superiores en Antropología Social).

Morelos, J. (1973), 'Fuerza de Trabajo', in Solís, L. (ed.), *La Economía Mexicana II Política y Desarrollo* (México DF: Fondo de Cultura Económica), 389–423.

Moreno, D. (1967), *El Congreso Constituyente de 1916–1917* (México DF: UNAM, Coordinación de Humanidades).

Movimiento Democrático de los Trabajadores de la Ford (1993), 'Testimonios de Ford: interview by Fernando Talavera y Francisco Muñoz', in *Síntesis de Coyuntura 8*, 2nd Edition (Mexico: Facultad de Economía Universidad Nacional Autónoma de México).

Movimiento Democrático de los Trabajadores de la Ford Negotiating Committee (1992), Interview by author, Mexico DF, 12 May.

Mujeres en Acción Sindical (1989), 'Mercado de Trabajo y Mano de Obra Femenina', in Tapia Fonllem, E. and Mercado, P. (eds), *Documentos de Trabajo 18* (México DF: Fundación Friedrich Ebert), 11–15.

Muñoz Rios, P. (1997), 'Perspectivas favorable tras los comicios: analistas. No saldrán capitales "mientras no haya populismo," advierten empresarios', *La Jornada*, 8 de julio.

Nash, J. and Fernández-Kelly, M.P. (1983), *Women, Men and the International Division of Labor* (Albany: State University of New York Press).

National Network on Gender and Economy (2005), *Women's Resistance and Alternatives to the Globalizing Model* (Mexico DF: National Network on Gender and Economy).

Navarro Delgado, E. (1989), 'La defensa del reglamento interior del trabajo frente a la ofensiva de los círculos de calidad', in Gutiérrez Garza, E. (ed.), *Reconversión Industrial y Lucha Sindical* (México DF: Fundación Friedrich Ebert-México).

Nevins, A. and Hill, F.E. (1954), *Ford: The Times, the Man the Company* (New York: Charles Scribner's Sons).

Niemeyer, E.V. (1974), Revolution at Queretaro: The Mexican Constitutional Convention of 1916–1917 (Austin TX: University of Texas Press).

Nissan Mexicana, SA de CV (1971), Letter to Comité Ejecutivo del Sindicato General de Trabajadores de Nissan Mexicana, SA de CV, 21 de octubre.

Ochoa Campos, M. (1976), *Calles: El Estadista* (México: Editorial Trillas).

Olcott, J. (2005), *Revolutionary Women in Postrevolutionary Mexico* (Durham: Duke University Press).

Olivo Solís, Á. (1983), 'Entrevista con Ángel Olivo Solís', In Coll, T. et al. (eds), *Lucha Obrera en México: La visión de sus Líders y Conceptos Fundamentales* (México DF: Editorial Popular de los Trabajadores).

Ortega Arenas, J. (1976), 'Notas sobre la situacion nacional e internacional', in *II Pleno Nacional* (Mexico: Unidad Obrera Independiente).

—— (1980), 'Ortega Arenas, el ayatola de las huelgas: Interview by Estela Osorio', *Contenido*, septiembre, 76–90.

—— (1984), *Instructivo Obrero* (Mexico DF: Costa-Amic Editores).

—— (1992), *Procesos de Cambio: Dialéctica Materialista* (Mexico DF: Editorial Claridad).

—— (1993), Interview by author, Mexico DF, 13 and 27 May.

Osorio, E. (1980), 'Ortega Arenas, el ayatola de las huelgas', *Contenido*, septiembre, 88.

Panitch, L. (1996), 'Rethinking the Role of the State', in Mittelman, J. (ed.), *Globalization: Critical Reflections* (Boulder CO: Lynne Rienner), 83–113.

Patroni, V. (1998), 'The Politics of Labour Legislation Reform in Mexico', *Capital and Class* 65, 107–32.

Paz, O. (1993), *El Laberinto de la Soledad/ Postdata Vuelta a el Llaberinto de la Soledad*, 2nd Edition (México DF: Fondo de Cultura Económica).

Pedrero Nieto, M. and Saavedra, N. (1987), *La industria maquiladora en México* (Ginebra: Oficina Internacional del Trabjajo).

Peterson, V.S. (ed.) (1992), *Gendered States: Feminist (Re)Visions of International Relations Theory* (Boulder CO: Lynne Rienner).

—— (1997), 'Dichotomies, Debates and New Thinking Spaces', unpublished paper.

—— (2006), 'How (the meaning of) Gender Matters in Political Economy', in Payne, A. (ed.), *Key Debates in New Political Economy* (London; New York: Routledge), 79–105.

—— and Runyan, A.S. (1993), *Global Gender Issues* (Boulder CO: Westview).

Piedrahita, R. (1992), 'Niega Jesús Valencia, intromisión de partidos y órganos extranjeros', *La Opinión*, jueves 13 de agosto.

Piore, M. and Sabel, C. (1984), *The Second Industrial Divide: Possibilities for Prosperity* (New York: Basic Books).

Pollert, A. (1988), 'Dismantling Flexibility', *Capital and Class* 34, 42–75.

Poniatowska, E. (1988), *Nada, nadie: Las voces del temblor* (Mexico DF: Ediciones Era).

Presidencia de la República, Dirección General de Comunicación Social. (1991a), *The Mexican Agenda* 11th Edition (Mexico DF: Dirección General de Comunicación Social).

—— (1991b), 'Pacto Para La Estabilidad y El Crecimiento Economico', Convenio por el que se extiende hasta el 31 de enero de 1993 el término de la Concertación vigente, Los Pinos, México, 10 de noviembre.

Punto Crítico (1972), 'Insurgencia Sindical', *Punto Crítico* 1:1, 28.

—— (1980), *Problemas y Perspectivas del Movimiento Obrero: 1970–1980* (México DF: Punto Crítico).

Ramírez, G. (1971), 'Sub-Gerente de Relaciones Industriales, Nissan Mexicana, SA de CV al Comité Ejecutivo del Sindicato General de Trabajadores de Nissan Mexicana, SA. de CV', 21 de octubre.

Ramírez, J.C. (ed.) (1988), *La nueva Industrialización en Sonora: El Caso de los Sectores de Alta Tecnología* (Hermosillo: El Colegio de Sonora).

Quintero Ramírez, C. (1990), *La sindicalización en las Maquiladoras Tijuanenses* (México DF: Consejo nacional para la Cultura y las Artes and Dirección General de Publicaciones).

Ramón Beteta, J. et al. (1969), *México Visto en el Siglo XX: Entrevistas de Historia Oral* (México DF: Instituto Mexicano de Investigaciones Económicas).

Ramos Escandón, C. (1987), 'Señoritas Porfirianas: Mujer e Ideología en el México Progresista, 1880–1910', in Ramos Escandón, C. et.al., *Presensia y Transperencia: La Mujer en la Historia de México* (México D.F.: El Colegio de México), 143–61.

Rappo, S. (1992),'Cláusulas modificadas del Contrato Colectivo de Volkswagen de México', *La Jornada de Oriente*, miercoles 8 de julio.

—— and Victoria, O. (1992), 'Estalló la huelga en la planta automotriz VW', *La Jornada de Oriente*, miercoles 1o de julio.

Reagan, R. 'Letter to Bob Packwood of the United States Senate, April 24, 1986' in Duncan Cameron (ed.) *The Free Trade Papers* (Toronto: James Lorimer and Co, 1986), 43–45.

Red Mexicana de Acción Frente al Libre Comercio (1992a), 'Memoria de Zacatecas 25, 26, 27 de Octubre de 1991', in *La Opinión Pública y las Negociaciones del Tratado de Libre Comercio: Alternativas Ciudadanas* (México DF: RMALC).

—— (1992b), 'Letter to Dr. Jaime Serra Puche, Secretario de Comercio y Fomento Industrial', México DF, 25 de julio.

Reding, A. (1991), 'Mexico: The Crumbling of the 'Perfect Dictatorship', *World Policy Journal* 8:2, 255–84.

Reygadas, P. et al. (eds) (1994), *La Guerra de Año Nuevo: Crónicas de Chiapas y México 1994* (México DF: Editorial Praxis).

Rocío, B. et al. (1989), 'La Industria Maquiladora Mexicana en los sectores electrónico y de autopartes', in Tapia Fonllem, E. and Mercado, P. (eds), *Documentos de Trabajo* (México DF: Fundación Friedrich Ebert).

Roman, R. (1976), *Ideology and Class in the Mexican Revolution*, unpublished manuscript, Sociology Department, University of Toronto.

Roxborough, I. (1984), *Unions and Politics in Mexico: The Case of the Automobile Industry* (Cambridge: Cambridge University Press).

Ruíz, E. (1976), *Labor and the Ambivalent Revolutionaries: Mexico, 1910–1923* (Baltimore: Johns Hopkins University Press).

Rupert, M. (1995), *Producing Hegemony: The Politics of Mass Production and American Global Power* (Cambridge: Cambridge University Press).

Safa, H. (1986), 'Runaway Shops and Female Employment: The Search for Cheap Labor', in Leacosk, E. and Safa, H.I. (eds), *Women's Work* (South Hadley MA: Bergin and Garvey), 58–71.

Salinas de Gortari, C. (1989), *Primer Informe de Gobierno* 1o de noviembre.

—— (1990), 'Reforming the State, *Nexos* 148.

—— (1994), *VI Informe de Gobierno de Carlos Salinas de Gortari* (México DF: El Gobierno de Mexico, Presidencia de la Republica).

Salzinger, L. (2003), *Genders in Production: Making Workers in Mexico's Global Factories* (Berkeley CA: University of California Press).

Sánchez Díaz, S.G. (1980), 'Sobre la Unidad Obrera Independiente', in *Memoria del Encuentro Sobre Historia del Movimiento Obrero* (vol 3; Puebla: Universidad Autónoma de Puebla).

Sanchís, N. (ed.) (2001), *EL ALCA en debate: Una perspectiva desde las mujeres* (Buenos Aires: Editorial Biblos).

Sandoval Godoy, S. (1990a), 'Conflictos laborales y relaciones capital- trabajo en la planta Ford de Hermosillo (1986–1989)', *Estudios Sociales* 1:1, 117–40.

—— (1990b), 'Los equipos de trabajo en la planta Ford', *Revista de El Colegio de Sonora* 2, 106–25.

—— (nd), 'Equipos de Trabajo: La Experiencia de Ford Motor Company en Hermosillo Sonora', unpublished paper, Centro de Investigación en Alimentación y Desarrollo, Hermosillo, Sonora.

Secretaría de Comercio y Fomento Industrial (1972), 'Decreto que fija las bases para el desarrollo de la industria automotriz', *Diario Oficial*, Artículos 10–11, martes 24 de octubre, 4.

—— (1977), 'Decreto para el Fomento de la Industria Automotriz', *Diario Oficial de la Federación*, 20 de junio.

—— (1989), *La Industria Maquiladora de Exportación* (Mexico DF: Gobierno de México).

—— (1991), 'Sector Automotriz', in *Monografía 10 Tratado de Libre Comercio en América del Norte* (México DF: Secretaría de Comercio y Fomento Industrial).

—— (1992), 'El ABC del TLC: El Tratado de Libre Comercio' México DF.

—— (1993), 'La Industria Automotriz y el TLC: Texto del Resumen de SECOFI', in *Tratado de Libre Comercio*, Resumen editado por la Secretaría de Comercio y Fomento Industrial.

Seidler, V.J. (2006), *Transforming Masculinities: Men, Cultures, Bodies, Power, Sex and Love* (London; New York: Routledge).

Sen, G. and Grown, C. (1987), *Development, Crises and Alternative Visions: Third World Women's Perspectives* (New York: Monthly Review).

Sepúlveda, B. and Chumacero, A. (1973), *La inversión extranjera en México* (México: Fondo Cultura Economico).

Seymour, A. and Wolfarth, T. (1990). 'Memo to Canadian Auto Workers' President Bob White', 17 October.

Shaiken, H. and Herzenberg, S. (1989), *Automatización y Producción Global: Producción de Motores de Automóvil en México, Estados Unidos y Canadá* (México DF: Facultad de Economía, UNAM).

—— (1990), 'Nuevas Estrategias de Modernización en la Industria Automovilística', in Álvarez Béjar, A. and Borrego, J. (eds), *La Inserción de México en la Cuenca del Pacífico* (vol 2; México DF: Facultad de Economía, Universidad Autónoma de México), 13–41.

Sindicato Independiente de Trabajadores de la Industria Automotriz, Similares y Conexos 'Volkswagen de México' (1991–1993), 'Estatutos del Sindicato Nacional Independiente de Trabajadores de la Industria Automotriz, Similares y Conexos, 1991–1993'.

—— (1992a), 'Cláusula No.25 Bis. De la Productividad', *Proyecto Revisión, 92–94.*

—— (1992b), 'Información a Nuestra Base Sindical Sobre los Resultados de la Revision Contractual', 6 de julio.

—— (1992c), "Comité Ejecutivo General: A la opinión pública...", *La Jornada,* lunes 17 de agosto.

—— (1992d), 'Información sobre el nuevo contrato colectivo', 24 de agosto.

—— (1992e), 'Información a los trabajadores sindicalizados', 26 de agosto.

Sindicato Nacional de Trabajadores de Ford Motor Company (1977), 'Estatutos'. CTM.

—— (1989), 'Estatutos'. CTM.

Sindicato Nacional de Trabajadores de Ford Motor Company Union Officials, CTM-Seccion Chihuahua (1992), Interview by author, 30 April.

Sindicato Nacional de Trabajadores de la Industria Textiles Morelos, Sección 51 (1972), '1972 Año de Juarez', Cuernavaca, Morelos.

Sintesis (1992), 'Hay la posibilidad de una nueva concertación: H. Barba', *Síntesis,* martes 11 de agosto.

Smith, R.F. (1972), *The United States and Revolutionary Nationalism in Mexico, 1919–1932* (Chicago: University of Chicago Press).

Smith, S. (1998), "Unacceptable Conclusions" and the "Man" Question: Masculinity, Gender and International Relations', in Marysia Zalewski and Jane Parpart eds. *The 'Man' Question in International Relations* (Boulder: Westview), 54–72.

Spaulding, R. (1982), 'Corporatism in Mexico', *Comparative Political Studies* 14:2, 139–61.

Spelich, J. (1988), 'Mexico imports jobs to boost exports', *ISLA*, 29 June.

Stanford, J. et al. (1993), 'Social Dumping Under North American Free Trade', Working Paper Series, Canadian Centre for Policy Alternatives, Ottawa.

Stidger, W.L. (1923), *Henry Ford: The Man and his Motives* (New York: George H. Doran).

Tacho, Comandante, EZLN (1994), Opening address, *Convención Nacional Democrática,* audiotape by author, 5 August.

Talavera, F. and Muñoz, F. (1993), *El Movimiento Democrático de los Trabajadores de la Ford, (1987–1991): Testimonios de Ford,* 2nd Edition (Mexico: Taller de Economía del Trabajo, Facultad de Economía Universidad Nacional Autónoma de México).

Talpade Mohanty, C. (1991), 'Under Western Eyes: Feminist Scholarship and Colonial Discourses', in Talpade Mohanty, C. et al. (eds), *Third World Women and the Politics of Feminism* (Bloomington; Indianapolis: Indiana University Press), 51–80.

Tecla Jiménez, A. (1992), *El Modo de Vida y La Clase Obrera en México* (México DF: Ediciones Taller Abierto).

Teichman, J. (1988), *Policymaking in Mexico: From Boom to Crisis* (Boston: Allen and Unwin).

Tello, C. (1990), *La política económica en México 1970–1976*, 10th Edition (México DF: Siglo Veintiuno Editores).

Thijssen, G. (1993), Interview by author, Cuernavaca, Morelos, 16 June.

Tickner, J.A. (1992), *Gender in International Relations: Feminist Perspectives on Achieving Global Security* (New York: Columbia University Press).

Traynor, K. (1992), 'The Origins of Free Trade Mania', in *Crossing the Line: Canada and Free Trade with Mexico* (Vancouver BC: New Star Books).

Trejo Delarbe, R. (1990), *Crónica del Sindicalismo en México (1976–1988)* (México DF: Siglo Veintiuno Editors).

—— (1991), *Los Mil Días de Carlos Salinas* (México DF: El Nacional).

Tuñón, E. (1982), *Huerta y el Movimiento Obrero* (Mexico DF: Ediciones El Caballito).

—— (1987), 'La Lucha Política de la Mujer Mexicana por el Derecho al Sufragio y sus Repercusiones', in Ramos Escandón, C. et.al. (eds), *Presencia y Transparencia: La Mujer en la Historica de México* (México DF: El Colegio de México), 181–9.

Unidad Obrera Independiente (1975), '?Anarquismo u Organization?' *Unidad Obrera Independiente*, 28 de julio, 6

—— (nd), *Politics* 23:3, 275–97.

United States Trade Representative (1994), 'Discussion Draft on Post-NAFTA Policy', *Inside NAFTA*, 23 February, 18–19.

Valdés Ugalde, F. (1994), 'From Bank Nationalization to State Reform: Business and the New Mexican Order', in Cook, M.L. et al. (eds), *The Politics of Economic Restructuring: State–Society Relations and Regime Change in Mexico* (San Diego CA: Center for US–Mexican Studies, University of California).

Valle Espinoza, E. (1970), 'Alegato de Defensa, 18 de septiembre 1970 antes Eduardo Ferrer MacGregor, Juez 1o Distrito Federal en Materia Penal', in *Tiempo de Hablar...: los procesos de México 68* (México DF: Editorial Estudiantes), 3–41.

Varley, A. (2000), 'Women and the Home in Mexican Family Law', in Dore, E. and Molyneux, M. (eds), *Hidden Histories of Gender and the State in Latin America* (Durham: Duke University Press), 238–61.

Vázquez, C.O. (1992a), 'Acepta Bueno Aguirre que una asamblea decida quien es el lider', *Uno Más Uno*, martes 4 de agosto.

—— (1992b), 'Destituyen a Bueno como líder de la VW', *Uno Más Uno*, domingo 16 de agosto.

—— (1992c), 'Reitera VW su pretensión de finiquitar las relaciones contractuales', *Uno Más Uno,* sábado 8 de agosto.

Velasco, E. (1997), 'Gran avance, aunque falta eradicar la coacción del voto: observadores', *La Jornada*, 9 de julio.

Velasco Arregui, E. (1993), 'Industrial Restructuring in Mexico during the 1980s', in Grinspun, R. and Cameron, M.A. (eds), *Political Economy of North American Free Trade* (Montreal: Canadian Centre for Policy Alternatives and McGill-Queen's University Press), 163–75.

Velásquez, C. (1998), 'El debate sobre LFT, coyuntura favorable a las trabajadoras', *DobleJornada*, 2 de junio.

Victoria, O. (1992), 'Nuevo Diálogo entre la VW y el Sindicato: Bueno Aguirre', *La Jornada*, miercoles 12 de agosto.

Villamar, A. and Atilano, M. (2005), 'World Trade Organisation: Gender Implications of its agreements and Regulations', in Aída, L. and Labelle, G. (eds), *Women's Resistance and Alternatives to the Globalizing Model* (Mexico DF: National Network on Gender and Economy), 4–9.

Villanueva, V. (1992), Interview by author, Mexico DF, February.

——— (1996), Personal communication with author, Toronto, August.

Volkswagen de México, *Administración de Salarios* (1992), *Grupos de Trabajo*.

Volkswagen de México (1992a)"Hogar dulce hogar", *La Jornada* 20 de Agosto de 1992.

Volkswagen de México (1992b), "Reingreso de personal de planta" 28 de agosto.

——— and SITIAVW (1989), 'Claúsula No. 16: Del Trabajo de Terceras personas', 28 de junio.

——— and SITIAVW (1992), Convenio No. 12, 28 de mayo.

——— and SITIAVW (1992), Contrato Colectivo, 18 de agosto.

White, R. (1992), 'Canadian Labor Letter on NAFTA', *Inside US Trade*, 31 July, 14–15.

Wilkie, J. and Michaels, A. (eds) (1969), *Revolution in Mexico: Years of Upheaval 1910–1940* (New York: Alfred A. Knopf).

Wilson, M. (1992), 'A Letter from Michael Wilson', in *The Global Trade Challenge*, Special Tabloid Supplement (Ottawa: Government of Canada).

Wolf, E.R. and Hansen, E.C. (1967), 'Caudillo Politics: A Structural Analysis', *Comparative Studies in Society and History* 9:2, 168–79.

Womack, J.P. et al. (1990), *The Machine that Changed the World: Based on the Massachusetts Institute of Technology 5-million dollar 5-year Study on the Future of the Automobile* (New York: Rawson Associates).

Women's Plan of Action (1992), 'Memoria Testimonial', Presented at Primer Encuentro Trinacional de Trabajadoras ante la Integración Económica y el Tratado de Libre Comercio, Valle de Bravo Toluca, del 5 al 9 de febrero.

Zalewski, M. and Parpart, J. (eds) (1998), *The 'Man' Question in International Relations* (Boulder: Westview).

Zapata, F. (1989), 'Labor and Politics: The Mexican Paradox', in Epstein, E.C. (ed.), *Labor Autonomy and the State in Latin America* (Boston: Unwin Hyman), 173–93.

Index

Gender in a Global/Local World